Growing the Next Generation of Researchers

Growing the Next Generation of **Researchers**

A handbook for emerging researchers and their mentors

Lyn Holness

UCT
P R E S S

Growing the next generation of researchers: A handbook for emerging researchers and their mentors

First published in 2015 by UCT Press
an imprint of Juta and Company Ltd
First Floor
Sunclare Building
21 Dreyer Street
Claremont
7708

PO Box 14373, Lansdowne, 7779, Cape Town, South Africa

© 2015, UCT Press
www.uctpress.co.za

ISBN 978-1-77582-085-7

Project Manager: Glenda Younge
Editor: Glenda Younge
Proofreader: Alfred LeMaitre
Typesetter: Red Setter
Cover designer: Paula Wood
Typeset in Minion Pro 10.5 pt on 14 pt

The authors and the publisher believe on the strength of due diligence exercised that this work does not contain any material that is the subject of copyright held by another person. In the alternative, they believe that any protected pre-existing material that may be comprised in it has been used with appropriate authority or has been used in circumstances that make such use permissible under the law.

This book has been independently peer-reviewed by academics who are experts in the field.

CONTENTS

Preface vii

Acknowledgements ix

Contributors ix

Introduction and background xiii

Part 1: Welcome to academia 1

Chapter 1: Understanding the terrain 5

Chapter 2: The research landscape: Internationalisation, quality
assurance and benchmarking 24

Chapter 3: Crossing research boundaries 42

Part 2: Developing a research profile: The art and craft of research 61

Chapter 4: Research information and its management 65

Chapter 5: Research integrity 79

Chapter 6: Planning your research 94

Chapter 7: Optimising research opportunities: Sabbaticals, conferences
and research visits 109

Chapter 8: Securing and managing research grants 129

Part 3: Getting research into the public sphere 145

Chapter 9: Scholarly publishing: From motivation to publication 149

Chapter 10: Scholarly publishing: Writing a book 165

Chapter 11: Research impact 175

Part 4: Doing and supervising a PhD 185

Chapter 12: Embarking on a PhD; Supervisor and student perspectives 189

Chapter 13: Writing a thesis: The preparatory stages 206

Chapter 14: The writing process: Submission and examination 219

Excursus: Complementary models of supervision 237

Conclusion 240

Appendix A: Memorandum of Understanding 243

References 245

Index 251

PREFACE

Becoming an academic has many parallels with moving to a new city. If you merely visit a city, you can mostly get by with basic information—a map indicating the most important places and a guide to using the public transport system will often be enough to facilitate a comfortable stay in an unfamiliar place. However, going to live in that city requires far more. To become a good and effective citizen requires a deeper understanding of its sociology, politics and the many complex systems that drive or influence daily life. Without the right advice and support, living in even the most desirable of cities can be a frustrating and debilitating experience to a newcomer; you see the road opening up before the established citizens as they go about their business with ease and confidence, while you often turn into blind alleys and stumble across unexpected obstacles. They don't know how to help you to settle in and to cope, and you don't know exactly what questions you should be asking them.

This book is an impressive *vade mecum* for both new citizens in academia and those who have the task of guiding them in respect of this crucial part of academic life, namely, doing good and meaningful research. Only someone with both experience and empathy could provide such guidance: as one begins to read the book, it is immediately obvious that the author has both of these qualities in abundance, and, as one progresses through the book, this initial sense is confirmed in every chapter.

I was fortunate to witness the Emerging Researcher Programme (ERP) grow from its inception in 2003 to what it is today. In those early days, I was Director of Research in the Law Faculty and I was looking for ways to help the new law lecturers grow as researchers. How lucky I was that, at that very time, the Research Office (under the leadership of its Director, Marilet Sienaert, and supported by the DVC responsible for research, Cheryl de la Rey) was just embarking on the most comprehensive programme of researcher development ever attempted at UCT—and at the centre of it all was the gentle hand of Lyn Holness, from whom I (and all those around her) learnt more than she will ever know.

With this book, Dr Holness commits the democratic act of sharing her knowledge beyond the borders of her own university's research enterprise. By doing this, she is making an important statement, namely, that if we are to be successful as a country and a continent, we have to pool our resources to grow a strong cohort of people who are able to produce the knowledge that will be necessary to ensure growth, development and prosperity in tomorrow's world; specifically in South Africa, sharing enabling information is vital to creating a transformed next generation of researchers.

The long list of people that Dr Holness acknowledges at the beginning of her book as having contributed in one way or another to the writing, and her description of the role that the Emerging Researcher Programme played in making it possible, emphasises two important things: (1) the enabling environment in the Research Office and (2) the willingness of so many academics in the various faculties who are willing to contribute to the development of our new researchers. Of course, the list of contributors does not include everyone who gives of their time to assist the researcher-development enterprise. It is important to say that the building of a strong research culture depends on individual researchers in the faculties, departments and research units, imparting the sense of excitement and satisfaction that the creation of new knowledge brings with it, but doing so while also bringing to the surface the challenges that confront everyone in their research life. This book enables every researcher to be more mindful of these challenges, but also more knowledgeable about how to overcome them.

In reading through the book, I found it difficult to think of any additional aspect that should have been covered. It is comprehensive and detailed, and it deals clearly and honestly with the various thorny issues that inevitably arise in the research environment; it imparts sensible advice on what to do and what not to do; and it is sensitive to the subtle differences between different research environments and the varying needs of individual researchers. Every person embarking on a research career and every person involved in developing researchers should read it—and keep a copy close at hand.

Professor Danie Visser
Deputy Vice-Chancellor, University of Cape Town

ACKNOWLEDGEMENTS

I acknowledge receipt of a generous grant from the South African National Research Foundation (NRF), which has made the publication of this book possible.

Many people have played a part, consciously or otherwise, in the production of this book, and I am deeply indebted to them. The preparation, co-ordination and writing process has taken me into terrain that is new to me, and I have learnt much from all those who have, in any way, participated. I am also grateful for the underlying matrix of support that has encouraged me in the execution of this task.

Dr Marilet Sienaert, in her capacity as Director of the UCT Research Office (now Executive Director) has been consistently supportive of the Emerging Researcher Programme (ERP), which lies at the heart of this book, and of me personally.

Professor Danie Visser has retained a constant interest in the work of researcher development, which has benefited from his wisdom and practical support, particularly in the process of awarding and managing grants. For this I extend my thanks to him, as I do also for the Preface he has written for this book.

It was the vision and prodding of Professor Evance Kalula that was the stimulus behind this project. For this I am grateful—and happy to present him with the final product.

My colleagues in the Research Office have shown generosity in sharing their skills and insights in various aspects of research management, and have provided the congenial atmosphere in which this project has thrived. In particular, I am indebted to my immediate colleagues in the Research Development cluster, for their extraordinary support, not least in assuming extra responsibilities to give me time to write. My deep thanks go to Dr Mignonne Breier, Dr Charles Masango, Mr Thando Mgqolozana, Dr Robert Morrell, Dr Gaëlle Ramon and Ms Judith Rix.

The experience, expertise and wisdom that Professor John de Gruchy and Professor Luigi Nassimbeni have brought to our work has been, and continues to be, invaluable. I am grateful to them both. John de Gruchy was also my PhD supervisor and has been my mentor for almost two decades.

Over the years many other colleagues in the broader UCT context have contributed in specific ways to the ERP, not least as seminar presenters. Although most are not named in the book, their collective insights have seeped into me and enhanced my grasp of many of the topics addressed in the pages that follow. For this I am grateful.

For the past 12 years much of my energy has centred on one-on-one interaction with those participating in the ERP. Strategies we have developed together to overcome hurdles and reach goals have enhanced my grasp of the issues involved in researcher development, and hence enriched what I have been able to bring to this book. My thanks go to each emerging researcher.

Various people, from their particular area of experience and expertise, have graciously made contributions that have been fed into chapters of this book. These contributions have enriched the content, thereby increasing the book's value to readers. I appreciate the graciously given time and effort that colleagues invested in the pieces they prepared, and the generosity of others who made their pre-existing material available.

Several colleagues offered critical insights on different sections in preparation of the manuscript. I extend my thanks to them, and particularly to Professor Jane English, who acted as internal reviewer of the entire manuscript. I am also grateful to the external reviewers, whose critique and suggestions have enhanced the quality of this book.

It has been a privilege to work with both Sandy Shepherd from UCT Press and Glenda Younge as editor and project manager. I thank them for their support and professionalism through the process of writing and preparing the manuscript for publication.

Lyn Holness

May 2015

LIST OF CONTRIBUTORS

The following people have in varying ways contributed insights from their areas of expertise and experience to sections of the book. Their contributions are acknowledged in the relevant sections.

From the University of Cape Town:

Dr Nelleke Bak (Director of Postgraduate Studies)

Dr Abongwe Bangeni (Academic Development Programme, Centre for Higher Education Development)

Dr Mignonne Breier (Cluster Manager for Research Development, Research Office)

Dr Shadreck Chirikure (Senior Lecturer, Department of Archaeology)

Professor Laura Czerniewicz (Director, Open-UCT)

Alexander d'Angelo (Humanities Information Services, UCT Libraries)

Emeritus Professor John de Gruchy (Senior Scholar, Research Office and Department of Religious Studies)

Associate Professor Karin de Jager (Library and Information Science)

Professor Tania Douglas (Director, MRC/UCT Medical Imaging Research Unit)

Associate Professor Jane English (Professional and Communication Studies)

Dr Freedom Nkhululeko Gumedze (Senior Lecturer, Department of Statistical Sciences)

Johannah Keikelame (Site Development Co-ordinator, Primary Health Care Directorate)

Associate Professor Azeem Khan (Department of Electrical Engineering)

Dr Charles Masango (Co-ordinator for Research Development, Research Office)

Dr Robert McLaughlin (Director, Office of Research Integrity)

Dr Robert Morrell (Co-ordinator, Programme for the Enhancement of Research Capacity [PERC] and NRF rating consultant, Research Office)

Emeritus Professor Luigi Nassimbeni (Senior Scholar, Research Office and Department of Chemistry)

Associate Professor Mary Nassimbeni (Library and Information Science)

Associate Professor Caroline Ncube (Head of Department, Commercial Law)

Professor Francis B. Nyamnjoh (Head of Department, Social Anthropology; until July 2009 Head of Publications for Council for the Development of Social Science Research in Africa [CODESRIA])

Professor Shirley Pendelbury (Children's Institute)

Professor Deborah Posel (Director, Institute for the Humanities in Africa [HUMA])

Dr Gaëlle Ramon (Co-ordinator for Research Development, Research Office)
Associate Professor Kanshukan Rajaratnam (Department of Finance and Tax)
Professor Alan Rycroft (Chair of Commercial Law)
Emeritus Professor Les Underhill (Senior Scholar, Avian Demography Unit)

From Research Access & Availability at International Network for the Availability of Scientific Publications (INASP):
Jonathan Harle (Senior Programme Manager)
Julie Walker (Programme Manager, Publishing Support and AuthorAID Director)

INTRODUCTION AND BACKGROUND

This book grew out of the Emerging Researcher Programme (ERP), launched at the University of Cape Town (UCT) in 2003. This was an institutional response to the concern that the majority of South Africa's research output was being produced by an ageing population of predominantly white, male academics. The challenge was then, and still is, to grow a new generation of researchers and to do this in a context of transformation.

Some of the material contained in this volume expands on an earlier publication, *The Emerging Researcher: Nurturing passion, developing skills, producing output.*[1] Approaches to researcher development have evolved over the years in response to wisdom gained, needs articulated by researchers, and ongoing changes and challenges in the higher education environment. For this reason, much of the material in this book addresses new insights and situations, including developments in the local and international research landscape.

These developments present challenges to research and researchers, notably novice researchers, and to the institutions of which they are a part. Some of them are specific to the South African and the broader sub-Saharan African context, while others are generic to all research development and therefore have more general relevance as well. There are trends in the global research environment that will have an unavoidable impact on the career paths of the upcoming generation of academics, and part of our concern is to raise awareness of and provide tools to respond to them. Among such trends is the increasing emphasis on 'engaged scholarship', which implies quality research that is accessible, is made available and has tangible impact.

Integral to the mandate of those conceptualising and implementing the ERP was to devise a programme that would optimally assist early-career academics in developing the research component of their academic profiles, enabling them, in time, to become established researchers, acquitting themselves nationally and abroad. Part of the vision was that a growing research-consciousness among staff would filter down to students as well. Early on we learned that a structured mentoring programme, which included attention to individual as well as generic needs, provided support, built confidence and capacity, and facilitated the desired outcomes. We realised also that its success depended on an institutional environment that promotes the research endeavour and nurtures new staff

---

1   De Gruchy, J.W. & Holness, L. (2007). *The Emerging Researcher: Nurturing passion, developing skills, producing output,* Cape Town: UCT Press.

members. Sections of the book therefore relate to the institutional responsibility to create this environment.

This book provides a resource to help emerging researchers navigate their way into, and in, the research world. It identifies skills that need to be developed and provides some of the necessary tools to do so; it raises awareness of possible challenges, such as information management through technology; and it demystifies the academic world. Along with this, our desire is to make this resource available and relevant to institutions beyond UCT, both nationally and continentally. Thus we focus on issues generic to academia and specifically to researcher development, all of which have a broad relevance.

The project is aligned with UCT's 'Afropolitan' vision, the aim of which is to establish mutually beneficial, productive and lasting links with higher education institutions across the African subcontinent.[2] This vision does not represent an alternative to internationalisation in higher education. Rather, it is an integral part of it.

UCT is a relatively well-resourced university, affording the privilege of having a dedicated programme to build research capacity. The programme is bolstered by a team of competent and supportive academics (several of whom have contributed to this book), and some who have been integral to the development of the ERP since its beginnings, in the role of Senior Research Scholars.[3] UCT acknowledges the responsibility to share these resources and the benefits accruing from them in the form of this book, at the same time acknowledging that the experience of being an academic will vary widely between institutions and even within institutions.

Although a scholarly publication in the traditional sense is not the aim of this volume, its very focus locates it in a new and growing field of study, namely, researcher development. Linda Evans, current editor of the *International Journal of Researcher Development*, defines researcher development broadly as 'the process whereby people's capacity and willingness to carry out the research components of their work or studies may be considered to be enhanced, with a degree of permanence that exceeds transistoriness.'[4] An interesting observation of Evans, and one aligned with the ERP model, is that researcher development incorporates both professional and personal development. This, she argues, is because the 'complex ecologies of people's lives' are being increasingly recognised as

---

2   The inspiration of the Vice-Chancellor of UCT, Dr Max Price, in an adaptation of a term popularised in 2005.

3   I refer in particular to Emeritus Professor John de Gruchy and Emeritus Professor Luigi Nassimbeni, who have played key roles in the Emerging Researcher Programme since its inception in 2003.

4   See Evans, L. (2012). 'Leadership for researcher development: What research leaders need to know and understand', *Educational Management, Administration and Leadership*, 40: 423. Originally published online, 25 April 2012. www.ema.sagepub.com/content/40/4/423. Accessed 12 August 2015.

the fusion of work and personal life.[5] We hope that this book, in providing strategies for growth in research capacity, will also reflect the fact that, since its inception, the ERP has worked intensely with individuals, taking each unique situation as a cue for strategising. A combination of personal interaction and group events, in the form of seminars, workshops and retreats, together with modest funding opportunities, has produced a viable and verifiable model of support for researcher development.

The milieu in which the Emerging Researcher Programme developed is UCT's Research Office, dedicated—as in other universities—to providing a broad range of strategic support for individual researchers and for the institution's research enterprise more broadly. This support is responsive to changing trends in the research environment, and covers a spectrum of initiatives ranging from the establishment of supportive and empowering relationships with academics, to more instrumental forms of strategic assistance, such as providing up-to-date research information and access to funding, brokering collaborations, etc. The ERP, working synergistically with other Research Office portfolios, as well as departmental, faculty and institutional initiatives, focuses intently on research capacity-building in the context of the other core academic responsibilities. This book is about the strategies that work in achieving this.

PERSPECTIVE

THE EMERGING RESEARCHER PROGRAMME (ERP)

I joined the ERP in 2004 when I was in the initial stages of thinking about registering for a PhD. I attended the research seminars, which focused specifically on preparing to register for a PhD. At this stage the seminar that I found most useful was the one that advised potential PhD candidates of the registration process and all the steps one should take in the process of registering.

This seminar addressed most of the issues with which I had been grappling (they seemed so minor but one never knows exactly who to ask and, when one does, in most cases, one is given contradictory information).

The seminars that followed after that always addressed challenges that I had or was encountering. For example, the seminar on planning and time management was invaluable. I learnt that one does not need to wait for a lengthy block of free time; 20 minutes can yield a coherent paragraph! I continued to make use of this bit of information as I wrote my thesis.

The ERP contributed significantly to my process of thinking, registering for, starting, and eventually finishing my PhD. Seminars like the one on Endnotes and writing for publication were very helpful and the research pack with all the necessary

---

5   Evans, 'Leadership for researcher development', 425, 426.

documents continues to be a useful resource. I am also grateful for the assistance with funding applications.

The programme has also made it possible for me to get funding to attend an international conference and to complete a longitudinal study that I started with a colleague when I joined the Language Development Unit. So far, three publications have resulted from this study, one of which was published in an accredited international journal.

During my PhD I was awarded a staff exchange scholarship to the US and the programme contributed by making funds available for me to attend a conference while I was there—thank you! It is a programme that caters to the diverse needs of all researchers; a resource that the university as a whole cannot afford to be without.

Abongwe Bangeni

When the ERP was launched at the beginning of 2003, our mandate was clear: to build research capacity in early-career academics (and those of longer standing who had done little research) in order to boost the production of sustained, high-quality research output. To this end, a group of senior academics were brought on board to share their research experience and skills through a combination of seminars and one-on-one consultations. Simultaneously, the programme co-ordinator (and later co-ordinators) was meeting with individuals who signed up for the programme, to assess where they were in relation to research, what they needed to do in order to develop research profiles, and what plan they would set in place to get there. The point of mentioning this is to draw attention to the *mentoring* dimension of researcher development.

Mentoring, coaching and counselling[6]

Writing some years back, Akilagpa Sawyerr cited 'the provision of a "soft landing" for young faculty' as one of the initiatives that could be effective in promoting research and research capacity development in African universities.[7] This, together with other strategies identified at the time, constitutes the core business of the ERP. As the programme took shape, a number of our instincts were confirmed, which have relevance for all new academics.

---

6 See Yallow, R. (n.d.). 'Responsible conduct research: Mentoring', www.ccnmtl.colombia.edu/projects/rcr_mentoring/foundation/index.html. Accessed 12 August 2013.

7 Sawyerr, A. (2004). 'African universities and the challenge of research capacity development', *Journal of Higher Education in Africa/RESA*, 2 (1): 211. www.codesria.org/IMG/pdf/8-SAW-YERR.pdf. Accessed 11 February 2013.

1   Researchers are people who work out of particular domestic, social, emotional and economic contexts, each of which needs to be taken into account when encouraging research development and setting realistic goals.

2   The amount and type of support required by individuals in this cohort of new academics varies considerably.

3   A support programme can never operate on a one-size-fits-all basis. Each person is met and offered support at the level of her or his particular need.

4   Allied to point 3 is that some people instinctively fit into a particular institution better than others.

The situation we encountered is not unique to UCT, and the spectrum of need for research support is probably more or less generic to most institutions, no matter where they are located.

Some people take up their academic appointments with the built-in departmental support offered by research groups (mainly in the sciences and health sciences). Others, coming from disciplines where individual research has historically been the norm, need to combat a sense of isolation in research. Still others are appointed to academic positions from situations in which they have not been adequately nurtured in basic research skills. Some find themselves in departments lacking in any research culture, so that PhDs and publishing (or other forms of research output) have been scarce, and colleagues, including some Heads of Department, have offered little encouragement. In other words, people come into their university posts from different research bases, some far better equipped than others.

I have consciously refrained from giving a name to the type of support offered through the ERP. Our brief has been a broad one: to assist academics with any need they have relating to research. Some needs are tangible, and up to now have been relatively easy to address: where to look for funding; how to select an appropriate journal; how to plan for one's first conference. Others are more existential: how to manage time in order to create a space for research; how to set personal research goals, and how to attain them in a non-supportive work environment. The reality is that the support needed by an early-career academic can range from mentoring to coaching to counselling—if one uses conventional understandings. Very often it involves features of all three: an experienced researcher working alongside a novice and empowering by example; the setting of strategic research goals and developing competencies; discussion of a personal circumstance that might be hindering progress with research. With few exceptions these support relationships with researchers are informal, while, at the same the time, the ERP provides a formal, dedicated structure to which queries and problems can be brought. These relationships are ongoing and progress is consistently measured. Just over a decade down the ERP line there are many emerging (or now emerged) researchers who cite emotional and practical support as key to their maturing as researchers and more general success as academics.

Mentoring for emerging researchers should not be confined to the generic assistance offered by any programme. There are disciplinary conventions and nuances that need to be learned, and for this there is no substitute for a mentor within one's department. There are some (by no means enough) departments in our university that routinely assign a mentor to each new staff member. The ability to work alongside a more senior colleague who 'knows the ropes'—not least the research ones—is indispensable. As with the rationale behind the ERP, this type of mentoring has to do with the transfer of skills from an older, more experienced generation to a younger, less experienced generation of academics, introducing them to the networks on which the wheels of academia turn. In essence, a critical component of such mentorship is the responsibility to induct new academics into a community of scholars through whom they will become familiar with current debate in their disciplines worldwide, and through whom, in time, they will establish fruitful collaborations. With increasing pressure for academics to compete globally, the importance of this cannot be exaggerated. But mentoring can come serendipitously too, and young academics do well to be constantly alert to strategies they can imbibe from any number of situations.

We encourage academics to draw support from other university capacity-building initiatives as well, acknowledging that research cannot and should not be isolated from other core activities, but should rather dovetail with them. UCT's New Academic Practitioners' Programme (NAPP), with its primary focus on developing teaching skills, is one such initiative in which we have routinely participated.

It has often been pointed out by older academics that the new generation is extremely fortunate to have on-tap support for research. In 'the old days' or 'when we were young' there were no such research support programmes and scant attention to things like appropriate supervision when engaged in graduate study. People had somehow to fend for themselves and did not have the opportunities afforded to their younger colleagues today. A few people seem to harbour a measure of resentment at this situation, but, in our experience, the vast majority of senior academics are very supportive of their younger colleagues, rising above any potential resentment that they did not have similar opportunities, and working co-operatively with the ERP. It is gratifying to see several past emerging researchers, who have been well mentored, now attaining leadership positions in their departments and faculties—and in turn mentoring junior staff.

The research development strategies discussed in Part 2 of this book presuppose, and are dependent on, a matrix of institutional support for emerging researchers. They presuppose also that such support is in part driven by efforts for both individuals and institutions to be or become internationally competitive without compromising on local relevance.

Apprenticeship[8]

One of the great losses in recent times has been the demise of the apprentice system, too often evident in the quality of work in the various building trades. In the past, a person who aspired to be a builder or carpenter would serve a lengthy apprenticeship with a master craftsman (at that time they were mainly crafts*men*), learning the craft through daily hands-on work over an extended period under the guidance of the master as role model, and sometimes coupled with formal tuition. At each step along the way, the apprentice would learn how best to accomplish the task at hand by observing and practising.

PERSPECTIVE

THE VALUE OF MENTORING: AN EMERGING RESEARCHER'S EXPERIENCE

The role of an academic in the Engineering Faculty has three main aspects: research, teaching and administration. The main role of mentorship in an emerging researcher's development is to facilitate exposure to the core aspects. This would ensure better preparedness to make career decisions later on, which could lead to greater career satisfaction. I had the privilege of being mentored by two incredible individuals, with distinct strengths. My first mentor was my direct supervisor, who had an astonishing focus on new scholarly research. He believed that the best teachers were often the best researchers, that is, individuals who enriched their teaching with their latest research. The interaction with him provided me with significant insight into the tireless effort required to becoming a world-class researcher and excellent teacher.

My second mentor was a senior colleague and HOD, who had been a consultant before joining the university. Interaction with him provided me with insight into contract negotiations and other important administrative skills required for running a large and successful research programme. In reflecting on the value that mentoring has had on my experience as an emerging researcher, I conclude that it allowed me to realise my own strength and inclination, as opposed to simply aspiring to become a clone of a particular mentor.

Azeem Khan

Mentoring of new staff members is the academic equivalent of the master–apprentice relationship, reflected in the fact that a Master's degree was, for centuries, the norm for all

---

8   Based on *The Emerging Researcher*, 105–106 and originally prepared by John W. de Gruchy.

who aspired to become university lecturers and professors.[9] A good mentor and supervisor is a role model for students, demonstrating good practice in his or her own research and helping colleagues and students to learn the craft in ways that are appropriate. Such mentors know by experience how to engage in research, and in the mentoring relationship they share this knowledge—knowing also when it is necessary for protégés to learn from others or discover things for themselves. In doing so, a good mentor avoids developing a relationship of dependency, and encourages students and younger colleagues to develop their own capacity and skills, and so to become, in turn, researchers in their own right and possible role models for others. We dare not let this 'apprenticeship' model disappear from the academy as we seek to grow a new generation of researchers.

The challenge presented in the pages that follow is therefore twofold. First, it is to encourage emerging researchers to familiarise themselves with the academic environment and understand what is required for them to succeed in it, and to employ specific strategies that will help them do so. Second, it is to assist institutional leadership at all levels to identify what emerging researchers require in order to develop and maintain healthy research profiles, and to provide an environment that supports this.

Target audience

The title of this book reflects its singular aim: to facilitate the growth of a new generation of researchers. The subtitle identifies the targeted readers, primary and secondary, who must necessarily come together to facilitate that growth: emerging researchers (primary) and their mentors (secondary).

The conversation throughout this book is pitched at those who are new to academia—or some perhaps not so new but still, in different ways, mystified by the environment. This 'new generation' includes PhD students (and in some cases Master's students), post-doctoral fellows, and early-career academic staff members, many of whom are completing higher degrees themselves. Some very basic issues are therefore addressed, many of them taken for granted by seasoned academics but often left unexplained to graduate students and less experienced staff members.

The relevance of the book to mentors lies in identifying the array of issues to be negotiated by early-career academics and in sharing some strategies to address them. The term 'mentor' is understood broadly to include all those (individuals and bodies; serendipitously or by intent) who have an impact on the oversight and growth of junior researchers in the overall context of the university and its academic agenda. University leadership, therefore, may also be usefully informed by some of the insights of the book,

---

9   Originally a Master's degree, based on the apprenticeship model, was a licence to practise
     theology, in other words, to make a living in the church. In time this was applied to other
     disciplines as well.

particularly the implications for new academics in understanding their institutions in the context of national and global trends and challenges.

While this book draws considerably on the experience of one institution, precisely because of its familiarity to most of the contributors, the aim is to be relevant in the broader southern African and sub-Saharan higher education environments as well. At the outset we acknowledge that not all institutions are equal and that early-career experiences and challenges differ widely from university to university and from individual to individual, even within a single institution.

Book outline

The book is divided into four parts, which inevitably overlap.

Part 1: Welcome to academia

This section focuses on the nature of the academic environment, locating research as a core academic function and setting the local research situation in its fast-changing wider context. This section provides an orientation to the academic world, locally and internationally, identifying and reflecting on some of its intrinsic features, contemporary challenges, and ongoing opportunities—all of which impact on the novice researcher.

Chapter 1:   Understanding the terrain

Chapter 2:   The research landscape: Internationalisation, quality assurance and benchmarking

Chapter 3:   Crossing research boundaries.

The eight chapters of Parts 2 and 3 discuss the development of a research profile in early-career academics, and strategies to build the necessary research capacity to facilitate this. A comprehensive seminar and workshop programme, work with individual researchers, and the challenge posed by changes in the local and global research environment inform this section.

Part 2: Developing a research profile: The art and craft of research

Part 2 introduces readers to a range of tools and targets for personal research growth.

Chapter 4:   Research information and its management

Chapter 5:   Research integrity

Chapter 6:   Planning your research

Chapter 7:   Optimising research opportunities: Sabbaticals, conferences and research visits

Chapter 8:   Securing and managing research grants.

Part 3:   **Getting research into the public sphere**

Part 3 focuses on the dissemination of research, mainly but not exclusively through publishing, and on the various strategies for, and measures of, research impact.

Chapter 9:   Scholarly publishing: From motivation to publication

Chapter 10:   Scholarly publishing: Writing a book

Chapter 11:   Research impact

Part 4:   **Doing and supervising a PhD**

Part 4 focuses on higher degrees, namely Master's and PhD. It combines the production of a graduate thesis from the perspective of both the student and the supervisor. To approach the topics together in this way was a strategic decision, based on our experience in running supervision workshops where many participants have been both students (doing their own PhDs) and supervisors (of Master's dissertations) themselves.

Chapter 12:   Embarking on a PhD: Supervisor and student perspectives

Chapter 13:   Writing a thesis: The preparatory stages

Chapter 14:   The writing process: Submission and examination.

A number of colleagues have contributed material for this book, some of them in particular areas of expertise and experience, and others in perspectives gained in the course of their overall journeys from being emerging researchers to competent, fully fledged academics. There are still others, not named, whose contributions to the ERP, either as ERP participants or as seminar and workshop presenters, have provided many of the insights communicated in the pages that follow.

There will be topics that merit more attention than they receive and others that some may consider laboured. We have aimed to achieve sufficient balance in the material for the book to serve the purposes for which it has been written: first, to inform and provide strategies for emerging researchers, creating in them a hunger to implement what they learn and to find out more for themselves; and second, to provide tools for those fulfilling mentorship roles in relation to early-career colleagues.

PART 1

WELCOME TO ACADEMIA

PART 1
WELCOME TO ACADEMIA

For most new academics, in particular those who have worked outside academia since completing their studies, the university is an unusual place. Returning as a staff member is a very different experience from being a student. While some come into academia from commerce, industry or other professions, there is another group of people who, without ever leaving university, make their way slowly up the ranks from being a student to a tutor, then perhaps a teaching assistant, and after this to a short-term teaching contact—all the while engaged in postgraduate study. So the transition to fully fledged academic staff member, when it comes, is not quite such a shock to this group.

Either way there is much to learn, not least in terms of the expectations placed on academics, and their corresponding responsibilities. Very often new staff members are not assigned mentors—people who will show them the academic ropes, spelling out those things that do not appear in the appointment letter and make little sense at the time of orientation, and which the Head of Department has forgotten to mention. Coming to grips with the university environment is usually achieved through a combination of trial and error, learning from colleagues and, over time, absorbing things by osmosis (often to the individual's cost).

Our local institutions and those of us who work in them are de facto part of the international academic community, with a set of basic, sometimes tacit, conventions that apply everywhere, creating and sustaining networks of co-operation and critique. This situation is not without problems. Many of the driving forces in academia, worldwide, have their roots in and are sustained by a Western colonial model, while higher education institutions in the 'Global South' (which includes the whole of the African continent) live with the tension created by the need to nurture a local identity with local relevance, on the one hand, and to compete globally, on the other.

Further to this is the reality of the highly differentiated institutional contexts in which academics work: the well-resourced, with adequate research funding, and the under-resourced (a particular problem in South Africa with its apartheid history and its legacy of historically disadvantaged institutions); those with a vibrant research culture and those with a more technicist approach; those where one is surrounded by research-active colleagues to 'show the ropes' and those finding themselves in a research vacuum, and so on. A limitation of this book, therefore—and especially Chapter 1—is that it cannot adequately address or reflect the conditions in which many academics find themselves.

But this does not invalidate the discussion, for its aim is to help readers understand both the *intrinsic nature* of academia, which applies no matter where one is located, and the *global research landscape* and the implications of this for the choices we make along the way.

The aim of Part 1 is to orient readers to the local, national and global academic terrain, with a particular focus on the research component of the academic portfolio.

CHAPTER 1

UNDERSTANDING THE TERRAIN

The networks of co-operation and critique that characterise the academic institutional environment are built around a number of features that are intrinsic to the terrain of academia. It is often taken for granted that the incoming generation understands this environment and knows how to function in it. But this is often not the case.

In order to set the stage for what follows in this book, at the outset we introduce these features and how they fit together, acknowledging that local realities might present a less straightforward picture than the generic one presented here. This chapter will address the following themes:

- The interplay between the core functions of the academic, with a focus on the relationship between teaching and research.
- The nature of the academic milieu, which includes the principles of academic freedom and academic citizenship, and manifests itself in:
  - peer review
  - collegiality
  - networking
  - online presence.
- Research integrity.

Core functions of the academic: Teaching, research, administration and leadership, and social responsiveness

Modern universities typically have three core functions: teaching, research and administration/leadership. In recent years social responsiveness has regained recognition as a core function.[1] Institutions differ in their use of terms to describe this function, which is most commonly associated with service of some sort that is based on, but additional to, work actually carried out in the research process. In a broad sense it refers to what is known as *engaged scholarship*. The weight given to these core functions may vary from institution to institution, and there may be opportunity for individual choice in prioritising. In many universities teaching and research are prioritised and equally weighted, and there may be a choice between administration/leadership and social responsiveness as a third category of assessment.

---

1 This marks a subtle shift from the three historic functions of universities: teaching, research and service.

The purpose of universities

A useful way to discern the relationship between the core activities is to look at why universities exist in the first place. Universities, or in some cases proto-universities, have their origins in China (third millennium BCE), Pakistan, India and Greece (first millennium BCE) and much later in Europe, where the first universities as we know them today emerged out of the learning kept alive in monasteries during the Dark Ages (fifth to tenth centuries, CE). Bologna (1088) is usually recognised as Europe's oldest university, followed by Paris (1150) and Oxford (1167).[2] In all cases they were concerned with scholarship or the promotion of learning, which in essence involves the generation, transfer and application of knowledge. The same holds true today, with this threefold dynamic being played out in a university's core functions, described above. The Latin origin of the word 'university' is: *universitas magistrorum et scholarium*, which in translation refers to a 'community of teachers and scholars'. Many of us are attracted to this idea of a community, to joining in its traditions which embrace curiosity and promote enquiry, and to sharing esteem for intellectual endeavours. This attraction translates into a range of ethical considerations that shapes the work of today's researchers and their encounters with new challenges.

The relationship between teaching and research

The relationship between teaching and research, or, to use a more contemporary term, the teaching–research nexus/interface, lies at the heart of a university. There is a substantial body of literature emanating from research in this area and grounded in varying understandings of the terms 'teaching', 'learning', 'research', and 'knowledge-production', and the relationships between them.

My own experience in working with academics is that most instinctively see research and teaching as two discrete, albeit sometimes related, activities. For some, these activities exist quite independently, research as knowledge production and teaching as knowledge transmission, and a research-active teacher is not a requirement for producing a love of learning in students. For others, teaching and research are more closely connected, forming part of the same activity. Here an assumption might be that good research produces good teaching and facilitates learning, and, conversely, that teaching undergraduate students is necessary for good research. In this view the outcomes of research provide or inform the content of teaching. This, however, is a flawed position: we all know that some of the most prolific researchers are appalling teachers, and among our best teachers are those with little or no interest in research.

---

2   www.cwrl.utexas.edu/~bump/OriginUniversities.html. Accessed 10 May 2014. There are scholars who argue that universities as we know them are uniquely European in their origin and defining characteristics.

The reality is that academic work is a more complex reality than any of these positions suggest.[3] In order to consider the relationships more meaningfully, it might be helpful to shift our attention from the *content* of research and teaching/learning to the *nature* of research and its relation to teaching and learning. A number of scholars in higher education provide insights that usefully inform this discussion.

Drawing on the theoretical positions of contemporaries, Chrissie Boughey brings teaching and research together in what she describes as the 'knowledge-making' task of all teachers within the areas in which they teach. This happens as they induct students into ways of knowledge-making that are grounded in the type of literacy that comes from apprenticeship to a particular discourse. Embedded in this understanding is the suggestion that university teachers do not teach knowledge but rather how knowledge is made.[4]

This position is supported in the work of Ernest L. Boyer, who calls for a return to an early meaning of the more inclusive term 'scholarship' as a way to move away from the teaching–research dichotomy and to bring legitimacy to the full scope of academic work. In the past, the integrity of one's scholarship was measured by the ability to think, to communicate and to learn, providing us with a useful way to understand more comprehensively the relationship between research and teaching.[5]

A third scholar, Angela Brew, makes some helpful distinctions to inform our understanding of the teaching–research relationship. She first identifies two conceptions of research:

1   *outcome-orientated* (concerned with knowledge generation and external-products; linked to the relationship between recognition and research)

2   *understanding-orientated* (internal research processes; holistic process of discovery, uncovering creating underlying meanings).

These conceptions are set alongside two models of teaching:

1   teaching as knowledge-transmission (teaching and research separate, independent from each other)

2   teaching as student-focused knowledge-production within a socio-political context.[6]

---

3   See the article by Smith, H. (2011). 'Relationships between teaching and research'. www.ucl.ac.uk/calt/support/cpd4he/resources/research_ teaching. Accessed 6 February 2014.

4   Boughey, C. (2012). 'Linking teaching and research: An alternative perspective', in *Teaching in Higher Education*, 17 (5): 629–635. Online 29 October 2012. www.dx.doi.org/10.1080/13562517.2 012.725528. Accessed 30 October 2014.

5   Boyer, E.L. (1990). 'Enlarging the perspective', in *Scholarship Reconsidered: Priorities of the Professoriate*, Ch. 2. Carnegie Foundation for the Advancement of Teaching: Special Report, 15–19.

6   Brew, A. (2003). 'Teaching and research: New relationships and their implications for inquiry-based teaching and learning in higher education', *Higher Education Research and Development*, 22 (1): 3–18.

These few perspectives confirm something crucial for every person setting out on an academic career: the relationship between teaching and research is both more complex and more important than many of us have been led to believe. It cannot be treated simplistically or dismissed as inconsequential. Contained in the sub-text of the different perspectives above is the importance of nurturing a spirit of enquiry among students that is only possible when both research and teaching are understood and practised holistically, taking into account content and process, intellectual endeavour and contextual reality.

In contrast to the past, many universities are now incorporating the teaching–research nexus into their institutional strategies. At an individual level, one way to implement this is for academics to make their research accessible to students by explaining it in a comprehensible way and gently introducing them to the idea of enquiry and, therefore, genuine learning. This might well generate in students an interest in research and in developing research skills early on, possibly leading to them sharing in research projects and even to contributing insights in the classroom, that is, to enquiry-based learning.

Common sense suggests that a healthy and productive relationship between these core functions and an expanded understanding of that relationship can only enhance the quality of knowledge production and communication in universities, to the benefit of both students and staff, and, ultimately, society as well. On the other hand, the dichotomising of teaching and research, especially at departmental level, is counter-productive at many levels, and for all.

Focusing on the *process of knowledge production* should not detract from the significance of the *research product* itself, nor should the two be mutually exclusive in teaching. But the opportunity to bridge the divide between the undergraduate teaching curriculum and the content of one's research and to invite student involvement is easier in some disciplines than others, and also in some contexts than in others. The iterative disciplines, for example, philosophy, history, literature and anthropology, where knowledge evolves and is theoretically grounded, offer greater opportunities for student involvement than disciplines grounded in experimental work. A student of history is likely to have greater opportunity to offer critical insights in a lecture than a student of anatomy, for example.

Most academics would like to teach in their areas of research interest. This lends itself to both an economic use of time and enthusiastic teaching. In reality this is seldom an option for early-career staff, but where it is possible, the opportunity should be grasped. Let us, however, consider this from the opposite perspective. Being required to teach a particular course can—surprisingly—generate a genuine interest in the area, in time becoming a serious research interest.

Another challenge faced by some junior staff members is how to manage the enormous institutional pressure to conduct research while in a departmental environment that does not value research and questions its relevance to teaching. In such a case, serious attention needs to be given to time management and careful planning.

These observations and comments do not provide answers but are designed to stimulate thought about possibilities for bringing together teaching and research, at departmental, faculty and institutional level. To consider these possibilities, some understanding of how academia works, both locally and internationally, can be useful for someone new to it. It is to this that we now turn our attention.

The nature of academia

Academia is a strange animal. It shares many features with other bodies or organisations, but its particular combination of functions and characteristics, and the weight they each bear, renders it unique. Academics of long standing tend to be blasé about their environment, forgetting that not everything is obvious to the newcomer. There are elements intrinsic to academia, the understanding of which is essential in order to become comfortably assimilated into this environment.

So, what are these? Until fairly recently there were at least three features that stood out: peer review, collegiality and networking. Now it is necessary to add another: online presence. These elements do not stand alone; they are interwoven, each sustained by the others, and there are particular ways in which they operate. Added to this is something fundamental and unique to university life and ethos, undergirding all else: the principle of *academic freedom*, which constitutes the matrix out of which universities have grown, and which needs to be held in creative tension with the other features of the environment and the challenges of the present.

If academic freedom undergirds the operation of universities, then its overseer is *academic integrity*—that is, activities carried out in an ethical manner. Many institutions now have an Office of Research Integrity. The career of a student, the granting of a degree, the reputation of an individual, a department or even a university can stand or fall on a single breach of ethical principles.

Academic freedom

Academic freedom has a long history and is not uncontested. This suggests that the principle of academic freedom, that is, the *freedom of enquiry essential to the mission of academia,* while widely embraced, is not without challenges.[7] What is academic freedom, what are its roots and why is it important?

The Dar es Salaam Declaration on Academic Freedom and Social Responsibility of Academics (1990)[8] defines academic freedom as 'the freedom of members of the

---

7   Some of these challenges, focusing mainly on the African higher education environment, are foregrounded in Ramola Ramtohul's article (2003). 'Academic freedom in a state-sponsored university: The case of the University of Mauritius, *Journal of Academic Freedom,* 3: 1–21.

8   This declaration was signed by delegates from six Tanzanian higher education institution staff associations. The full declaration, with a Preamble explaining the context that gave rise to it, is available at www1.umn.edu/humanrts/africa/DARDOK.htm. Accessed 6 August 2013.

academic community, individually or collectively, in the pursuit, development and transmission of knowledge, through research, study, discussion, documentation, production, creation, teaching, lecturing and writing'. This captures the original medieval sense of academic freedom in Europe, which was to ensure freedom of thought, ideas and expression to all those within and those visiting (passing through) universities. The concept is teased out further to include the requirement that such free pursuit of knowledge should take place without 'unreasonable interference or restriction from law, institutional regulations or public pressure'.[9]

In South Africa, Section 16 of the Constitution offers specific protection to academic freedom, despite some notable breaches in certain institutions here. But not all countries and institutions embrace the concept as comprehensively as this, making the scholarly pursuit difficult at times for academics. In many contexts universities exist and their business is carried out in the midst of social, political and economic challenges, and at times they must contend with state authoritarianism as well. There are situations in which university autonomy does not exist, where academic promotion criteria equate with those in the public service (years of service, for example), and where the state determines what research can be undertaken (and hence financed) at universities.

Having said this, it is equally true that for many African countries independence came with a determination for a particular type of academic freedom, 're-appropriating knowledge and history'.[10] While there is caution about a concept so closely linked to Europe, and while subsequent historical developments have complicated and sometimes compromised conditions at higher education institutions, it remains that the principle of academic freedom is critical for the production of the type of knowledge that will enable our continent and subcontinent to flourish. This, however, needs to be exercised within the parameters of what has been described as a complementary concept: *academic citizenship*.

For Bruce Macfarlane, academic citizenship refers to the obligations of academic staff in relation to the overlapping communities they serve: students, colleagues, institution, discipline and profession, and the public. The importance of academic citizenship, as understood alongside academic freedom, is self-explanatory: it serves an ethical function, namely to avoid using academic freedom for achieving political rather than intellectual goals. Furthermore, academic citizenship is central to the success of the university as an entity rather than as a collection of individuals set on achieving personal goals.[11]

---

9   www.britannica.com/EBchecked/topic/2591/academic-freedom. Accessed 6 August 2013.

10   Khelfaoui, H. (2009). 'The Bologna Process in Africa: Globalization or return to "colonial situation"', *Journal of Higher Education in Africa*, 7 (1&2): 23. www.codesria.org/IMG/pdf/1Introduction_Eng.pdf. Accessed 6 August 2013.

11   Macfarlane, B. (2007). 'Defining and rewarding academic citizenship: The implications for university promotion policy', *Journal of Higher Education and Policy Management*, 29 (3): 261–273. Drawing on the work of colleagues such as Schils, E. (1997). *The Calling of Education: The academic ethic and other essays in higher education*. Chicago, IL: University of Chicago Press.

UNIVERSITY OF BIRMINGHAM

BENCHMARKS FOR ACADEMIC CITIZENSHIP

MAY 2012

'Academic citizenship takes many forms and is guided by the principle of conscientious and responsible institutional involvement that extends beyond immediate colleagues, students, discipline or university to include obligations to society at large. At a formal level it involves the assumption of leadership and management at an appropriate level. At an informal level academic citizenship embraces responsibilities to colleagues, whether inside or outside the institution, such as helping, nurturing and supporting their work, especially that of younger or newer colleagues. It includes generous, mutually respectful and supportive working relationships with academic, administrative, technical and support staff. In all, the best acts of good citizenship demonstrate personal commitment towards the best interests of the institution.'[12]

Against this backdrop we turn to consider some other distinguishing features of an academic environment, beginning with *peer review*.

Peer review

Peer review may be described as evaluation of work by an individual or, more commonly, a group of people who are of similar or higher competence or ranking in the same field as the person or group producing the work.[13] Peer review may also be about the assessment of a situation by a group. At its best, peer review is primarily about quality assurance, the process aimed at maintaining or enhancing the quality of work in a particular field (academic or otherwise), and providing accurate assessment of it. It should also be about ensuring fairness.

In other words, the work or situation is subject to independent scrutiny in order to detect weaknesses or errors to which the producer/s of the work or those involved in the situation may have blind spots. Because peer review is frequently associated with a reward of one sort or another, it can be a powerful incentive to produce excellence. Conversely, peer review can also lead to disgrace, hence from a negative perspective as well it is used for moderating behaviour and performance. Peer review is present in many contexts, from children's playgrounds to the business world, but it is something associated particularly with academia.

In a work context reviewers (also sometimes referred to as referees) are usually not selected from among close colleagues or others with a special relationship to the

---

12 www.intranet.birmingham.ac.uk/hr/documents/public/pdr/academic/citizenship-benchmarks. pdf. Accessed 28 October 2014.

13 'Peer' refers to a person of equal standing. However, in the peer-review system it is usually, although not always, persons of higher rank or greater expertise that evaluate the work.

producer of the work, or from among a group who may have vested interests one way or another. The object is to obtain, as far as possible, unbiased evaluation of the piece of work or the situation under scrutiny. Reviewers of another's work are often anonymous to the producer/s of the work, and in some cases, notably in the review of written work for publication, the review is 'double blind'. That is, neither party knows the identity of the other.[14]

Up to this point the comments have been deliberately non-specific. Those with any experience of academia will immediately connect the term with the publishing process and the evaluation of other, non-textual, forms of research output. In reality, however, peer review permeates every aspect of academic life. It is going on all the time; it is built into the system. In striving for excellence, the reputation of a university stands or falls partly on the efficiency or otherwise of its various peer-review mechanisms. In Chapter 5, I shall consider in more depth peer review in publishing, but for now let us consider a number of areas in which it functions in the academy.

Procedures may differ between institutions, but the principles of academic peer review remain intact. They are put into effect every day in classes, committee meetings, review panels, conflict management situations, disciplinary hearings, research colloquia, and so on. This is not to suggest that peer review is the only or most important thing happening. It is not the end product. But, all the while, peer review is at work. It happens within institutions and across institutions. Below are a few examples of peer review in action.

Think about *conferences* and the levels of peer review operating in these.

+ First, if you intend presenting a paper at a conference you submit an abstract. On the basis of a review process your abstract will be accepted or turned down, determining whether or not your piece of work is deemed appropriate for presentation at the conference.

+ If it is accepted, the next stage is the presentation itself with questions and comments afterwards—another process of peer review, providing feedback that will, hopefully, enhance the quality of your work.

+ Once you are home, and particularly if your institution provided funding for the conference, you will incorporate any useful feedback into your paper and transform it into an article for publication, inviting further peer review.

+ Once it is published the process continues because each time your paper is read and cited, whether positively or negatively, it is effectively being reviewed by peers.

Next, I consider *funding applications,* using an illustration from my own institution. Early-career staff members who participate in our Emerging Researcher Programme are eligible to apply for specially designated research development grants. The most obvious

---

14   Some of this material is sourced from The Linux Information Project. www.linfo.org/peer_review.html. Accessed 17 April 2013.

goal of the application process is to enable a cohort of inexperienced academics to obtain the funding necessary to make progress with their research. But the application process itself is used to build research capacity.

- ◆ Applicants are invited to submit draft proposals for pre-submission review. Comments and suggestions for improvement are provided and implemented.
- ◆ Final drafts are submitted and scrutinised by a review panel, who, in making awards, sometimes request further refinement before final approval of the grant.

This whole peer-review process is geared towards habitual excellence in the quality of proposals produced by the academics.

The peer-review process is not without problems; it is not a perfect system. Nowhere is this more evident than in the academic publishing world, where it is easily abused to promote particular individuals, groups or causes. It is also manipulated to promote business interests of the monopolies controlling academic publishing, worldwide. The problems (and temptations) of peer review manifest themselves at a local level as well: biased committee members, reviewers with a personal grudge against a grant applicant, ideological conflicts that cloud scientific merit, and incestuous journal boards, to name but a few.

The reality is—and this is the refrain—that, despite its faults, *peer review is the best system we have* to promote fairness, opportunity, efficiency and excellence in the academy, and this has implications for everyone. The responsibility of each academic is to play her or his part in ensuring that the peer-review system works as effectively as possible, and this means playing a part in the various review processes, both within and beyond one's own university. Serving terms on institutional committees and boards is one of the most important, and certainly the most immediate, examples of participation in peer review. Other examples are the reviewing of articles for journals and acting as an external examiner of dissertations, both of which are closely related to a second hallmark of the academic environment: *collegiality*.

Collegiality

When one agrees to examine an 80 000-word PhD thesis from an unknown student in a foreign country, it is not because of what it pays, nor because one has spare time or expects to derive much benefit from the task. The same applies to reviewing articles for a journal. And when a colleague goes on sabbatical and asks you to assume temporary responsibility for supervising a graduate student, you agree despite already having more dissertation students than you can manage. Why do academics do this? The answer is at least partially contained in the word 'collegiality'.

Academia is built on a creative blend of collaborative teamwork and independent investigation, where mutual respect between colleagues is paramount. It is this combination that defines the term collegiality and leads to the suggestion that 'A campus culture that values collegiality and civility is among the most important contributions a university can make'.[15] Collegiality creates an environment conducive to successful execution of the core academic functions identified earlier: teaching, research, administration and service (social responsiveness), as well as to the allied professional and supportive functions in a university, and effective institutional leadership.

The concept of collegiality goes back at least to Roman times and has always been associated with shared governance in contrast to hierarchical managerialism (frequently more effective in decision-making but less democratic). From the perspective of a new academic staff member, the issue of shared governance is significant, taking us back to each individual's responsibility to participate, as appropriate, in the committees and on boards and panels that reflect the devolved and democratic nature of leadership in a well-functioning university. It would be a mistake, however, to give the impression that in contemporary institutions 'hierarchical managerialism' is not a threat. Sadly, the contrary holds true as shifts in this direction are the reality of modern universities *at a cost to collegialism*.

New academics need to understand the values that are threatened by these shifts, and use their academic freedom to protect them, where necessary. A unique characteristic of universities—closely related to shared governance and academic freedom—is that they are among the only remaining places where people can hold and share divergent ideas and thoughts.[16] This is where collegiality is crucial, allowing for a respectful yet robust exchange of ideas, rigorous debate and constructive conflict.

There are, of course, certain dangers inherent in an operation heavily dependent on collegiality. In some circumstances the idea of collegiality lends itself to the exclusion of people on the basis of differences from the perceived norm, so that those invited to serve on a committee, for example, are restricted to individuals who will not 'rock the boat'. Linked to this is the danger of collegiality being identified with blind loyalty, where a colleague is protected or defended regardless of the situation under scrutiny. Another danger lies in confusing collegiality with the trio of enthusiasm, dedication to the task and fostering harmony—forgetting that free thought, conflicting ideas and idiosyncratic behaviour belong to the terrain of academia. Succumbing to these dangers, among other consequences, jeopardises the principle of academic freedom.

Collegiality in academia is not limited to relationships within an institution. As with peer review, it crosses institutions, countries and continents. It is one of the reasons why a department will agree to host a visiting academic; it is what makes international intellectual debate possible; and—to return to the point at which we started—it is the reason

---

15   Cipriano, R.E. (2012). 'Faculty collegiality as a synergistic agent', *Faculty Focus*, 15 August. See also Bart, M. (2013). 'To promote a congenial workplace, invest in people', *Faculty Focus*, 5 October. www.facultyfocus.com/articles/academic-leadership. Both accessed 2 May 2013.
16   Cipriano, 'Faculty collegiality as a synergistic agent'.

we agree to review articles or externally examine dissertations. And it works both ways: collegiality breeds reciprocity. This leads into a third and critical characteristic of academic life, dreaded by some and warmly embraced by others: *networking*.

Networking

The mention of academic networking tends to divide people into two groups: the ones whose faces light up at the news that effective networking is critical to academic success and those whose countenances contort into a look of undisguised horror. There are problems with both extremes. For the former, networking can become obsessive and all-consuming, crowding out actual research productivity and effective teaching in the pursuit of establishing the relationships that are going to make it all possible. Among the latter are those whose academic careers are destined to remain in the starting blocks because they lack the freshness that comes with the flow and exchange of scholarly ideas and experiences.

The reality is that while networking is second nature to some, it is extraordinarily difficult for others. Accepting that these poles exist, it remains true that well-managed networking is critical to success in academia, and certainly to the development, over time, of a robust research profile featuring mutually productive research collaborations. In this way networking affects not only individuals but can also have a positive and cumulative impact on institutions.

What is academic networking? It is something closely aligned with both collegiality and peer review and can be described as 'the use of both formal and informal connections between groups of colleagues to develop your career'.[17]

- These connections may be local (within an institution or even a faculty) or more distant (national or international).
- They may venture beyond academia to facilitate partnerships—with industry, for example.
- Networking is part of the groundwork underlying professional relationships that operate to the mutual benefit of the parties concerned, and where reciprocity is a key feature.
- Academic partnerships become more complex in their nature and scope at a senior level, but the skills that make them possible have been honed over the years and most often began with an individual taking the small step of making contact with someone they did not know before.

Academic networking, then, is a skill or craft that needs to be developed and honed no matter where one is situated on the 'natural networker' spectrum. It makes sense,

---

17 Armstrong, C. (2007). *How to Develop Successful Networking Skills in Academia*. www.jobs.ac.uk/careers-advice/working-in-higher-education/573/how-todevelop-successful-networking-skills-in-academia. Accessed 6 May 2013.

therefore, to identify a colleague who does it well—your PhD supervisor might be a good place to begin—and to note their strategies and ask for advice.

Effective networking cannot simply be left to chance. Some people struggle with this idea because they are concerned that strategising for the establishment of academic networks seems unethical. The idea of planned encounters and conversations at conferences, having worked out which buttons to press in order to evoke a positive response from an individual, and of having a private longer-term agenda … all sound deceptive and manipulative. But within academia itself it is not considered so. As with peer review and collegiality, it is the way in which the system works, and works well. Everyone does it. Everyone *needs to* do it. Networking has evolved in the academic world as one of the cornerstones of effective knowledge production, transmission and application. In its purest form it is not self-seeking and it is reciprocal, bringing about greater good than individual effort can provide. It makes knowledge production a community endeavour in which all stand to benefit and nobody should stand to lose.

Have clarified this, let us consider some of the networking opportunities available to academics and the conditions that make them fruitful. Most contemporary networking opportunities can be broadly divided into two categories: face-to-face and electronic. They are equally important and frequently work together. However, electronic networking is becoming increasingly common and complicated, and this is addressed separately in the following section, where I consider our online presence.

Conferences present unique opportunities for networking. One small, tentative approach at a conference can, in time, snowball into a fruitful, high-level collaboration involving academic exchanges, visiting scholars, postgraduate students and international agreements. Networking begins small and spreads. It is in its nature to do so. It may very well begin with a conversation and listening to each other's presentations that leads to a joint paper and then to a research visit to plan a collaborative project. And so it goes on ...

Among the strategies for effective networking are the importance of planning ahead and following up. Potential networking opportunities should be built into short- and medium-term research plans (Chapter 4). Consider the following scenario: a visiting academic is to spend part of her sabbatical based in your department, so you find out as much as you can about her in advance. You may discover that her research is relevant to your own and you might want to make prior contact with her in anticipation of her visit. This is the type of forward planning that bears fruit.

There is no substitute for face-to-face encounters, but afterwards details of the conversations can become blurred. As soon as possible, you should record the main points of each conversation and follow up with an email saying how good it was to meet, how useful you found their paper, insights, etc. and then allude to points raised in the conversation, particularly in terms of potential co-operation. Not all networking encounters are worth pursuing and some networks, which you may think are well established and show promise, come to an abrupt end. Do not be discouraged. This belongs to the terrain, and such experiences will be less frequent as you gain experience and develop skills in discernment.

There are many other opportunities for networking besides conferences. The point in exploiting them is to *get yourself on the research radar screen*, both nationally and internationally. This leads to things like becoming aware of funding opportunities; building up a reservoir of potential examiners for your students; receiving invitations to give lectures or present at conferences; becoming involved in collaborative research projects; and so on.

For now, as an early-career academic, these simple principles of networking may be useful: be strategic, be discerning, be timely and be generous!

PERSPECTIVE

DOING RESEARCH AND BEING AN ACADEMIC AT UCT

I joined UCT in January 2005 as a lecturer in the Commercial Law department. In that same year I registered as a doctoral candidate, with the intention of completing a draft thesis that I had begun working on at another institution. I began teaching Company Law to students in the Commerce Faculty—my first experience of 'service course' teaching. In May 2005, our second son was born. Looking back, I see how, to use a cliché, 'the rubber really hit the road' that year. I was a full-time member of staff, juggling teaching, doctoral research, a move to a new city and job, as well as a baby! As the years passed, my teaching diversified and now includes LLB and LLM teaching, as well as postgraduate research supervision.

Working with my new supervisor at UCT, who took early retirement and was replaced by another, I completely recast my doctoral thesis and I finally completed it in 2011. At the same time, I continued to research beyond my doctorate and publish articles and book chapters and attend conferences in South Africa and abroad. I found being a part-time doctoral candidate extremely pressurised as I had my other research and teaching to contend with at the same time. I relied extensively on UCT's formal support structures and participated in both the New Academic Practitioners' Programme (NAPP) and the Emerging Researchers' Programme (ERP). In addition, I did the Short Course on Teaching offered by CHED. I found these programmes especially useful as they provided information, which a new academic is expected to know—perhaps 'by osmosis'.

I read something online about 'taking your mentors where you find them'. The piece emphasised that the classic model of a formalised mentorship scheme—where one was allocated a mentor to whom one looked for extensive all-encompassing guidance—was over-rated. Often these relationships faltered for various reasons. It urged readers to appreciate mentors for a reason or a season; one could have a once-off conversation with a colleague on a particular issue, teaching strategies perhaps (a mentor for a reason), or have short-term support from a colleague on a particular aspect such as authoring a book chapter (a mentor for a season). I took the author's advice and took my mentors where and as I found them. For example, a chance meeting in the tearoom with a colleague led to a discussion of a substantive legal issue that had been bothering me and was the spark for a journal paper.

Peer support has also been invaluable. Several years into my doctoral research, two colleagues and I began exchanging thesis chapters, reading them and meeting to discuss them. It didn't matter that our fields were disparate (one was writing on Tax Law, the other on Muslim Personal Law and fundamental freedoms, while I was writing on Intellectual Property Law). We read each other's work for logic and coherence. The opportunity to explain and defend our positions to each other was very useful. In many instances I also discussed my work and writing with colleagues outside my faculty.

My involvement in international research projects has meant that I belong to a network of like-minded scholars who have been an amazing support and inspiration. These experiences have shown me that, to cannibalise another cliché, it takes a scholarly community to make an academic. If I can give any advice to anyone else it is this: *take your mentors where and as you find them, don't overlook your peers and don't confine yourself to your faculty or university*.

Caroline Ncube

I move on now to discuss electronic networking, its scope and the importance of managing your 'online presence' as an academic.

Online presence: A new dimension[18]

Every academic develops a professional persona as their reputation grows. What that persona looks like is determined by the nature, quality and expression of the academic work.

How the work and the researcher appear in the world is relevant, especially now that a new dimension to a professional existence in the academic enterprise is your representation online. This is inescapable because of the sobering reality that everyone already has a presence online, whether you are conscious of it or not, through online activities and through the actions of others. The trace of your online activities is sometimes called a *digital shadow* or your digital ghost. You cannot do much about this shadow as you do not control it, but you can create for yourself a *digital footprint* that you can control.

---

18   Prepared by Laura Czerniewicz.

Academics need to shape and imprint a digital footprint in a form over which they themselves have influence.

How can academics shape their online presence? There is very little to be done about negative representations online (online shadow) other than to ensure that the positive representations are overwhelming.

A watchful brief is essential, and not a form of vanity. Search engine alerts to your name and academic outputs are a minimum so that you are always aware of what is out there in the digital space. Keeping an eye on how your work is being used or saved on social media spaces (such as Mendeley or Twitter) is important too. Ensuring a unique name may be necessary, through the inclusion of a middle name, or by using initials only, for example.

Every academic needs an online profile, and you need to make a decision as to which is your main profile, that is, where it is located, whether it be the profile on the university departmental website or a profile on a general social media site (such as LinkedIn) or an academic-oriented social media site (such as academia.edu). It is difficult to keep several profiles up to date so one profile can be selected for regular updating. It is a good idea to be virtually present on multiple sites, with a link provided to the most up-to-date profile. In addition, every academic should have a Google Scholar profile, as this is where citations are collected and can be easily viewed. Some promotional processes require a Google Scholar profile to demonstrate citations.

While presence as an individual is a good idea, the online availability of all your scholarship is essential. Researchers are known to search largely online, and expect to be able to access the object itself. It is up to individual academics to ensure that their work is made available online. It can be helpful to get assistance from librarians or other professionals to ensure that objects are properly described and curated, thus ensuring discoverability by digital searches.

Social media offer opportunities for extending online presence at every stage of the research process. Online references can be saved on book marking sites (such as Delicious and CiteULike), and individuals can become known as collectors of useful links in particular subject areas. Platforms such as Mendeley and Zotero enable comments and discussions as well as curation of content. Data can be shared. Conversations about links happen on sites such as Twitter and Facebook, where retweeting and commenting on others leads to reciprocity and engagement with scholars with shared interests. And for those who are able to find a 'voice', blogging is an excellent way to create a presence as an academic and a public intellectual. These activities all take time, and you need to make decisions about where to focus your energy because no one can do it all. Yet, investment in your online presence is essential.

While many people will be familiar with the opportunities and challenges posed by the Internet, other readers will not. In addition, it cannot be presumed that all readers of this book have equal access to the electronic media. This is where university libraries play a crucial role. Indeed, every academic, regardless of experience or location, should acquaint her- or himself with the range of services provided by the university library. (See also Chapter 4: Research information and its management.)

Easy access to information facilitated by the electronic media, the equal ease with which this information, not least an individual's online presence, can be manipulated and misused, points to the next topic for consideration: integrity in research.

Research integrity[19]

The explosion of new challenges for academics—whether, for example, to brand your own mind and body through social media, or to be branded by your institution of employment—brings new light to longstanding, important conditions of possibility for academic success: the conditions of intellectual integrity and ethics.

The field of research integrity is a broad and complicated one. It concerns responsibility and care for the relationships on which the discovery and dissemination of knowledge depends, and the resonance between the conduct of research and the contexts in which research takes place and/or has effect. The topic has, in recent years, become regarded as increasingly important and serious. Scholars today have the resources of institutional oversight committees, training, policies, professional associations with the guidance afforded by them, and a growing professional class of administrators to support research endeavours. Until relatively recently, these resources did not exist in such recognised and accessible forms. When American anthropologist Franz Boas, for example, discovered evidence that, during World War I, four American anthropologists had used their status as academics for espionage in Central America, he wrote a public letter, published in *The Nation*, in which he declared that the four anthropologists had compromised their own integrity and that of the nascent scientific field of cultural anthropology itself.[20]

In response, the American Anthropological Association (AAA)—itself heavily influenced by anthropologists who worked within the US federal government—censured Boas. By the time the censure was rescinded by the AAA in 2005, more than one generation of social scientists had been trained to understand that a lack of forthrightness in the self-positioning of a researcher is a form of deception and is, with few exceptions, unacceptable. The world has changed, and normative expectations for academic research have been enhanced by it. Common principles documented in sources, including the

19 Prepared by Robert McLaughlin.
20 Boas, F. (1919). 'Scientists as spies', *The Nation*, 797, 19 December.

Belmont Report, Helsinki Declaration and, more recently, the Singapore Statement and the Montreal Statement, attest to enhanced consciousness of ethical considerations and specific techniques by which to ensure the appropriateness of your research conduct.[21]

Even more broadly, the International Covenant on Economic, Social and Cultural Rights, promulgated in 1966, declares the right of *everyone*:

◆ to take part in cultural life

◆ to enjoy the benefits of scientific progress and its applications

◆ to benefit from the protection of moral and material interests resulting from any scientific, literary or artistic production of which she or he is the author.[22]

Despite the potential conflicts between culture and science, this expression of the rights to culture and science within the same provision of the Covenant suggests an embeddedness of scholarship within human communities. These may be diverse, varied, large or small, and may exist in the relationships on which the discovery and dissemination of knowledge depends. Against this background, most scholars benefit from the relatively discrete classifications of subtopics associated with research integrity. These include:

◆ the protection of human subjects and research participants

◆ the ethical treatment of animals used in research

◆ the absence of fraud, falsification, plagiarism, misrepresentation of the replication of one's own work as 'original', and misappropriation

◆ the identification and management of both financial and other conflicts of interest that might influence scholarly work.

New areas of concern include bio-safety and environmental impacts of research. Each of these areas relates to particular ethical considerations and debates, and scholars bear a responsibility to be informed about how their work is to be structured in relation to these considerations.

Unfortunately, too many young scholars experience research integrity procedures by way of anxiety about senior colleagues sitting in closed-door meetings to stand in harsh judgement of early, best efforts at the crafting of a grant application, protocol or manuscript.

---

21 Belmont Report. (1979). www.hhs.gov/ohrp/humansubjects/guidance/belmont.html; Helsinki Declaration. (1964, amended 1975, 1983, 1989, 1996, 2000, 2002, 2004 and 2008). www. wma.net/en/30publications/10policies/b3/. Singapore Statement on Research Integrity. (2010). www.singaporestatement.org/statement.html; Montreal Statement on Research Integrity in Cross-Boundary Research Collaborations. (2013) www.wcri2013.org/Montreal_Statement_e. shtml.

22 UN General Assembly, *International Covenant of Social, Economic, and Cultural Rights*, Art. 15, Section 1, adopted and opened for signature, ratification and accession by UN General Assembly Resolution 2200A (XXI), 16 December 1966, reproduced in: Center for the Study of Human Rights. (1994). *Twenty-Five Human Rights Documents*. New York: Columbia University Press.

In fact, such committees tend to attract champions of research, individuals who become advocates for the projects they review, even if they observe small grammatical errors, offer critiques and demand modifications. They serve because they believe in research and seek to approve the best protocols that can be written, both for the purposes of the discovery and dissemination of knowledge, and for the ethical posture of research in their chosen fields of expertise. Committee members are, in most cases, fellow researchers.

At present, the field of research integrity is dominated by questions including the following:

- Will the identifiability (or re-identifiability) of genomic data determine the use of these data?
- How does one assess the moral standing of animals?
- What does authorship mean in an era of 'Big Science' in which hundreds of investigators collaborate in streams of incremental findings?
- How does one work with novel funding sources and private interests (including the prospective financial interests of corporations, foundations, and individuals) in terms of managing actual and potential conflicts?
- How does one maintain intellectual independence against such powers as subpoena, institutional research agendas, and new burdens like blogging about one's area of expertise?

The issues present both theoretical and practical challenges and they relate to methods and to ethics simultaneously. Where the issues blur traditional black-and-white distinctions between these things, they beg for a new paradigm in which scholars find energy, insight and nuance in the shifting grey margins that define research.

Universities and the intellectual enterprise[23]

I have described some of the interplaying features of an academic environment. Together these comprise the milieu that has grown up to nourish the fundamental task of a university: the intellectual enterprise. This plays itself out in a variety of ways in different disciplines and different contexts, each facing ever more complicated challenges, particularly in terms of relevance to society. But it is the pursuit and production of knowledge in an intellectual community that remains the central and distinguishing feature of a university. The success of this endeavour is premised on a number of features, which include acknowledgement of the following:

- The value of the intellectual community as being one that is non-hierarchical, accommodates independence and even unruliness, but is also energising and collegial, offering support as well as critique.

---

23   This section draws on a presentation by Deborah Posel.

- The value of confronting big questions, looking beyond the minutiae of individual research projects to keep an eye on the broader context or big picture.

- The creative power that exists in unsettling things: in questioning them and making the familiar strange, in such a way that we are forced to revisit our assumptions and look for solutions in a broader sphere. In an institution this generates and sustains, among both staff and students, the spirit of enquiry referred to earlier.

Let us open up this idea of the intellectual enterprise. What is it that excites academics? The answer is simple: playing with ideas, and revitalising them in a way that brings something new and relevant. This is the ground on which academic futures are built. But we need to recognise and hold in tension two propositions:

1   Academics are a particular kind of people: free-thinking; not compliant; independent; going down routes that are not clearly mapped out and doing so with a high degree of personal autonomy.[24]

2   At the same time the future of the university in the world lies in its connection with others and responsibility towards them. The university does not exist for itself. This applies across the entire spectrum of knowledge: from technologies to new forms of management, from history to development of student curricula, and so on.

The tension between these two propositions is necessary and can be creative. It avoids unhelpful excesses in either one, and requires intellectual and not bureaucratic ways of bringing academics together for effective collaboration that can have real impact.

Conclusion

In this chapter I have considered the immediate environment in which the academic task—for current purposes, notably research—is executed. The focus, therefore, has been on the individual academic's place in an institution and as part of the wider academic community. In Chapter 2 we broaden our focus on academia to the international higher education landscape.

---

24   Quantum physics, after all, suggests that discovery and newness are dependent on a measure of unpredictability and chaos.

THE RESEARCH LANDSCAPE

INTERNATIONALISATION, QUALITY ASSURANCE AND BENCHMARKING

The new generation of academics finds itself in a mutating and potentially bewilder-ing environment. Much of what emerging researchers do will be closely linked to the local situation—their institutions, projects, immediate aspirations and challenges. But they cannot avoid an encounter with the rapidly changing nature and increasing com-plexity of the wider environment in which they work, a leading feature of which is the phenomenon known as *internationalisation*.

This is particularly so for those of us in the Global South, not least in Africa, where universities are trying to balance multiple demands, which include the need to address 'new challenges of knowledge production and dissemination, of Africanising global scholarship and globalising African scholarship'.[1] Because of the powerful impact of knowledge production and flow in the Global North, and how it affects internationalisa-tion, new researchers need to understand the contribution they can and should make from the perspective of the South to knowledge production in the 'global village'. (For further discussion on North–South perspectives see Chapter 3, International research collaboration from an African Perspective, page 55.)

Closely linked to internationalisation is the place that *quality assurance and bench-marking* now have in higher education. In order to attract funding and to be both com-petitive and relevant, institutions and individual academics are required to comply with high standards of competency and levels of collaboration as international benchmarking and relevance measures are applied.

The need for such global competitiveness filters down to early-career academics in a number of ways: increased pressure to obtain PhDs; the unrelenting drive not simply to publish but to publish in the 'right places', that is, in highly esteemed, sought-after journals; meeting the requirements of potential funders, whose quality assurance and research impact demands are tightening; and the need for meaningful exposure to the international research community. Along with this come challenges to conventional ways of measuring research quality and impact.

It is important that we do not speak about internationalisation uncritically. We will see, for instance, how some of the criteria for playing competitively in the global game,

---

1   Zeleza, P.T. & Olukoshi, A. (2004). Prelude to *African Universities in the Twenty-first Century,* Vol. 1: *Liberalisation and Internationalisation*. Dakar: CODESRIA.

(recruiting and nurturing top students, for instance) could challenge local priorities, for example, in terms of South Africa's transformation and development agenda. Such a situation complicates a university's striving for both global competitiveness and local relevance.

However, the flourishing of our universities is contingent on locating ourselves favourably within the global environment, so we need to find ways to work constructively with the dialectic we face. The agenda of this chapter, therefore, is to familiarise the reader with the current international research environment and how this relates to the Global South, and then to introduce a benchmarking strategy employed in South Africa in the form of its research rating system, to keep the national research endeavour at an internationally competitive level. The chapter ends with suggestions as to how some of the imperatives identified in this conversation might be fruitfully adapted to serve the individual research agendas of emerging researchers.

The international research landscape[2]

Phrases such as the 'knowledge economy', 'internationalisation' and 'global competitiveness' abound in the literature on higher education. They represent dynamics that we cannot dismiss and are not unambiguously positive, but which we can seek to understand and employ to our advantage. What lies behind these thrusts in the context of the modern university?

Evolving functions of universities

On one level the perceived functions of universities are contextually determined. They might differ, for example, depending on whether one is in Africa or North America, or on an individual's situation in either of these contexts. On another level, functions will be identified in terms of the personal agendas and resources of staff and students:

- where and what you want to study
- where you want to work
- what resources are available to you
- how you conceive of your intellectual home.

These are important issues in affecting choices made by academics. But as local dynamics they are, nevertheless, caught up in a global higher education environment characterised in part by the evolving functions of universities, and this involves de facto every academic.

Despite a much older history of universities outside of Europe (noted in Chapter 1), it is the European model, notably that which began in the late nineteenth century, that has shaped the higher education environment which dominates globally today. The

---

2   This section was prepared by Marilet Sienaert and Lyn Holness.

model itself goes back to the medieval university and encapsulates certain core functions and values, namely the training of professionals and general education for all (Latin: *studium generale*), aimed at preserving and ordering knowledge. In the late nineteenth and early twentieth centuries the natural sciences, in which great strides had been made from the sixteenth to eighteenth centuries, were brought into universities, where they assumed and have maintained a dominant position into the twenty-first century.

In contrast to earlier visions, which focused on knowledge production for the sake of knowledge, universities are now faced with so many competing demands that they run the risk of becoming overloaded with multiple missions.[3] They have to produce new knowledge and train students, but they are also held accountable for their responsiveness to local, national and global challenges. Universities are therefore charged more than ever before with community needs and social expectations (but not necessarily greater resources), while worldwide there is a risk of universities becoming overwhelmingly directed by imperatives of the state, not least in Africa. The quest for internationalisation is often in binary opposition to the demand for local responsiveness and for locally grounded knowledge production, which compounds the challenge, particularly for institutions in the Global South:

Advancing the knowledge project from a southern perspective involves grasping the opportunities provided by globalisation whilst simultaneously breaking new conceptual ground.[4]

Internationalisation

Internationalisation, while it may be a contemporary term, in fact has a long history in universities. A particular form of it was operational in the 'settler universities' established under British colonialism in Australia, New Zealand, Canada and South Africa. Its impulse came from a mix of colonial expansionism and revolutions in transport and communication, both of which facilitated links with 'universal' learning. One reflection of this was the introduction of science, law, medicine and engineering into curricula, and the admission of women.[5]

Internationalisation is therefore not new. It is its current form, the impulses behind it and the far-reaching implications of it that are new. Although scholars are not completely agreed on the meaning of internationalisation, the term is used here in the broad contemporary sense of *the practice of pursuing knowledge and delivering learning in the context of a globalised world*. It is the inevitable result of a number of factors:

---

3   Michael Gallagher, Executive Director, Group of 8, Australia.
4   Kotecha, P. (2012). 'Introduction: Making internationalisation work for higher education in southern Africa', *Internationalisation in Higher Education: Perspectives from the Global South*, SARUA Leadership Dialogue Series, 4 (2): 2.
5   Pietsch, T. (2013). 'Academic networks, internationalisation and empire', *ACU Bulletin*, 179, June: 18 & 19. See also Pietsch, T. (2013). *Empire of Scholars: Universities, networks and the British academic world, 1850–1939*. Manchester: Manchester University Press.

◆ increasing costs of research

◆ pressure from governments for research that produces 'other public goods' in addition to good scholarship

◆ new technologies and advances in communications.

From a southern perspective, internationalisation has understandably been met with a measure of scepticism, but this new situation is here to stay and the challenge, suggests Piyushi Kotecha, is for us to shape an international agenda rather than grasping at ad hoc opportunities identified by countries and institutions in the North.[6]

Internationalisation is having a number of effects, many of them positive and others less so:

◆ Universities have been *forced out of their ivory towers*, so that research is becoming more closely tied to the needs of society rather than being the private property of the intellectual. Reflecting the call of the early twentieth-century visionary, Richard Bourne, universities need to be 'thoroughly re-imagined'.[7]

◆ The last century has seen a move in research *away from discipline-based questions to focus on complex problems* that require input from a broad range of disciplinary backgrounds. This will hopefully issue in more comprehensive solutions in critical areas such as climate change, food production and security, conflict and violence, and health, where research will have a tangible impact. Such transdisciplinary solutions, increasingly *reflected in the requirements of funders*, require a move beyond existing paradigms with universities, to remain competitive, becoming more flexible in terms of their current—mostly disciplinary—structures and their rigid operational practices.

NOTE

There is an important caveat here. New academics should not overlook the fact that fruitful collaborative research that addresses complex problems is contingent on the participation of individuals well-rooted in discrete disciplines, and who have honed areas of expertise. It is the experience and skills accruing from this that will in time contribute to the complex solutions to the equally complex problems being addressed in collaborative research.

◆ The new order requires a *rethinking of staff conditions*. This means a change from tenured positions in one institution to 'models of life-long learning and

---

6 See Kotecha, 'Making internationalisation work', 3. See also in the same volume, Zeleza, P.T. (2012). 'Internationalisation in higher education: Opportunities and challenges for the Knowledge Project in the Global South', 18.

7 Gibbons, M. (2013). 'Change and reflection', *ACU Bulletin*, 179: 3.

adaptation as the most competent and flexible individuals move from one research environment to another'.[8]

This point requires further unpacking. There are many who consider this trend to reflect a neoliberal university model which, on careful reflection, effectually disadvantages many academics. For example, 2014 statistics show that in South African universities more than half the academics were not permanently employed. Whatever other reasons exist for this situation, it is a cost-cutting measure, which ultimately affects both job security and knowledge production.

* Internationalisation poses a *challenge to university management* where traditional structures of *discipline-based research and peer review are no longer adequate* for the management and review of interdisciplinary work carried out on the edges of established disciplines, and where the nature, complexity and impact of the work may require high-level monitoring.

* *Staff and student mobility* is another feature of the new situation, where it has become an educational imperative to prepare students and staff for these new realities. This includes introducing graduates to a global community of scholars in their field and inserting them into well-informed networks that will strengthen their chances of success.

In this respect it is interesting to follow the response of African universities to the challenge of internationalisation. Reporting on the 2011 conference of the African Network for Internationalisation of Education (ANIE), James Otieno Jowi notes the aim of the meeting: *for African universities to reposition themselves to respond to internationalisation and to identify areas that require support in order to benefit from internationalisation.* Going back several years, the conference noted and endorsed African universities' initial response to the challenges of globalisation, namely to begin with intra-African internationalisation in order to increase student and staff mobility within Africa and to enable African universities to develop a common framework for engaging with other parts of the world.[9] This requires the forging of 'stronger intra-regional links, South–South co-operation, and connections with the African diaspora in the North'.[10] The intra-African initiative issued in a number of partnerships, among which are the successful USHEPiA programme and the more recent EU-sponsored ACP programme, ARISE.[11]

The principles of the Bologna Process, initially regarded with reservation by some in the Global South, have played their part on the African continent in stimulating

8   Gibbons, 'Change and reflection', 3.

9   Jowi, J.O. (2011). Report on ANIE conference: 'Africa: Universities rethink internationalisation', *University World News*, 86, 10 November.

10   Zeleza, P.T. (2012). 'Internationalisation in higher education', 19.

11   USHEPiA = University Science, Humanities and Engineering Partnerships in Africa; ARISE = Africa Regional International Staff/Student Exchange.

greater attention to developing regional higher education spaces with goals and strategies consistent with 'cultural, historical, political and economic contexts all with their own higher education priorities'.[12]

These global trends are having an impact in other ways too: increasing competition, including for talent (which for universities means good staff and students) and for access to resources for research; an increased awareness of public accountability, in turn leading to a renewed focus on value for money and quality control, emphasising the importance of quality assurance; and a rethinking of practices in higher education, in turn opening the way for effective benchmarking against peers.

Among the most significant outcomes of these international trends has been the development and increasing influence of the university rankings system(s).

University rankings

Some readers may be unfamiliar with the term 'rankings'. The growing focus on quality control in higher education has inevitably resulted in universities measuring their performance against that of others. Such benchmarking against peers led to international comparisons as the obvious next step. Out of this were born a number of university rankings systems. Beginning in Shanghai, China, in 2003 as a means to assess national progress against global benchmarks (specifically in the hard sciences), there are now three main rankings systems:

1 Shanghai system (also known as the Academic Ranking of World Universities [ARWU] and based at the University of Shanghai Jiao Tong's Centre for World Class Universities)

2 Times Higher Education World University Rankings (powered by Thomson Reuters)

3 QS World University Rankings.

These systems gauge university performance across a university's core functions, each according to the system's own set of carefully selected and calibrated criteria.

While some institutions, notably (although not exclusively) those in the Global North, fit neatly into the ranking system(s) and consequently score highly, in many other cases ranking has effectively, in terms of criteria, led to apples being compared to pears. The rankings are perceived as skewed in favour of some countries, institutions and disciplines, and to the disadvantage of others, namely, those in contexts of developmental, social and economic challenges and those facing the need for historical redress in terms of knowledge and knowledge production.

The primary critique of ranking systems from the perspective of the South, and notably South Africa, is that they ignore and thereby reduce focus on the university as a space for transformation. While the social justice and transformation project underpins

---

12   Background document to call for papers for the 5th ANIE Annual Conference, Addis Ababa, October 2013.

most higher education policy in South Africa, it is entirely absent from ranking processes, so that a focus on improving rankings subtly forces a shift in focus from the university as a public good.

Among other criticisms levelled against the rankings systems are the following:

◆ The Shanghai system, in particular, is focused on the 'heavy sciences', favours research over teaching and learning, and gives inordinate recognition to Nobel Prizes.

◆ The Times Higher Education and QS systems tend to favour Anglo-Saxon institutions, with the great majority of top rankings coming from the US and the UK.

Having acknowledged this, it is nevertheless possible to put a positive spin on the rankings and other benchmarking and quality assurance mechanisms by drawing selectively and sensibly from their practices to serve as a catalyst for self-evaluation, self-reflection and strategic planning—in other words, to focus on the criteria for measurement rather than on the tool itself.

Bibliometric analysis

Internationalisation has also manifested itself in the increasing sophistication of systems of bibliometric analysis. An example is *Scopus*, the world's largest abstract and citation database of peer-reviewed literature, featuring smart tools to track, analyse and visualise research happening worldwide. Scopus is thus able to deliver a comprehensive overview of research across a spectrum of disciplines, much of it collaborative and inter-disciplinary. Thomson Reuters' *Web of Science*, another powerful research information and bibliometric tool, is similarly engaged in measuring research, especially trans-disciplinary research, for its distribution, output and impact.

This is a contested area and is considered by some to have become an obsession in recent years. As commercial ventures, access via these companies to bibliometric information requires an enormous financial outlay by institutions. Despite valid criticism, however, these analyses have many positive effects:

◆ They are able to increase the visibility and impact of research publications co-authored with international partners, which, in turn, increases the likely application in society of research findings.

◆ They provide a means to pinpoint where, across the globe, specific research collaborations are in place.

◆ Bibliometric analysis also increases the chances of your work having an impact on the less tangible world of ideas.

Bibliometrics has, in addition to managing research information, played a leading role in the assessment of research. Measures such as impact factor have—in a process that is not always transparent—been the principle tools to assess the value and impact of research. Although long criticised for its inadequacies,[13] not least as a gauge for research in law, the humanities and social sciences, it (together with more recent measures such as the h-index) has long been widely accepted as normative in science.

The situation is changing, as demonstrated quite dramatically by the launch in 2013 of the San Francisco Declaration on Research Assessment,[14] emerging from within the scientific community itself and challenging the adequacy of impact Factor and other stand-alone measures to assess the value of research.[15] This demonstrates another dimension of change in the international research environment: the call, not to replace existing metrics, but to:

◆ Complement them with other measures that accommodate other types of output.

◆ Assess research on its own merits rather than on the basis of the journal in which it is published.

◆ Capitalise on the opportunities provided by online publications (relaxing various limitations routinely placed on conventional journal articles).

International partnerships

Findings of a World Bank study[16] show that universities that are globally most successful at recruiting and retaining top academics and students have the following characteristics:

◆ They are *research-intensive.*

◆ They have *carefully defined goals.*

◆ Their strength lies in brilliant individuals coupled with *group capacity* and *strategic collaboration.*

◆ They are *grounded in the local.*

As long as these priorities remain, internationalisation in the form of partnerships can help to address several challenges. On the 'power of partnerships' John Hearn suggests that:

◆ Without compromising existing research activities, there is benefit in jointly tackling global challenges that affect us all.

---

13 See, for example, Alberts, B. (2013). 'Impact factor distortions', Editorial, *Science,* 340, May; and Shekman, R. & Patterson, M. (2013). 'Reforming research assessment', eLife, 2: e00855.
14 www.ascb.org/SFdeclaration.html. Accessed 13 April 2015.
15 See Chapter 10 for further discussion.
16 Altbach, P. & Salmi, J. (eds). (2011). *The Road to Academic Excellence: The making of world-class research universities.* Washington, DC: The World Bank.

◆ Formalised partnerships can be a platform for forging alliances with funding agencies, business and NGOs to leverage third-party funds.

◆ Much can be gained from joint governance of higher degrees, 'exchange, trust and team work'.[17]

Consider the African context of dwindling resources and a shortage of supervisors, yet the persistent need to increase both research funding and the number of doctoral graduates. Global research partnerships with PhD training embedded into strategically selected, interdisciplinary research collaborations with selected international partners would provide a number of things: co-supervision resources, enhancement of the student experience, and assistance in leveraging third-party research funding through collaborative bids. Ideally, such collaboration would include partners from both the Global South (specifically other countries in Africa) and from developed economies in the Global North, with a number of positive spin-offs:

◆ Students gain 360-degree exposure while engaging from the vantage point of their home location (geographical and historical).

◆ It raises awareness of the way in which tackling the challenges that face our own cities and regions can be brought to bear in our engagement with the rest of the world.

    • There are multiple examples of research on unique local characteristics (geographical, cultural, historical) that bring new perspectives to global debates and challenges. Examples from South Africa are in the areas of:

      - Marine biology, where access to the Indian, Atlantic and Southern oceans position us uniquely to collaborate in international research on the effect of climate change on the oceans.

      - Astronomy/cosmology, where the southern skies are an ideal location for the international SKA telescope initiative.

In support of both international partnerships and adapted staff conditions, Graeme Hugo, Director of the Australian Population and Migration Research Centre at the University of Adelaide, makes a case for international migration in higher education, which would permit academics from the developing world to work across borders by having joint appointments, thus mitigating some of the negative effects of the brain drain often resulting from international staff and student exchange.[18]

---

17 See also Hearn, J. (2013) regarding the launch of the Australia Africa Universities Network, in the *ACU Bulletin*, 179, June.

18 Report on comments by Professor Graham Hugo in his ACU Perspectives speech on 'International migration and higher education in Australia' (published 27 March 2013); www.acu.ac.uk/news/view?id=49. Accessed 13 March 2013.

The global and the local

There is a danger that focusing on internationalisation and foregrounding its (positive) potential obscures a very real flipside, especially pertinent to the altered South African higher education context. The drive to international competitiveness raises a number of issues. First, it suggests a focus on securing and nurturing the top students and the most promising academics, deflecting attention from the challenges facing us in the need to accept and develop weaker students and less prepared academics. Second, in South Africa there are effectively only five out of our 23 universities currently able to compete at this level. This creates a dialectical situation, where the tension between competing demands makes the situation in South Africa—and in the whole African subcontinent— far more complex that an introductory discussion of internationalisation might suggest.

This section has introduced the global research landscape. Its aim was threefold:

1   To expose readers, notably those entering academia, to the dynamics at work in the international academic community and how these dynamics impact on universities and individual researchers.
2   To suggest that, while not all aspects of global trends are warmly received or necessarily appropriate to our southern context, we can nevertheless draw on them to identify principles to assist in the self-evaluation and ultimate success of both institutional and national research efforts.
3   To act as a prompt to emerging researchers when planning their academic careers.

In the section that follows, the aim is to build on the awareness created by the previous discussion on the international research landscape to focus on the local and individual research endeavour. Although the discussion will be grounded in the South African benchmarking model, the process and principles should have relevance beyond this context.

Academic benchmarking: South Africa's researcher rating system[19]

In 1984 the South African National Research Foundation (NRF) introduced a hierarchical, peer-reviewed ranking system of South Africa's research-active scientists. For South African universities, NRF ratings testify to the quality of their staff, while for individual researchers a rating affirms research status and provides access to funding. The system, involving international peer review, provides a useful tool for benchmarking the quality of our researchers and our national research system against the best in the world.

Research benchmarking in South Africa has historically been associated with two national imperatives: the development of local research capacity and the funding of

---

19   Prepared by Robert Morrell.

research. To address both these needs and to acknowledge research quality, the rating system was inaugurated at a time when universities were becoming research-active, and it was acknowledged that teaching could and should be enhanced by energetic research agendas. Hitherto, university-based research was constrained by the lack of available funding and the absence of any co-ordinating national body to direct and organise national research activities.

The rating system distinguishes between:

- world-leading (A)
- internationally recognised (B)
- nationally established researchers (C)
- P and Y, for which younger academics are eligible, accommodate similar distinctions.

Initially the system was for only the 'hard' scientists, but in 2002 it was extended to include the social sciences and humanities, including the creative disciplines. This increased both the number of rated researchers and interest in the system, so that at present approximately 10 per cent of the country's institutionally linked researchers and those based in research centres are rated. While access to funding has increased interest in the rating system, universities themselves attach importance to it as a form of quality assurance and benchmarking, which *inter alia* attracts the best students.

Other features of the system include the following:

- The benchmarking it affords is also about measuring your achievements against those of competitors in the field, serving as a point of reflection and a spur to improvement.
- It is the only national system in South Africa that is able authoritatively to show the performance of universities relative to one another based on clear, explicit and transparent criteria and processes.
- Universities themselves give legitimacy to the system by participating in it.
- It is universities, not individuals, who formally apply for research ratings for their staff. And it is universities that choose to devote resources to the process of obtaining ratings, some investing heavily in the system, others less so.

We turn now to how the rating system works, reflecting briefly on its benefits (intended and unintended) and acknowledging criticisms and weaknesses, especially when viewed as a benchmarking mechanism.

How the system works

The NRF issues an annual call, directed through South African universities and research institutes, inviting researchers to apply for rating. Applicants complete an online form, which includes listing all publications and other educational and employment details, and completing four narrative sections. So, if you are applying, you will need, in sequential order, to supply the following:

- your biographical information
- description of your completed research
- self-assessment of your research
- your future research.

Taken together, these narrative sections require you to write introspective historical accounts of your research achievements, including a description of the key research contributions you have made. You need to show that your research:

- is coherent (has a clear focus)
- has had impact
- provides evidence of 'quality'.

Your university, through a team of senior scholars, reviews the application and recommends a particular rating. Universities may decline to forward applications to the NRF if they doubt their potential for success, thus avoiding unhappiness among aspiring applicants.

While researchers are preparing their rating applications, the NRF specialist committees, which will preside over the peer-review process, are being constituted. There are over 20 specialist committees comprising invited scholars, who are established and usually fairly senior in their fields, to cover the full spectrum of research activity. Working under a convenor, it is a committee's task to select reviewers and then assess the reports that these reviewers submit to the NRF—tasks vital for the integrity and legitimacy of the rating process. Ultimate rating is based solely on the reports that peers (reviewers) submit and not on the opinions of the specialist committees or any other part of the NRF apparatus. The role of the NRF is to source the peer-review reports and then to interpret them.

Each applicant nominates a number of reviewers, three or four of whom will be chosen to complement an equal number of reviewers of the specialist committee's own choice and whose identity is not known to the applicant. These reviewers are approached by the NRF and invited to write reports on the applicant's work. They are expected to read at least the submission of the applicant plus the five best identified research outputs produced in the preceding eight years.

Towards the end of the year, each specialist committee meets to consider the rating applications. Their jobs now are to make two sets of judgements:

- Are the reviewer reports excellent, good or unsatisfactory (and therefore unusable)?

◆ Do the reports suggest that the applicant is a world leader (A), internationally recognised (B) or an established researcher (C)? Applications in the young researcher category are similarly assessed.

When all the reports have been processed, a successful applicant is awarded a rating, which is arrived at by considering all the reports and reaching a conclusion.

At the end of the process each applicant receives a feedback letter indicating the rating awarded and the reasons for the rating, including feedback from the reviewers and their response rate. Unsuccessful applicants are similarly informed, and those who wish to contest the outcomes may appeal in a process formally endorsed by their own university. The duty of the appellant is to indicate the grounds for dissatisfaction and then to approach the NRF Ratings Appeal Committee, which meets a number of times each year to consider such cases.

The rating system has both strengths and weaknesses and faces a number of challenges.

Strengths

◆ As a national system it creates a single measure for all researchers across disciplines.

◆ It is a merit-based system with criteria clearly stated and processes visible and transparent, rendering it credible and fair.

◆ The use of peer review makes the rating system a robust measure of quality, neatly dovetailing with other existing measures of performance for individuals and universities in a competitive global research environment.

◆ At the level of the individual researcher, the system
  • allows you to check your status relative to colleagues and others working in the field
  • can act as an incentive to improve the quality of your research and increase quantity, and
  • provides a perspective on your career progress and becomes an instrument for career planning with strategic research choices.

◆ The system remains essentially unchanged and is thus a mature system, developed over time to high levels of sophistication and efficiency.

◆ The system does not favour one type of research over another, and has managed to retain an apolitical position.

Weaknesses

Many of its weaknesses are recognised and attempts are being made to address these.

◆ The system depends on the expertise and willingness of reviewers, and, as the system has grown, reviewer fatigue has threatened the viability and credibility of the system.

- ❖ There is frequently lack of familiarity, especially among overseas reviewers, with the rating system itself. For example, reviewers' understanding of the system as being one requiring a testimonial, rather than an evaluation, may render their reports unusable.
- ❖ There are weaknesses internal to the system, such as disentangling an applicant from a research team:
  - Specialist committees are obliged to make a finding about the individual's contribution.
  - Reviewer discrepancies may arise in interpreting terms such as 'a leading international scholar in their field' (A category requirement).
- ❖ A strong research focus demonstrating coherence is a requirement for a good NRF rating, favouring those with a narrow focus and working against those doing inter- or transdisciplinary work, for which no evaluative provision is made.

Limitations and challenges

Apart from overt weaknesses, there are also limitations to what ratings can say or do:

- ❖ Reviewers' reports are intended to safeguard against arbitrary or skewed outcomes, yet the choice of a particular reviewer may well tilt a rating one way or the other, despite a sophisticated system of scrutiny.
- ❖ Because the rating system operates in an environment in which there are other measures in place to evaluate research—the various bibliometric measures, for example—there may be a discrepancy between the NRF rating and the profile of the researcher gauged by other measures.
- ❖ The rating system emerged in order to promote scientific research, in the narrow sense. It was 18 years before it was extended to the humanities and social sciences, leading to a concern that the system is biased against the humanities. This perception stems in part from the ease with which journal articles are counted and weighted and, by comparison, the difficulty in counting and weighting books and book chapters (which are more commonly produced by scholars in the humanities).

But a steady increase in the number of humanities ratings in recent years, not least in the A category, indicates that the system may be normalising. In one notable humanities case some years ago, an A rating was awarded primarily for a single monograph.

Moving on

Having introduced the South African NRF research rating system we move on to consider what may be gleaned from the process by those for whom the system is not relevant (those from outside South Africa); those who are new researchers; and those who, for various reasons, opt not to go 'the rating route'.

Adapting the rating application for personal research benchmarking

Some of the exercises required for a rating application are useful for any researcher wishing to assess his or her own research, and could be adapted by institutions as part of internal research quality assurance and benchmarking exercises.

There are three sections of the application that are particularly useful:

1   a brief description of your completed research

2   a self-assessment of your research

3   a plan for ongoing and future research.

Each of these sections requires a *narrative* description, meaning that far more thought needs to go into the exercise than would be the case with lists, bullet points and graphic representations of your research story. For some academics, in whose disciplines writing is not a central activity, this poses quite a challenge. The challenge is intensified by the word limit imposed: approximately 800 words, or two A4 pages, for the description of completed research and 400 words each for the impact (self-assessment) and planning sections: not only a story, but a succinct one too! The word limit poses a different sort of challenge to those who love writing: it keeps the narrative focused and prevents rambling.

In evaluating research, reviewers look mainly for three things: *coherence, quality* and *impact*. Quantity of output is obviously important, but it is subsidiary to these other features. In each of the three narratives the onus is on you as the researcher to demonstrate these elements in your research. The exercise, when done for a rating application, invites assessment of the past eight years of research, but, for newer academics wishing to gauge their progress to date, it can be adapted accordingly.

Brief description of completed research: Your research story

In an earlier section of the rating form you are required to list your research outputs over the past eight years. You are now invited to *engage* with that completed work in telling the story of your research, highlighting your *best achievements* along the way. A story necessarily has links between one stage and the next, demonstrating how the plot *holds together* and unfolds. Your research story (*verified by your outputs*) needs to do likewise, demonstrating how you moved from one stage or project to the next, and how your present work is connected to what went before. In other words, you are showing the *coherence* in your research. If you cannot do this, you have a problem. It suggests that you may be jumping from one topic that holds your interest to another, without seeing any project through to the next level.

This task causes panic among some researchers, who find it difficult to identify the thread running through their research. In a minority of cases there *is no thread* and this is a wake-up call to reassess where you are going with your research. It may require some guidance from a more experienced colleague and it certainly requires some serious research planning. Over the years, many people have consulted us in a panic about this very issue, but, for the majority, some careful thought and digging beneath the surface helps them to discern the thread. The point is that usually there is something sparked off by a project, perhaps in doing research for an article, which leads into a new but related area for the next one. The link is there, even if it is not immediately obvious. Frequently this is in the form of some *underlying theme* that opens itself to development in a number of ways, the one thing leading to the next. It is the underlying theme—which should, however, not be too broad to make it meaningless—that is critical for demonstrating coherence or connectedness in the research.

In telling the story of your completed research, you should desist from referring to anticipated outputs, for example, an article still under review or an exhibition scheduled for later in the year. The object of this exercise is to reflect on what has *already appeared*, not that which is still to come.

Self-assessment of research outputs: Best outputs and their impact

Having engaged with your research journey, you are now asked to *assess* what you have produced. The self-assessment should also be in the form of a *narrative*, with special emphasis on those contributions listed among the best research outputs. This is an opportunity to provide an account of how these outputs reflect the development and growth of your research during recent years, and what *impact* they have had. Mention should be made of instances where you have, in your view, made noteworthy contributions to the *extension of knowledge in your field*, as well as to how your work *relates to other work* being done in your field. For a rating application the self-assessment should relate to research done during the last eight years, but again, for less experienced researchers who are doing this as a personal assessment exercise, this time period can be adjusted.

Where more than one person has contributed to the research outputs you have listed, in this section you should indicate *your own contribution to the team effort*. This draws attention to a good practice: keeping a log of your research, noting all the details that you might need ready access to later. In team projects with co-authored articles you should carefully note your role in the project and the publications.

Another important issue concerns the replication/duplication of outputs, for example, a conference proceeding that has been reworked into a full journal article. In the self-assessment exercise, separating the two pieces of work is discouraged, although the practice itself is acceptable. At another level, a fairly common but dubious practice is to use essentially the same material for a number of publications, with the aim of increasing your research output. This is done by repackaging and perhaps tweaking the material, and giving articles different titles. It is self-delusory to imagine that in this case quantity equates with quality, and ultimately the practice will work against you. So, in assessing your work, *be honest with yourself.*

Ongoing and planned future research: Where to from here?

In Part 2 of this book we look in more detail at the need for research planning, which components should feature in it, and the interplay between them. One of the keys to success as a researcher is to '*keep the ball rolling*'. This means getting into a rhythm where there is always something about to be completed, something midway, something being started, and something else being envisioned—in a way that demonstrates coherence and continuity in your research. This requires careful planning.

A third exercise required in an NRF rating application is to provide a *narrative* of your *ongoing and planned future research*. This should include your research vision for the *next five years* as well as a concise discussion of your *envisaged research activities* during this period, showing how your completed research will be carried forward. The plan should confirm your research *trajectory*: the direction in which the research is headed.

Although *anticipated outputs* are precluded from the other narrative sections, this is the place to mention them: planned exhibitions; articles 'in press', 'accepted' or 'submitted'; a patent that has been applied for; pending PhD registration/graduation, etc.

A mistake made by many early-career academics is to equate *conference presentations* with research output. This is not the case. The presentation is part of the journey *towards an output* but it is not the product itself. If conferences are mentioned in your narrative plan, they should always be *tied to an anticipated, peer-reviewed output*: a publication, a PhD proposal, a thesis chapter, etc.

The value of the exercises

These three exercises can become useful tools in assessing your research status and development. They can be used as *documents-in-process*, updated each year and providing content for a number of research 'tick boxes' with which to gauge your progress.

> **PERSPECTIVE**
>
> I wrote my NRF rating application four years after graduating with my PhD. This, together with the fact that I was within the relevant age bracket, meant that I was eligible for a young scientist rating, and the idea of securing some funding for my research was my main motivation. I was also aware that my profile as a researcher

was going to be inspected and assessed, something I did not particularly look forward to. In fact, I dreaded it! Fortunately, my university had a process in place to help me. It was good to know that all candidates would receive dedicated attention to ensure we were putting our best foot forward: both the 'green shoots' and the 'well-rooted' were being accompanied on this journey.

Being a natural scientist and foreign, words in English are not my strong suit! I prefer to use graphs and tables to put my point across, which is encouraged by a rather dry and factual writing style in my discipline. So there I was facing a daunting task: writing four lengthy narratives to give a good account of my work. I had to use the right type of vocabulary in order to inspire confidence in the reviewers with regards to my skills, my completed work and my future in research. It was a real balancing act to write about my achievements without sounding either overly arrogant or too modest.

I wrote a first 'naïve' version of my application at the beginning of the process. When I submitted the polished application four months later, it had transformed into a professional, sharp, yet true assessment of who I was as a researcher. Through reviews and advice given by my research colleagues and the university task team, I developed a better sense of my identity as a researcher, my skills and my shortfalls, and it allowed me to project myself and identify a trajectory for my research and career. Looking at these narratives boosted my confidence and helped me to focus and prioritise.

In the end, I secured a successful rating, but, in view of all I had gained from the process, this was just the cherry on top of the cake.

Gaëlle Ramon

Conclusion

This chapter has sought to highlight challenges we face in the higher education environment, largely as a result of the internationalisation process. In tandem with the challenges, other issues surface, such as the need for things like quality assurance measures. Another is the imperative to develop strategies that meet the mutating demands of research funders, one of which is the call for more interdisciplinary research, capable of addressing complex issues. This is the subject of Chapter 3.

CROSSING RESEARCH BOUNDARIES

Sooner or later every academic will find her- or himself in a conversation about the nature, merits and challenges of research that in some way or another crosses disciplinary boundaries. You may in time be invited to join, or serendipitously find yourself involved in, a project that involves engagement with colleagues from outside your discipline, department, faculty or institution. By definition, interdisciplinary research (the term is used here, for convenience, in its loosest sense) presumes two basic applications.

First, there is participation by at least two parties (two people from different disciplines or a single person working in more than one discipline). Second, it results in some level of cross-fertilisation. Where more than one party is involved, the term collaboration is also applied. Beyond this the territory is not so clear and the agenda of this section is to explore the nature of these pursuits.

There is no universally agreed-upon definition of interdisciplinarity, nor of the terms used to describe the different types of disciplinary exchange. The aim is not to provide categorical definitions and distinctions. Rather it is to begin a conversation about:

- the reality that there is more and more interaction between disciplines
- the ways in which disciplines interact with each other
- the possibilities and limitations of each level of interaction
- the growing global awareness of accountability to society and the need for tangible impact, both of which lie behind interdisciplinary research.

Academic disciplines and their breach

Most of us enter academia via a particular discipline. In this sense the term 'discipline' refers broadly to a body of knowledge or branch of learning that has its own defining elements, of which we are all tacitly aware: specific origins and intellectual history, epistemology, ways of organising itself, vocabulary, a set of assumptions around which it develops, rules for asking questions, methods used for investigation and building a body of knowledge, and perhaps most significantly, a community of scholars committed to learning and teaching in that defined field.

In the early European universities there were four areas of study: medicine, philosophy, theology and law. Academics were versatile thinkers, polymaths in the truest sense, forerunners of Renaissance thinkers. Categories of knowledge were broader, more general, and hence less specialised than today—and more holistic. The passing of time saw increasing specialisation, which led, in response to the Enlightenment, to a multiplicity of disciplines, that is, mono-disciplines, specialisations in isolation.[1] The Western origin of academic disciplines raises issues for those in the Global South—for our purposes notably Africa—where a colonial past has frequently had a controlling impact on knowledge production, something that is now beginning to be addressed.

Among the positive spin-offs of this intense concentration of expertise, which continued through the twentieth century, were the development of the scientific method and major strides in understanding, both in science and technology and across the spectrum of disciplines. Application of this knowledge has wrought radical changes in almost every area of life, many of them positive. For this reason knowledge production at ever-deepening levels within discrete disciplines remains critical, and emerging researchers do well to make sure that they are solidly grounded in their home disciplines. This provides a firm and authoritative basis from which to engage in conversation with those in other disciplines.

But this very knowledge, and what humankind is able to do with it, has raised other questions and led to the realisation that life itself is not as siloed as individual academic disciplines are, and seldom are unidimensional approaches to an issue adequate. This is particularly relevant in the African context, where life and knowledge are intuitively understood more holistically. In a word, researchers in all disciplines are slowly coming to realise two fundamental things:

1   Disciplines are often not quite as unrelated as was supposed in the past, nor should they be, and

2   Many problems are too complex to be addressed from only one perspective.

At this point it is appropriate to mention a very pragmatic reason, arising out of the points made above, for engaging in interdisciplinary research: access to research funding. Increasingly funders, pushing for tangible impacts on society, that is, with specific deliverables, cite interdisciplinary collaboration as a criterion for funding.

How the disciplines and stakeholders come together and how we describe their interaction is complex and not undisputed. What is more important for our purposes than precise definitions of these exchanges is to understand what was mentioned earlier: the types of interaction, and the possibilities and limitations presented by its different forms.

---

1   Max-Neef, M.A. (2005). 'Foundations of transdisciplinarity', *Ecological Economics*, 53: 6.

PERSPECTIVE

IMPORTANCE OF THE HUMANITIES IN INTEGRATING SCIENTIFIC DATA

There seems to be a prevalent but misinformed perception that the humanities are not that important within a modern African context, either as a career option or as a solver of contemporary societal problems. This view is inaccurate because the humanities deal with society and human beings, and it is impossible to understand science, technology and society, either in the past or in the present, without considering humans. Indeed, Africa is at an advantage here because it has always recognised that culture and technology cannot be bifurcated in any academic endeavour.

Based on observations in non-Western contexts, sociologists have long argued that technology is a total social fact, for it is about humans and how they interact with a range of variables to eke out a living. In the nineteenth and parts of the twentieth centuries, the dominance of science and technology in Western thought made it seem as if the sociological or cultural elements of technology, often collectively grouped under the rubric of magic, were unimportant. The technology of indigenous iron smelting in much of sub-Saharan Africa is an example. This technology reduced iron ores to usable iron in charcoal-fuelled furnaces of varying sizes and forms—a direct method markedly different from the indirect method of the blast furnaces in Europe, which are now in universal use.

In the late nineteenth century, when European men and women of science visited Africa, what caught their eye most were the cultural aspects—labelled 'magic'—associated with iron production. Researchers interested in the humanities in Africa realised that iron smelting was metaphorically associated with human copulation and gestation. An iron-smelting furnace symbolised a woman, who fell pregnant and gave birth to a 'child iron'. This made smelting a highly transformative technology, which changed raw ore from nature through a heat-mediated process to create usable iron. Indeed, smelting furnaces in Bantu Africa were decorated with female anatomical features such as breasts and genitalia. The process of smelting was also associated with rituals and taboos, and the iron was used to forge decorative and utilitarian items. From this dominance of cultural and sociological factors, it is clear that any study of pre-industrial smelting in Africa that fails to consider these critical aspects is doomed to be incomplete.

By the 1960s, researchers interested in the application of chemical, earth and engineering sciences to study the technology of pre-industrial African metal production were fascinated by the complementarity between rituals and purely technological factors such as the quality of ore used in reduction. Iron smelting re-enactments were carried out in Cameroon, Tanzania, Zimbabwe, South Africa and other countries.

Africa has always been ahead in recognising the disadvantages of separating technology from cultural context and the significance of the humanities in explaining technological processes. But perhaps Africanist researchers ought to have been louder to enable them to take up research leadership on a global front.

Shadreck Chirikure

Towards an understanding of interdisciplinarity

The word 'towards' is important. The reality is that there is no general consensus on the definition, meaning and scope of 'interdisciplinary' and its associated terms, 'multidisciplinary', 'cross-disciplinary' and 'trans-disciplinary'.

There are at least two broad understandings of interdisciplinarity. On the one hand, the term is used loosely by many people to refer to any and every level of encounter and dialogue between two or more disciplines in the context of research. Such an approach is sometimes described as 'generalist'; it is the less complicated and serves a useful instrumental purpose as a generic term. But on its own it fails to take sufficient account of the many nuances in the way researchers from different disciplinary backgrounds work together, or of their engagements beyond academia and the impact this has both on the process and final research product. For a less experienced researcher it poses the risk of making incorrect assumptions about other disciplines and their relationship to one's own.

On the other hand, there is the 'integrationist' approach to understanding interdisciplinarity, where the coming together and blending of disciplinary insights, resulting in 'integrative knowledge',[2] is the critical factor in true interdisciplinary work. Such work takes seriously the reality of complexity, and is built on the following premises:

- Integration between different perspectives becomes the primary focus of such research.
- No problem presents itself in one neat disciplinary area. Rather,
  - there are different angles from which a problem can be viewed and questions asked
  - it is combined wisdom that will come closest to a solution, precisely because it takes into account the challenge of complexity.
- Interdisciplinarity is a theory-based research process, involving a description of how it operates.
- The result of such research is something altogether new, featuring new theories and questions and new methods of addressing them.

---

2   'Defining interdisciplinary studies' in Repko, A.F. (2008). *Interdisciplinary Research: Process and Theory*, 2nd edition, Ch. 1. London: Sage Publications. www.sagepub.com/upm-data/43242_1.pdf. Accessed 23 October 2013.

Transdisciplinary research

Transdisciplinary research takes interdisciplinarity to a new level. This is because its defining feature is the *transgression of academic boundaries into the non-academic world.* Partnership with industry or sectors of the community are examples, as they reach 'outside of the academic research environment to undertake activities in partnership with non-academic collaborators in a co-productive manner'.[3] Here scientific research is combined with decision-making capacity for other stakeholders.[4]

> **EXAMPLE**
>
> **TRANSDISCIPLINARY RESEARCH IN ACTION: HIV/AIDS MANAGEMENT**
>
> We take an example from our continent. In Africa, not least South Africa, the HIV/AIDS epidemic requires urgent and ongoing attention. Although it manifests as a health issue, an exclusively medical approach is inadequate for this multifactorial problem. The syndrome's prevalence and management require attention to issues such as poverty, education, nutrition, mother-to-baby transmission, culture and medication. This requires input from those with expertise in a range of both medical and non-medical areas, involving various academic disciplines. In addition, it requires collaboration with the non-academic sector as well—government, pharmaceutical companies, social workers, NGOs and local communities—in effectively addressing the problem. In parts of Africa, work is being conducted on traditional medicine and HIV/AIDS, with increasing collaboration around issues of culture-bound programmes and the use of an ethnographic approach.[5]

Almost poetically, Helga Nowotny describes what happens to knowledge in such a dynamic:

> *Knowledge seeps through institutions and structures like water through the pores of a membrane. Knowledge seeps in both directions, from science to society as well as from society to science. It seeps through institutions and from academia to and from the outside world. Transdisciplinarity is therefore about transgressing boundaries.*[6]

---

3   New, M. & Morrell, R. (2013). 'Draft report on the URC Task Team on Interdisciplinary and Transdisciplinary Research at UCT', University of Cape Town.

4   Stock, P. & Burton, R.J.F. (2011). 'Defining terms for integrated (multi-inter-trans-disciplinary) sustainability research', *Sustainability*, 3: 1090–1113; doi: 10.3390/su3081090; 1098. www.mdpi.com/journal/sustainability. Accessed 25 October 2013.

5   See Kessel, F. & Rosenfield, P.L. (2008). 'Towards transdisciplinary research: Historical and contemporary perspectives', *American Journal of Preventative Medicine*, 35 (2), Supplement: S225–S234.

6   Novotny, H. (2006). 'The potential of transdisciplinarity'. First published in *Interdiscipline*, May 2006. www.helga-novotny.eu/downloads/helga_novot_b59.pdf. Accessed 13 April 2014. See also, Thompson Klein, J. (2004). 'Prospects for transdisciplinarity', *Futures*, 36: 515–526.

This is integrated research transcending itself. First, drawing on knowledge and methods not available within a single disciplinary field, it is integrated from the beginning and produces outputs that would not otherwise have been possible. Second, because of its stakeholder reach (that is, into non-academic partnerships) it has the potential for genuine impact beyond academia, extending, inter alia, to issues of the magnitude of climate change, food security and sustainability, yet not excluding more modest and local challenges as well.

Cross-disciplinary and multidisciplinary research

There are other ways in which people of different disciplines engage with each other at meaningful levels, endorsing the fact that a single perspective cannot provide all the insights available on a particular issue.

Cross-disciplinarity

This might be understood as viewing one discipline from the perspective of, and using insights from, another to inform a study. Allow me to draw on my own discipline, theology, for a simple example.

One of the theologians whose work I have studied draws extensively on musical imagery (for example, *cantus firmus,* art of fugue, counterpoint) to illustrate theological concepts. This led a group of us to engage with a musicologist to explore the place and function of these concepts/techniques in music itself, in order to better understand the points this particular theologian was making. There are many other examples, some at a much more profound level, of studies in one discipline being informed by insights from another. The critical thing is that the study remains grounded in one discipline, drawing on another for greater understanding in a particular area. It is therefore essentially a consultative process.

Multidisciplinarity

In other types or levels of research, people from different disciplines, each drawing on their own discipline's canon of knowledge, and as equal and discrete stakeholders, address a common challenge. This type of research has been described as 'thematically based investigation with multiple goals', where parallel studies 'co-exist in a context'.[7] Such studies often have relevance for innovation where the development of a new product or system or process is dependent on specific disciplinary insights for its success. For example, more effective land use in a rural community might require the development of an affordable sewage-processing mechanism to generate organic fertiliser for the land. This would involve, inter alia, social scientists, civil engineers and chemical engineers.

---

7   Stock & Burton, 'Defining terms', 1095.

From what has been said above, notably about the complexity of the terrain, there are certain things inherent to the crossing of research boundaries which academics with limited research experience could usefully bear in mind.

Early-career researchers and interdisciplinarity

1 Remain rooted in your own discipline. The more rooted you are, the more equipped you will become to enter into conversation with colleagues in other disciplines.

2 Remember that in all high-level interdisciplinary research the expertise of specialists in specific areas is crucial.

3 It is usually unwise to embark on interdisciplinary study for a higher degree unless
   • you have considerable prior experience in working with other disciplines
   • your supervisor/adviser has experience in supervising such work
   • you are a team member in an interdisciplinary project.

   One reason for this caution is the difficulty in finding competent and sympathetic examiners. Another is the risk of superficial and inaccurate application of insights gleaned from other disciplines, compromising the authority of the study.

4 When you are starting out in postgraduate supervision, it is unwise to agree to student topics that require work across disciplines. This should not preclude students from having consultative conversations with those whose disciplinary perspectives might enhance their grasp of the topic.

5 Each discipline has its own vocabulary, and terms used in one may have a different meaning in another. The lack of shared vocabulary is a major challenge, even to the most basic level of cross-disciplinary interaction.

6 Educate yourself about high-quality studies across disciplines in your own institution, learning to assess the nature and potential of different types of disciplinary exchange.

7 In time, possibly try to become involved as a team player in a project that works on some level across disciplines in order to get a hands-on feel for what is involved.

PERSPECTIVE

DEPENDENCE ON SKILLS OF OTHERS, WELL TRAINED AND ROOTED IN THEIR OWN DISCIPLINES

Modern-day knowledge production is becoming increasingly multi-, inter- and transdisciplinary. Yet it is extremely important that we develop and exploit our own strengths. We must first become experts in our fields and then seek strategic alliances with those who have skills and equipment that we lack.

I am an archaeologist whose research area is the history of farming communities and their development and interaction at the local, regional and international level. In archaeology there is little room for generalists, and I chose to specialise in the study of pre-industrial metal production and use, and the nature of its impact on society. This specialisation falls within a sub-field known as archaeometallurgy. Theoretically, an archaeometallurgist should appreciate basic chemistry, mineralogy, geochemistry and material science; he or she must also understand history and anthropology as well as basic archaeology. Clearly, it is difficult to master all these subjects with their complexities and although I have learnt and employ the scientific methods of earth and engineering subjects, I am aware of my limitations. This means that in any research project I collaborate with expert geochemists, expert material scientists and expert anthropologists. These specialists bring in the much-needed depth which takes my research to different levels.

This highlights a critical factor in interdisciplinary collaboration and co-operation: *individual expertise is the pivot of any collaboration.* Such specialisation becomes our selling point as we seek partnerships and collaborations. It will take me a very long time to become a good geochemist, material scientist and even historian. I am an archaeologist and will use that to leverage my collaborations with anthropologists, environmentalists, geologists and historians. This way I achieve more impact than if I try to do everything myself. At the end of the day, it is subject specialists who gain more prominence than generalists.

Shadreck Chirikure

Research collaborations (or collaborative research)

Dictionary definitions of collaboration stress two features: the *working together* of individuals to achieve a *common goal.*[8] This sounds straightforward but gives no indication as to how closely together individuals should work or what roles they should play for their work to be considered collaborative. In some sectors this may not be such

---

8   This section draws on Katz, J.S. & Martin, B.R. (1997). 'What is research collaboration?' *Research Policy*, 26: 1–18. www.sussex.ac.uk/Users/sylvank/pubs/Res_col9.pdf. Accessed 3 March 2015.

an issue, but in academia generally and particularly for those of us in the Global South, the constitution of genuine collaboration is indeed an issue.

Early-career academics soon become aware of the enthusiasm for research collaborations and the concern to foster them. Such enthusiasm is frequently grounded in certain assumptions, summarised as follows:

- The concept of research collaboration is well understood.
- It is essentially the same phenomenon, whether involving individuals, groups, institutions, sectors or nations.
- The level of collaboration is always measurable.
- More collaboration is automatically better.

Why does collaboration occur?

Here are some of the motivating factors in research collaborations, which apply on various levels, from loose, informal arrangements to sophisticated, cross-sector partnerships:

- **Research funding.** Escalating costs of research, and the inclusion of collaboration as a requirement of funders for awarding grants, signifies a general shift in funding patterns.

- **Travel and communication.** The ease of international travel for conferences and research visits, together with the impact of electronic media, facilitates networking, which in turn encourages collaborative research efforts;

- **Social nature of knowledge production.** Most collaborations begin informally, often over conversations at conferences, and grow from there, leading at times to formal collaborations or ongoing informal links and networks.

- **Specialisation needs.** Specialisation needs range from simple research projects requiring the input of a specialist, for example, a statistician, to the need for complex equipment in high-level scientific research.

- **Interdisciplinary research**
  - The growing number and importance of interdisciplinary projects and fields requires collaborative research efforts.
  - Scientific advances are frequently the result of integration or fusion of previously separate fields, leading to new or emerging fields and technologies, for instance, biotechnology.
  - There is a general move towards cross-fertilisation between disciplines as awareness of complexity and the need for different perspectives grows.

❖ **Political factors**

- Some research collaborations develop to build strategic links between nations, such as those between nations of Western Europe post World War II, and between East and West following the lifting of the Iron Curtain.

- Particularly significant in Africa are collaborative initiatives by countries looking for African partners (sometimes for access to local knowledge) as a requirement of funders or for other reasons (see also the final section of this chapter, 'Research collaboration from an African perspective')—all political in the broad sense.

❖ **Scholarly visibility.** There is evidence that in some disciplines scholarly visibility and recognition increase where there are multi-authored papers emerging from collaborative work.

❖ **Research training**

- Some research collaborations involve a senior researcher wishing to build capacity in a junior colleague or protégé, or train apprentice researchers; or a researcher may need to gain experience her- or himself by working in a collaborative project.

- Many funders include research capacity development as a criterion for grants.

What is collaboration and who are collaborators?

Because collaboration is intrinsically a social process, it is difficult to establish boundaries between what constitutes research collaboration and what does not:

- ❖ At one extreme (minimal) anyone providing input into a piece of research is a collaborator.

- ❖ At the other extreme (maximal) only those scholars contributing directly to all the main research tasks over the duration of the project are considered collaborators.

There are obvious problems with both extremes, and it is far more realistic to suggest that research collaboration lies on a spectrum, somewhere between these two poles.

Collaborations involve co-operation between individuals. But they can equally involve research groups within a department; between departments, faculties or institutions; or between academics and other sectors, for example, health, industry, business or politics—as we have seen in considering interdisciplinary and transdisciplinary research. They may be local or across regions or countries. There may be two partners or 20. Many universities have established formal collaborative research links, based on Memoranda of Understanding, with other institutions. Individual institutions will have their own criteria for defining research collaboration, often reserving the term for formal and intensive forms of working together and excluding less formal, lower-level interactions.

Collaborators, as distinguished from other researchers, might then include the following:

- Those working on a research project for its duration or for a large part of it, or who frequently make a substantial contribution.
- Those whose names and positions appear on the proposal.
- Those responsible for one or more main elements of the research.
- Sometimes those responsible for a key step in the research—the original idea, theoretical interpretation or definitive breakthrough.
- Sometimes the original project proposer or fundraiser (even though this is more a project management than a research function).

Co-authorship and collaboration

The complications arising from the 'fuzziness' in deciding who is a collaborator become obvious in the issue of *co-authorship as an indicator of collaboration*. Increasingly it is acknowledged that co-authorship is no more than one indicator of genuine collaboration: although it is often used as a measure, it cannot be assumed that multi-/co-authorship and collaboration are synonymous. Below are some of the factors that need to be considered when using simple bibliometrics, where authorship is a key factor, as an indicator of collaboration:

- The precise activities of all persons involved need to be known in order to establish the respective contributions.
- Because of the complex nature of human interaction over time, the nature and extent of collaborative activity is difficult to assess.
- Not all aspects of a collaborative piece of work can be quantified, and sometimes even qualitative assessment is difficult, for example, the impact of a brilliant suggestion or protracted laboratory or archival work.
- Co-authorship does not always result from collaboration; collaborators from different disciplines may choose to publish separately.
- On the other hand, a co-authored paper may simply represent a pooling of individual research findings that do not emerge from collaboration.

What are the costs and benefits of collaborative research?

As with most undertakings, collaborative research has costs and benefits. A few simple questions in response to invitations to participate in a collaborative project might be helpful:

- Is it worth it for me, in my context and at this stage of my career?
- What costs, financial and otherwise, will it involve for me?
- At the end of the day, will the effort I put into it be worth it in terms of my own research agenda?
- What extra time commitment will be necessary? Can I afford it?
- Will I be acknowledged, at the end of the day, as a genuine collaborator or is my participation opportunistic on the part of those inviting me?

There are certain benefits that accrue from collaborative research projects and in answering the questions above they should be borne in mind:

- **Sharing** of knowledge, skills and techniques:
  - Research is becoming increasingly complex, placing ever-greater demands on researchers in terms of knowledge and skills, which take time to acquire. One of the benefits of collaborative research is shared responsibility and a skills pool to draw on in the execution of research.
- **Transfer** of knowledge, skills and techniques:
  - Collaboration is useful in transferring tacit knowledge, where not everything is documented.
  - For an emerging researcher, participating in collaborative research facilitates a tapping into the expertise and skills of more senior colleagues, thus growing your own capacity as a researcher by developing expertise in the field.
- **Cross-fertilisation** of ideas leading to new insights:
  - Collaboration is more than the sum of its parts and frequently leads to new insights that might not have emerged otherwise.
- **Intellectual companionship:**
  - Research collaboration facilitates the networking that has the effect of 'plugging' the researcher into a network of contacts in the scholarly community.
  - This leads to greater potential for the visibility of one's work.

Bibliometric information on collaborative research

(Refer to comments in Chapter 1 on *Scopus* and *Web of Science*.)

With this introduction to the concept and practicalities of collaborative research, we close the chapter with a reflection on international collaborations through a southern, and particularly an African, lens. Historic power imbalances between South and North have often affected the focus and design of collaborative work, the resources available for it, and the respective roles played by partners from different parts of the world.[9] Francis B. Nyamnjoh[10] interrogates the situation in what follows, contextualising many of the issues raised in the preceding conversation.

International research collaboration from an African perspective

When Lyn Holness arm-twisted me with her charming persistence into agreeing to share my thoughts on international research collaboration from an African perspective, I did not think much at the time about what I was committing myself to. Now that I am actually about to put down a few thoughts, I am full of questions on and around the following keywords: research collaboration, international *and* African.

Francis B. Nyamnjoh

Research collaboration

The mention of research collaboration immediately raises a number of questions, foregrounding issues that need to be interrogated when speaking of the subject from an African perspective. These are summarised as follows:

1   **The meaning of research collaboration.** One might ask what research collaboration actually entails, given that every research process involves conceptualisation, elaboration, implementation, analysis and interpretation, and dissemination of findings. The critical issue here is the amount of collaboration in this process that would qualify as genuine, equal or participatory.

2   **The weighting of a contribution.** If one is not involved from the very conceptualisation and elaboration of a given study, questions arise about whether one's contribution can be weighted in the same way as the contribution of the initiator of the project and/or of those who fund it.

3   **The position of research assistants and students.** This group often gets co-opted or involved primarily because they need the money. This raises the issue of whether they can or should be considered part and parcel of the research in the same way as the principal researchers who see themselves as originators of

---

9   Kotecha, 'Making internationalisation work', 2.

10   Francis B. Nyamnjoh joined the University of Cape Town in August 2009 as Professor of Social Anthropology from the Council for the Development of Social Science Research in Africa (CODESRIA), where he served as Head of Publications from July 2003 to July 2009. He has taught sociology, anthropology and communication studies at universities in Cameroon and Botswana, and has researched and written extensively on these countries.

the big idea(s) at the heart of the process.[11] This is a challenge, especially in the social sciences and humanities, where the tendency is for lone-ranger scholarship and single-authored publications.

4   **Negotiating interests in the collaborative process.** Many research projects involve collaborators from outside of the academy, whose interests may not always intersect or coincide with the academic interests and ambitions of scholars within universities and research institutions. How do they fit into the research process and the negotiation of the collaboration? How to provide for or contain their power and influence might require a careful balancing act, and prove challenging, particularly for researchers dependent on or desperate for the financial support of such collaborators.

5   **Decisions and democratisation.** When it comes to decision-making, tensions easily arise around the democratisation of the project. This often hinges on the willingness and readiness—or otherwise—of the grant winner or the funder to involve non-grant winning collaborators who are far more knowledgeable about the scientific issues and research questions than is he or she.

6   **Publications and the ordering of names.** When publications for legitimacy and credentialism are part of the bargain—as is usually the case—questions arise about the extent to which the ordering of authors' names reflects the actual work done. Situations arise where the head of the laboratory or the principal grant-holder insists on their name coming first and therefore being weighted more, merely because of their laboratory ownership or fundraising abilities. The situation is worse in institutions where well-placed academics who have sacrificed research for administration and management positions insist on being
included as authors of publications without evidence of direct participation in the research process.

7   **Implications of co-production and co-publication.** A number of potentially contentious issues arise where collaborative work results in co-production or co-publication, among these being where the copyright or patent lies (that is, with whom?). It also questions the meaning of co-production, co-publication and ownership in a genuinely democratic or egalitarian participatory context— where paid pipers are, nonetheless, allowed to call their tunes.

8   **Hierarchies and collaborative work.** There are different hierarchies to be accommodated in collaborative work. First, given the hierarchies of disciplines within the same university institutions—ones where disciplines in the natural

---

11   Editorial note: it should be noted that, usually, paid assistance for research does not require acknowledgement.

sciences often get weighted and valorised more than the social sciences and humanities—questions arise as to what form interdisciplinary, multidisciplinary, transdisciplinary and faculty research collaboration takes. Second, we might ask who takes for granted their worthiness to be a collaborator and who considers themselves fortunate to be included. Who is a natural winner and who is a perpetual runner-up? Other factors that inform hierarchical relationships in collaborative work include race, place, class, gender and generation.

9   **Speaking and listening.** Who is ready, compelled or expected to listen to whom, and why? The success or failure of any collaboration might depend on the type of communication model adopted in the process by the institutions or scholars involved. If there is much *talking at, talking on, talking past, talking around and talking to, but little talking with* the one collaborator by the other, the collaboration in question is jeopardised.

These same issues apply to collaboration between institutions within the same country, especially where such institutions are of unequal status—between the Ivy and non-Ivy League universities in the USA, for example, or in the case of South Africa, between the historically advantaged and the historically disadvantaged universities.

The questions raised are not to suggest that every collaboration should be at the same level, but rather to argue that where and how in the research process you are brought in as a collaborator speaks to how seriously your contribution is weighted. In some cases certain collaborators are considered to be equipped only for data collection, and their contributions often earn little more than a token mention in the acknowledgements page or in a footnote on 'hired hands'. Frequently the divisions between the mind and the body, the intellectual and the emotional, the rational and the irrational, the natural/hard sciences and the social/soft/human sciences are all too obvious and present in various guises. Here, the power dynamics and hierarchies in the research process are also indicative of internalised hierarchies of humanity, and of the interconnections between the global and the local. Many researchers have been schooled in and are very much a part of these dynamics, often seeking to reproduce them, even when their rhetoric is one of creative innovation.

International research collaboration

International collaboration raises further questions as to what it presupposes or suggests, and whether its logic and challenges are different from the logic and challenges of research collaboration at the local and institutional levels. Beyond funding as an incentive, we need to ask about other factors that propel the need to collaborate internationally on matters of research, which may include the following:

1   The belief that different countries have different research cultures and traditions, and that interlinking cultures and traditions through international collaboration in research design and implementation would yield better results.

2   An underlying belief in human progress as a linear pursuit, in which those higher up the evolutionary ladder are necessarily superior to those lower down, and should serve as models to be adopted. That there are countries and regions of superior attainments and those with inferior achievements, and that the 'superior' partners are seeking to share their achievements or the fruits of superior intellects and technologies with their lesser counterparts, whose role in the collaboration is confined to learning, and not to teaching or questioning what they are taught.

If the modus operandi of the collaboration were to be otherwise informed and not based purely on conventional wisdom with its evolutionary logic of hierarchies of humanity, collaboration could assume a different shape. It would be something that does not presuppose, take for granted or define *a priori* who is who in the process and in what capacity they are there. Such collaboration would have a number of features. It would be open-ended, democratic and participatory; underpinned by the belief that in research and science no single race, place, culture, gender or generation has the monopoly of innovative ideas and wisdom, and that everyone learns from everyone else; a model of research and science that is an exercise in humility founded by collective efforts with an open and genuine quest for the truth.

If one accepts that few cultures, races and geographies have escaped the entanglements and co-mingling brought about by imperial and colonial encounters and by global consumer capitalism, then all dreams and aspirations for pure and unbiased work are illusory. This suggests that international research collaboration that takes for granted difference in research culture and tradition in a given context is problematic from the outset. And if, indeed, there is no such thing as 'purity', and differences in research tradition or culture are more imagined than real, what could be the justification for research collaboration of an international nature?

It is important to contemplate these issues in order to know exactly what we mean by, and seek from, international research collaboration. Unless we approach it with this presence of mind, we run the risk of rehashing outdated and contested evolutionary thinking—the type of thinking that pushes us to explain differences with assumptions and stereotypes rather than employ science to open up possibilities for deeper understanding of our world and of humanity.

African perspective

Considering international collaboration through an African lens brings a range of additional issues into focus. We would need, for example, to interrogate the following:

- What added value is provided by an African perspective?

- What makes a perspective African?

- Is the perspective sensitive to predicaments, experiences, aspirations or ambitions that are African, or is it a perspective by someone who identifies or is identified with a particular racial category or geography?

- What is the identity of those doing the qualifying, and their rationale behind it?

- Is there a possibility that a perspective projected as 'African' may not be taken seriously by those who contest the Africanity that supposedly informs such a perspective?

- The ideas of 'being African' that carry the day raise questions about with whom and why, where and when international research collaboration is being discussed, considered or contemplated.

- Is the capacity to carry the day empirically substantiated or ethnographically grounded in lived experiences, histories and realities of being and becoming African, or informed by a stubborn insistence on the conveniences of contested encounters and unequal relationships?

There is the risk that those seeking international collaboration may be in an all-powerful position—having both the yam and the knife as Chinua Achebe would put it[12]—able to call the shots both financially and in setting research agendas. And what if they were, in addition, to adopt age-old and long discredited evolutionary perspectives of humanity and progress in which Africa is confined to a particular geography, peopled by the black race—a geography and people that could never outgrow nature, and that could be claimed by others, without these others being necessarily claimed by Africa and Africans? What would collaboration entail, with a continent and people trapped in the state of nature, and governed more by superstitions, traditions and the forces of darkness, from which civilisation is meant to free humanity? Civilisation here is seen as the progression away from raw nature and its unpredictabilities, as well as from raw emotions and its dangerous irrationalities.

What form would such collaboration take? Even if the collaboration were to be initiated by the African partners, the tendency would be for the supposedly superior collaborators,

---

12   See Achebe, C. (1964). *Arrow of God*. Oxford: Heinemann African Writers Series. See also Nadine Gordimer's review of Chinua Achebe's *Anthills of the Savannah*. www.nytimes. com/1988/02/21/books/a-tyranny-of-clowns.html. Accessed 10 May 2014; Rao, J.V. & College, A.V.N. (n.d.). 'Culture through language in the novels of Chinua Achebe' in *African Postcolonial Literature in English: In the postcolonial web*. www.postcolonialweb.org/achebe/jrao1.html. Accessed 10 May 2014.

in the purportedly more civilised (often Western, increasingly Chinese), non-African institution and country to dictate the terms of the collaboration. This would be on the assumption that s/he who pays the piper calls the tune. Or, if indeed nothing good comes from darkness—albeit as a continent and as humans—the non-African partner could assume for themselves, almost uncritically, the role of harbinger and bringer of enlightenment.

It is these unfounded assumptions underpinning international research collaboration that many scholars and research institutions within Africa have attempted to challenge.[13] Those who embrace collaboration without scrutinising the underlying assumptions of their collaborating partners are—even as Africans with Africa's best interests at heart—likely to continue to perpetuate the same evolutionary fallacies, which are detrimental to Africa and Africans.

The Council for the Development of Social Science Research in Africa (CODESRIA), headquartered in Dakar, is one of the leading institutions in the struggle against unequal partnerships in research collaboration involving Africa. Since its creation in 1973, CODESRIA has served as the mouthpiece for many universities and intellectuals throughout the continent. It insists on those desirous of collaborating with African researchers and research institutions to channel core funding either directly to the individuals and institutions involved, or through CODESRIA as a pan-African enabler or facilitator of predicament-oriented scholarly conversations. In core funding, African institutions and individual researchers have the advantage of elaborating research projects in tune with a local sense of priorities. It is CODESRIA's preferred form of collaboration, as opposed to the more common practice of a non-African individual or research institution elaborating their own research agenda—often without consultation—and then seeking to co-opt African collaborators, with money as the main enticer. How can this be fulfilling as research collaboration, when the research agenda is set before the collaboration is established? One fallacy in international collaboration involving African institutions is the claim that Africa lacks capacity, and that capacity-building should thus be privileged in various collaboration initiatives.

If the idea of research collaboration at local and global levels is to be informed not by fixations with binaries and evolutionary ideas of race, place, cultures and humans, but by histories of mobility and interconnections, then such collaboration should be founded on a permanent investment in challenging hierarchies and inequalities at every level of the research process. This entails, among other things, thinking of research as an ongoing conversation (among researchers and between researchers and research participants or subjects) in which people opt in, opt out or rejoin from different vantage points; a conversation that is not linear, but circular in the way it unfolds. Could we consider

---

13 See Costello, A. & Zumla, A. (2000). 'Moving to research partnerships in developing countries', *British Medical Journal*, 321: 827–829. www.bmj.com/content/321/7264/827. Accessed 12 February 2015.

research as a marketplace of ideas, truly open and receptive to all that come questing, and where practices such as protectionism are embargoed? Such a marketplace allows for all sensitivities and sensibilities, and for the importance of context, without the impulse to import and impose a hierarchy or a sort of Jacob's ladder of contexts. This, to me, is the sort of international research collaboration to which we should aspire.

PART 2

DEVELOPING A
RESEARCH PROFILE
THE ART AND CRAFT
OF RESEARCH

PART 2

DEVELOPING A RESEARCH PROFILE
THE ART AND CRAFT OF RESEARCH

The development of a research consciousness is of the essence of being an academic.[1] This should not be seen as something opposed to the development of teaching skills and commitment, but rather as complementary to them. Good teaching and good research belong together, even though some may choose or be required to place more emphasis on the one than the other. Most academics will be required to undertake research, and for this it is necessary to develop a research consciousness and to cultivate certain research skills and disciplines. A helpful place to begin is to consider research as both an art and a craft. This highlights the need for research to be driven by both creativity and skill.

Some key terms that describe the *art of research* are: passion, identifying gaps, flying kites, innovation, curiosity, thinking laterally, exploring ideas, inspiration, and, of course, creativity itself. There are certain values that accrue to the researcher in this regard. For example, there is enjoyment in research when it breaks open fresh ground; when a creative insight provides a way beyond an impasse; when we imaginatively turn mistakes to our advantage, and when a surprising result requires that we revisit our original premise.

Some key terms that describe the *craft of research* are: technique, becoming informed, strategising, planning, developing and honing specific skills, and innovation. The craft of research means knowing about the material you will be using, where you will find it, what it can do, how best to use it for the particular project, how to finance it, and how to manage it. It means identifying appropriate methods and knowing how to use them. It is the craft of transforming imagination into outcomes and harnessing creativity in a way that is productive.

Research design is where the art and craft of research intersect.

Like others engaged in art and craft, there are some academics who are remarkably imaginative in designing research projects but who do not have the capacity and skill to bring them to fruition. Likewise there are those who have capacity and skill, but whose research vision is pedestrian. They cannot envisage possibilities and thus get stuck at the initial conception stage and/or along the way. Some academic disciplines may seem more favourable to the art of research and others to the craft. For example, the humanities,

---

1   This introduction draws and expands on material from De Gruchy & Holness (2007). *The Emerging Researcher*, 37, 38.

where concepts and theory play a prominent role, may depend more on creativity and imagination than do the natural sciences which necessarily depend on adherence to certain rules and procedures.

The reality is that all cutting-edge research—that is, research that breaks fresh ground—depends on developing both the art and the craft of research. Someone engaged in the fine or performing arts is likely to have a finely tuned creative ability, but without the practical skills to bring that creativity to reality, little can be achieved. So, too, a physicist or biochemist would of necessity have highly developed technical skills, but in order to break fresh ground both need to be sensitive to possible new perspectives. Few, if any, great scientific developments have come about without this combination. In addition, the current move towards interdisciplinary research demands both the creative bent implicit in an openness to crossing disciplinary boundaries and the craft that is necessary to make the endeavour productive.

Developing the skills for the craft in which you are engaged will occupy much of my attention in the chapters that follow, but in anticipation of this there are two issues critical to successful research that must be discussed: managing research information and research integrity, the subjects of Chapters 4 and 5.

PERSPECTIVE

STRATEGIES FOR PERSONAL RESEARCH DEVELOPMENT

- Find a good mentor or mentors, who has/have achieved what you aspire to achieve.
- Pay attention to your university environment, understand it and understand what role you do and can play in it; this helps you to identify collaborative opportunities.
- If you see an opportunity, pursue it.
- Don't be afraid to aim high when applying for grants.
- Don't be discouraged when your grant application is rejected—try again.
- Understand the funding landscape, pay attention to what's hot and likely to be funded.
- Be flexible and willing to tweak your research focus to suit funder priorities.
- Don't limit your 'research' to your science—your research skills can be useful in finding solutions to various professional challenges.
- Nurture your professional relationships.
- Take advantage of every opportunity for personal and professional development.

Tania Douglas

CHAPTER 4

RESEARCH INFORMATION AND ITS MANAGEMENT

It is a truism to talk of living in the 'information age', but the plethora of information available to academics, its daily increase, and learning how to manage it, is something that cannot be ignored and poses a challenge to many. The electronic media are largely, albeit not solely, responsible for this information surge and it is in this area that most assistance is needed—to access, assess and effectively use it. In order to become or remain competitive, nationally and globally, it is in the interests of every academic to be aware of what is available. Many academics are disempowered by ignorance with regard to information management.

But 'information' must be understood more broadly. The Internet is not the only source of information. In most disciplines, texts—books and articles, whether digital or printed—remain the primary source of information and using them efficiently and ethically is critical. In many disciplines, information is gathered empirically, and effective management of this data is paramount. What is available in terms of funding and access opportunities also comprises 'information'.

The aim of this chapter is to gather together material on various aspects of research information and its management. The content represents no more than a sample of what is out there, but hopefully it will be useful.

The place of university libraries

The importance of services offered by university libraries, and the resources that avail through them to support researchers, cannot be overstated. Novice researchers are encouraged to acquaint themselves with what is available and get to know their subject librarians as soon as possible. Librarians are there to help. They are trained and willing to do so.

Access to research information in Africa[1]

One of the fundamental difficulties reported by African researchers—early-career and more established—is a lack of access to the latest journals and other resources for their work. This frustrates the ability to develop new research and win funding, or to publish new work informed by the latest data or thinking. But while it is a commonly reported problem, access to leading academic journals is actually much better than many researchers realise.

---

1   Submitted by Jonathan Harle, Senior Programme Manager, Research Access and Availability at International Network for the Availability of Scientific Publications (INASP).

What follows is designed to help in obtaining access to e-journals and other online resources via access initiatives and other routes.

- ◆ Academics, researchers and students in universities and research institutes across sub-Saharan Africa, South Asia and Latin America now have access to *many thousands of journals*, in full-text, and free at the point of use. This includes both the latest issues and extensive back-issue collections.

- ◆ Access initiatives typically operate on an *institutional basis*, with access usually arranged through libraries with the provider of the scheme, or through membership of the national library consortium, where this exists.

- ◆ In some cases resources are made available *free of charge*, while in other cases *affordable pricing models* have been negotiated, often resulting in discounts of up to 95 per cent of basic institutional subscription rates.

- ◆ Open access resources are available to anyone and will not require payment to access or registration.

BEING PART OF THE GLOBAL INFORMATION ENVIRONMENT

'The way in which information is produced, shared, and consumed is now so heavily mediated by information technology that a university depends on the quality of its connections to both the commercial Internet and the global research network.'

'African universities are pivotal to development in Africa through research and education and their libraries are the engine[s] facilitating these developmental process[es]. Being part of the global information environment is not negotiable.'[2]

In our 11 African partner countries we work with national library consortia, who collectively raise funding and purchase electronic resources at appropriately discounted prices, which we have secured with publishers. In 2011 we calculated that, as a result, their researchers had about 70 per cent of the leading international journals available, free at the point of use to any researcher. As more and more is published open access, the level of high quality material from leading academic journals that is freely available to African academics is growing.

While there are many smaller or disciplinary-specific initiatives, some of the major initiatives are listed in the table opposite:

---

2   Echezona, R.I. & Ugwuanyi, C.F. (2010). 'African university libraries and Internet connectivity: Challenges and the way forward', *Library Philosophy and Practice*, September. www.webpages. uidaho.edu/~mbolin/lpp2010.htm. Accessed 4 March 2012.

Table 4.1: Major access initiatives of African Library Consortia

Research4Life

An umbrella for four schemes

Check your institution's registration and eligibility status: www.research4life.org/institutions/

To register an institution for access: www.registration.research4life.org/register/default.aspx

Access to these resources is via a dedicated password-controlled site. Librarians must register and are then provided with a password to distribute to their users.

AGORA (agriculture) provides a collection of more than 3 000 journals in the fields of food, agriculture, environmental science, and related social sciences:

HINARI (medicine and health) provides a collection of over 11 400 journals, up to 18 500 e-books, and up to 70 other information resources in biomedical and health subjects.

OARE (environmental science) provides over 4 000 resources in environmental studies and related fields

ARDI (technology and innovation) provides nearly 10 000 journals, books and reference works on science and technology:

www.aginternetwork.org

www.who.int/hinari

www.unep.org/oare

www.wipo.int/ardi/

International Network for the Availability of Scientific Publications (INASP)

Offers discounted subscriptions.

Works with more than 50 publishers and aggregators to make their resources available within low-income countries in Africa, Asia and Latin America.

Over 23 000 full-text journals are available and over 7 000 e-books, as well as citation and bibliographic databases. Twenty-two partner countries benefit from the widest range of resources, where discounts have been negotiated, while an additional group of network countries benefits from resources to which INASP has secured free access.

Access to these resources is via the respective publisher's platform. Registered institutions

Register:
www.inasp.info/en/training-resources/e-resources/dash-board/

Resources available through INASP:
www.inasp.info/en/network/publishers/

INASP e-resources and other support available in your country (click 'show publishers')
www.inasp.info/en/network/country/

Accessing online journals and other e-resources in developing countries: A brief guide for academics, researchers and students: www.inasp.info/en/training-resources/e-resources/access-support/

INASP (cont.)	provide their IP address range to each publisher, enabling campus-wide access. INASP has negotiated national-level licensing, and in many cases subscriptions are managed as part of the national library consortia, which manage funding on behalf of their member institutions.	
Electronic Information for Librarians (EIFL)	Negotiates centrally with publishers to secure highly discounted prices and fair terms of use for libraries in more than 60 developing and transition countries in Africa, Asia, Europe and Latin America.	Further details: www.eifl.net. Full list of resources: www.eifl.net/list-of-resources
The Essential Electronic Agricultural Library (TEEAL)	A digital library, developed by Cornell University, and supplied on an external hard drive and DVDs, with no need for Internet access. African universities and research institutes can purchase this for an initial base cost and subsequent annual updates.	www.teeal.org
Global Development Network (GDN).	Research institutes which are part of GDN can access a range of high quality resources through document delivery, by email or in print, via the British Library for Development Studies.	www.gdnet.org/cms.php?id=blds_document_delivery_service
JSTOR (acronym for 'Journal Storage')	Waives or offers a reduced participation fee for any academic or not-for-profit institution in developing countries (and all of Africa). Access is for all JSTOR Archive Collections.	www.about.jstor.org/libraries/developing-nations-access-initiative
Association of Commonwealth Universities (ACU) Africa Desk		www.africadesk.ac.uk/pages/research-resources/access-journals

Open Access resources	More and more journals and other resources are now being published open access. This means that they can be freely accessed from any computer with an Internet connection. Below are some of the recommended resources:	www.doaj.org
	Directory of Open Access Journals (DOAJ) includes over 9 000 Open Access journals	www.doabooks.org
	Directory of Open Access Books (DOAB) contains over 1 400 academic books from 35 publishers	
	WorldWideScience enables you to search across a number of national scientific databases and portals	www.worldwidescience.org
	Bioline International is an aggregator of Open Access journals from across the world	www.bioline.org.br
	INASP also maintains a directory of Open Access materials and programmes	www.inasp.info/en/training-resources/external/open-access-resources/
	Directory of Open Access Repositories (OpenDOAR) allows you to search the contents of repositories across the world. Many universities now have their own institutional repositories, which allow academics to upload copies of their articles and make these freely available.	www.opendoar.org

A number of regions and countries have developed their own **online journal platforms**.	These platforms include:	
	African Journals Online (AJOL) hosts several hundred African-published, peer-reviewed, academic journals, including many in the humanities and social sciences)	www.ajol.info
	Bangladesh Journals Online (BanglaJOL)	www.banglajol.info
	Latin America Journals Online (LAMJOL)	www.lamjol.info

Online journal platforms (cont.)	Mongolia Journals Online (MongoliaJOL)	www.mongoliajol.info
	Nepal Journals Online (NepJOL)	www.nepjol.info
	Philippine Journals Online (PhilJOL)	www.philjol.inf
	Scielo provides access to over 200 Brazilian journals	www.scielo.org
	Sri Lanka Journals Online (SLJOL)	www.sljol.info
	Vietnam Journals Online (VJOL)	www.vjol.info

Simply securing online subscriptions is only part of the solution. Access also means that reliable Internet connections are required, and sufficient access to computers. Both are steadily improving—the former as a result of the undersea fibre-optic cables and projects to build high-speed terrestrial networks across countries. Researchers need to be able to find and locate these, and to be able to judge what is appropriate for their work. This means both good search skills, and the skills to critically appraise sources and the quality of information.

It is here that information skills training, which many libraries are developing, could prove particularly valuable in helping you to understand what is already accessible to you, and how to go about finding this. But whether this support is provided or not, remember the following:

- Understand that a great deal is freely available to you—so be proactive, raise your expectations and don't fall into the trap of assuming it probably won't be available.
- If you know what you want—a particular journal or article—access it via your library website. The library manages a range of journal databases and the librarians will ensure that you are directed to the right access point.
- If you don't have a particular article or title in mind but just want to know what is out there that may be relevant, put some thought into your search strategy. A Google search is useful, but it won't answer every question. Google Scholar offers more. Your library will have specialist academic databases you can search and these are likely to be much more powerful than Google. Some will be specific to an individual publisher, some multi-publisher but within a specific subject area. Search in a few of these.

AuthorAID[3]

AuthorAID, a pioneering INASP programme, offers support and mentoring to researchers in developing countries to publish and otherwise communicate their work. By introducing researchers free of charge to an international research community, it provides a wider global forum to discuss and disseminate research. With international support, AuthorAID offers the following:

◆ a community space for *discussion and questions*, where researchers can benefit from advice and insights from members across the globe

◆ access to a range of *documents and presentations* on best practice in writing and publication

◆ worldwide *training workshops* on scientific writing

◆ a chance to network with other researchers

◆ *personal mentoring* by highly published researchers and professional editors.

Participants in AuthorAID may be:

◆ emerging researchers in developing countries who could benefit from mentoring and discussion, and

◆ seasoned academics with a strong research track record who may like to plough back into the research community.

To find out more: www.authoraid.info/en/about/
To register: www.authoraid.info/accounts/register

Locating journal lists

Details of listed journals can be obtained either by doing a straight Google search ('ISI listed journals'), or by accessing the lists through your university website. In addition to the international lists of approved scholarly journals, South Africa has an extra one: the Department of Higher Education (DHET) accredited journal list. The relevant lists are:

◆ **ISI (Institute of Scientific Information)** listed journals

   www.library.up.ac.za/journals/docs/ISI.pdf

◆ **Arts and Humanities Citation Index**

   www.thomsonscientific.com/cgi-bin/jrnlst/jlresults.cgi?PC=H&Alpha=T

◆ **Science Citation Index Expanded**

   www.ip-science.thomsonreuters.com/cgi-bin/jrnlst/jlresults.cgi?PC=D

◆ **Social Sciences Citation Index**

   www.ip-science.thomsonreuters.com/mjl/publist_ssci.pdf

---

3   Submitted by Julie Walker, Programme Manager, Publishing Support and AuthorAID Director, Research Access & Availability at International Network for the Availability of Scientific Publications (INASP).

Also:

- List of approved DHET South African journals (a Google search brings up the relevant web pages of the various South African universities)
- IBSS (International Bibliography of the Social Sciences) listed journals
- The DHET gives accreditation to certain conferences that meet the required criteria. There is a list of conferences whose proceedings are peer reviewed and are approved for accreditation and subsidy purposes. This list is reviewed regularly and is available through university websites.

Some pointers to effective Internet use[4]

Academics in institutions that offer information skills training, often through libraries, should avail themselves of this opportunity.

Types of Internet material

Assessing a source

It is no secret that the Internet offers an extraordinary range of material and for the novice researcher, it is difficult to distinguish between a good and bad source. A few simple guidelines will help:

- ◆ Look for 'edu' and 'ac' in the URL. This indicates that the source is a university or associated institution. Similarly, be cautious about '.com' sites, where the primary interest is commercial rather than scholarly.
- ◆ Google Scholar is an excellent source for locating reliable material. Bear in mind that locating it via your own institution's library website enables access to far more full-text articles than accessing via the web.
- ◆ Very often the number of citations of the article in which you are interested will be shown. This, together with the source of the citations, is an indication of the article's worth.
- ◆ A URL may include the name of a reputable academic publisher or organisation linked to your field and can therefore usually be trusted.
- ◆ Sites like Britannica or Wikipedia. It is not usually wise to include these as references in a scholarly piece of work, but they can be very useful in providing an aspect on or general idea of the terrain in which you are interested if it is new to you. If academics were honest, many would confess that this is frequently their starting point! However, do not remain here. Move on to a deeper search once you have gained an overall idea.

---

4   What follows is informed by a presentation in 2013 by Alexander D'Angelo entitled 'Alex's guide to researching in the library', UCT Libraries.

Specialised reference works

There are many of these that can be reliably used. Features of a good subject encyclopae-dia include the following:

- It is narrowly focused and with each section written by an expert in that field.
- It provides a background history of research trends (that is, *the history of academic thought on that subject*).
- It outlines likely issues for current and future research.

  Example: 'African legal systems':

  - A short discussion alphabetically on pages 229–232 of *International Encyclopedia of the Social & Behavioral Sciences*/editors-in-chief, Neil J. Smelser, Paul B. Baltes. (Amsterdam: Elsevier, 2001.) Vol. 1.
  - The four-page article is broken up into a range of helpful headings.
  - It contains a bibliography of 13 major sources.
  - The article is signed and you can check the author's affiliation, and the articles are overseen by section editors and editors in chief, also with affiliations listed.
- It will have a short bibliography which usually lists the seminal works, or the most commonly sought works, on that subject. This can form the core of a research bibliography.
- It will often suggest a set of critical search terms appropriate to that topic or define a term, as it is used in that area of specialisation. This is particularly important for cross-disciplinary research.

  Example: *paternal* or *maternal* as used in anthropology have much to do with kin structures and bloodlines, and little to do with fathering or mothering be-haviours, as they might in sociology or psychology.

Most university libraries will have some online encyclopaedias. Oxford Reference Online is one source across all disciplines (but has lately begun to include some books, which require payment).

Referencing Internet material

The ease with which online material is accessed often leads to carelessness in referenc-ing. Online sources should be referenced as meticulously as print sources are, and should contain:

- publication details (author's names, name of book or article, publisher, issue number for journals, date and place of publication, page numbers (if provided) web address
- date on which the material was accessed.

Boolean searching

It is possible to create very precise searches by simply using keywords and combining them with *Boolean Operators, wildcards and brackets*, which work across most databases. Knowing how to use these can save hours of fruitless and frustrating searches! The guide below is based on an EBSCO database help file:

- **Boolean Operators (*And, Or, Not*)**

  And combines search terms so that each search result contains all of the terms. For example, *education and technology* finds articles that contain *both terms*.

  Or combines search terms so that each search result contains at least one of the terms. For example, *education or technology* finds results that contain *either term*.

  Not excludes terms so that each search result does not contain any of the terms that follow it. For example, *education not technology* finds results that contain the term *education* but **not** the term *technology*.

  Caution: the **not** operator can cause problems if 'not' is part of the title of a book or article. It will exclude in its search the word following 'not'!

- **Wildcard (?, #) and truncation (*) symbols**

  Both are used to create searches where there are unknown characters, multiple spellings or various endings. Neither the wildcard nor the truncation symbol can be used as the first character in a search term.

  - **Wildcard question mark (?)**

    - Enter your search terms and replace each unknown character with a ?. EBSCO*host* finds all citations of that word with the ? replaced by a letter. *Example*: type *ne?t* to find all citations containing *neat, nest* or *next*. EBSCO*host* does not find *net* because the wildcard replaces a single character.
    - When searching for a title that ends in a question mark, the symbol should be removed from the search in order to ensure results will be returned.

  - **Wildcard pound sign (#)**

    - Enter your search terms, adding the # in places where an alternate spelling may contain an extra character. EBSCO*host* finds all citations of the word that appear with or without the extra character.

    Example: type *colo#r* to find all citations containing *color* or *colour*.

  - **Truncation**

    - Represented by an asterisk (*).

- Enter the root of a search term and replace the ending with an *. EBSCO-*host* finds all forms of that word.
  Example: type *comput** to find the words *computer* or *computing*.
- Truncation symbol (*) may also be used between words to match any word.
  Example: *a midsummer * dream* will return results that contain the exact phrase, *a midsummer night's dream*.

◆ **Grouping terms together using brackets**

Brackets may also be used to control a search query:

- Without brackets, a search is executed from left to right.

- Words that you enclose in brackets are searched first.

- Brackets allow you to control and define the way the search will be executed.

- The left phrase in brackets is searched first; then, based upon those results, the second phrase in brackets is searched.

  Example:
  Generalised search: dog or cat and show or parade. (Result: everything on cat and dog shows *and* everything on parades generally.)
  Focused search: (dog or cat) and (show or parade). (Result: articles about shows and parades that reference cats and dogs.)

Terminology and spelling

◆ Differences in American and British standard **spelling**.
Examples: behaviour/behavior or colour/color, or axe/ax. This can radically affect your search results. Use wildcards for these.

◆ **Differences in terminology** between American and standard British English.
Example: 'corn' where we would use 'maize'.

◆ **Social taboos which vary from country to country**
Examples: terms for race, poverty or social class. These can vary, between databases, journals of different national origins or different disciplines within a database.

Searching for theses

Accessing theses is useful for a number of reasons:

◆ to see what similar work has been done on your topic and what is being written at the cutting edge of unpublished research

◆ to help you identify and explore a different angle on a topic

- to give you access to a body of material that is available nowhere else
- to use a thesis's references and bibliography as a starting point for you to research more literature and thus take the research further
- to allow you to check that your exact thesis topic has not been or is not currently being written at another university.

In many institutions theses not in the library can be ordered by inter-library loan. A fair number of more recent ones are available on the web, so putting the title into a Google search can often be rewarding.

African and South African theses are available as follows:

- **Database of African Theses and Dissertations (DATAD)** is a project of the Association of African Universities (AAU), Accra, Ghana. This represents a co-ordinated attempt to preserve, index and make available African theses as a local and international resource.[5] (www.aau.org/datad/database)
- **Nexus** database from the National Research Foundation (www.nrf.ac.za) is fairly up to date, provides better abstracts than others *but* does not take Boolean operators very well (see discussion below) and requires a password, hence institutional registration is a prerequisite for access.
- **Union Catalogue of Theses and Dissertations (UCTD)**
- **Africa-Wide Information via EBSCOhost**, which holds records of theses, as well as book chapters and journal articles, is also helpful in bringing up South African theses.

International theses may be found as follows:

- **ProQuest Dissertations and Theses—A&I** is a good tool which claims to be 'the single, central, authoritative resource for information about doctoral dissertations and master's theses', and dating from 1861 to the present.
- **WorldCat Dissertations and Theses** provides access to the dissertations and theses available in Online Computer Library Center (OCLC) member libraries, as well as links to theses which are *available free* on the web.

There are pros and cons—limitations—to each database. For example, WorldCat does not supply abstracts but it does do key-term searching. The secret is to begin by consulting the relevant librarian to set you on course for an effective search.

Other databases

There are a number of platforms that contain a large number of databases where it is possible to search for articles, books, etc. **EBSCO**, for example, is the platform for many very

---

5   See Materu-Behitsa, M. (2003). 'The Database of African Theses and Dissertations (DATAD)'. www.codesria.org/pdf/mary_Materu_Behitsa.pdf. Accessed 12 February 2013.

good interdisciplinary databases, as well as a number of specialised ones for particular subjects—PsycInfo for psychology, EconLit for economics, MLA for literature, SocIndex for sociology being among them.

There is one database that every early-career researcher should become familiar with: **Google Scholar**—a reliable source of research information, with topics ranging from scholars themselves, to publications, to citations and others.

Bibliographic data management

These are programmes for keeping electronic track of references and building bibliographies. They are an asset to researchers, removing much of the tedium associated with accurate referencing. There are a number of such products available: RefWorks, Reference Manager, Citation and Mendeley being among them. A good comparison with referencing software options can be found at:

www.en.wikipedia.org/wiki/Comparison_of_reference_management_software.

Most of these programmes are expensive for individuals, but in some cases institutional licences have been obtained, making the product free for staff and students. Mendeley is available via a free download on the Internet. In addition to bibliographic data management, it offers a variety of other functions which make it extremely attractive to users.

Other Internet functions

The material covered in this section offers a mere sample of what is available to researchers through the Internet. There are several topics that were not covered and with which librarians will be able to offer assistance, for example, searching for books and journals, slimming down results with a Visual Search option, and citation searching. Please avail yourself of services offered by your library.

Research Professional Africa (RPA)

Research Professional Africa (RPA) is a comprehensive and versatile database providing details of international funding opportunities for which those doing research on the African continent are eligible. All disciplines are covered. An institutional subscription is required, and this entitles every staff member and student access to RPA. In addition to information about funders and funding opportunities, RPA offers other research information services, enabling the subscriber to set up e-mail alerts, create shared funding resources, and become informed about the African funding environment.

Subscribers also receive free access to two searchable database e-libraries:

- the NEPAD STI policy e-library containing every African country's STI policy documents

- the ACU university R&I policy e-library containing downloadable documents from the universities of many African and other Commonwealth countries.

Further information can be obtained as follows:

- visit www.researchresearch.com/africa
- call +27 (0)21 447 5484
- email info@research-africa.net.

Conclusion

With this introduction to various facets of research information and the need for its management, researchers are encouraged to avail themselves of the opportunities open to them, beginning with institutional libraries. Underlying the obtaining and use of information—and indeed at the heart of the whole academic endeavour—is the imperative that research be conducted in an ethical manner. It is therefore to the subject of research ethics or integrity to which we turn in Chapter 5.

CHAPTER 5

RESEARCH INTEGRITY

Chapter 1 introduced the idea of research integrity as a backbone of the academic enterprise and identified some of the issues at stake in conducting research in an ethical manner. I now draw attention to specific issues, teasing out down-to-earth implications of the principles of research integrity. The mention of research ethics obviously brings to mind research involving human and animal subjects. But doing research in an ethical manner also goes beyond this to incorporate issues such as plagiarism, manipulation of statistics, selective gathering and use of data, etc.[1] I begin with some preliminary observations.

Preliminary observations

The following points are useful to set the stage for this conversation:

- *Ethical issues permeate every human activity*, and this applies no less to research. Whether it has to do with experiments with animals, fieldwork with human subjects, data analysis and interpretation, citing literary sources, relations with colleagues, business dealings, administration of funds, or confidential commissioned research, ethical decisions and constraints are involved.

- There is *the need to raise awareness of research ethics* with all its permutations, particularly in disciplines where ethics traditionally have not been part of the conversation.

- *The abuse of power relations with subjects must be avoided.* In South Africa, apartheid history is replete with the abuse of vulnerable sections of the population.

- Following a proper protocol for ethics in research serves *to protect researchers* as much as it is designed to protect the subjects of research. Having the appropriate and necessary permission to pursue research may well provide you with the
indemnity should legal action be threatened. Not to follow such protocols is a risky business, quite apart from being ethically irresponsible.

- Following appropriate ethical procedures *enhances the professional and moral standing of the researcher.*

- *Potential problem areas in research ethics include:*

---

1   I acknowledge the input of Solly Benatar, Linda Haines, Jennifer Jelsma and Ingrid Schloss in seminars held on this subject.

- The use of racial groups to define research topics.
- Involvement in secret research, as well as the use of data given in confidence.
- Unintended side effects of research.

A set of relationships

Ethics has to do with *the construction of bonds and values* within any community, which involves a range of activities in which we, consciously or unconsciously, are required to make choices. Much of it can be understood in terms of *a set of relationships* that need to be established and maintained, four groups of which are identified by Johann Mouton as follows:

1 relationship to the practice of science (professional ethics), for example, ethical publishing practices
2 relationship to society, for example, no secret or clandestine research
3 relationship to the subjects of science, for example, the right to anonymity and confidentiality; the rights of vulnerable groups
4 relationship to the environment.[2]

Code of ethics/guides to ethics in research

The various university websites and research organisations have guides to research ethics (requirements and processes), a sample of which is included here. It is interesting but not surprising that there is much common content in these documents, showing how seriously the issue of research carried out within agreed ethical parameters is regarded. Ethics clearance is required for all research involving human and animal subjects. Different universities may use slightly different descriptive terms, for example, '*Application for Approval for Scientific Projects with Human Participants, Biological Samples of Human Origin or Vertebrates*',[3] with variations in their requirements and procedures for granting clearance for research. But the aim is generally consistent.

Ethics websites of some universities and research organisations

The following sample of universities' ethics webpages provide a cross-section of requirements, highlighting many similarities.

Human Sciences Research Council (HSRC)
www.hsrc.ac.za/en/about/research-ethics/code-of-research-ethics

North-West University
www.nwu.ac.za/sites/www.nwu.ac.za/files/files/i-research-support/ResearchLinkdocs/SetswanaPDFs/ethicsinfo.pdf

---

2 Mouton, J. (2004). *How to Succeed in Your Master's and Doctoral Studies: A South African guide and resource book*. Pretoria: Van Schaik, 238–248.
3 North-West University.

University of Pretoria

www.ais.up.ac.za/research/docs/code_ethics.pdf

University of the Witwatersrand

www.wits.ac.za/academic/researchsupport/19111/code_of_ethics.html

University of Zululand

www.unizulu.ac.za/wp-content/uploads/2014/06/Research-Officer-ETHEKWINI.pdf

Research with human subjects

Procedures for gaining ethics approval in most institutions are rigorous, as indicated by the following example drawn from a health sciences faculty:

Procedure for obtaining ethics approval

- The protocol is approved by the Departmental Research Committee.
- Full proposals are sent to three reviewers.
- A synopsis is sent to all committee members.
- All committee members receive reports of reviewers and debate the issues raised.
- Comments are returned to the researcher with suggestions as to how objections can be addressed.
- Amended submission is sent to the original reviewers for final approval.

Requirements for approvals

The following documents have to be provided before approval:

- a well-developed protocol
- a well-structured synopsis
- details of funding and any conflict of interest
- approval from HOD and Faculty Research Committee Chair
- a completed information sheet
- completed and signed informed consent forms.

Requirements for informed consent

An information sheet should be given to each subject. This should clarify:

- the justification for the study and research design
- the possible risks involved
- the possible benefits
- what will be required in terms of their time, behaviour and subjection to different procedures

- payment
- their right to withdraw with no penalty.

All of this presupposes that communication is conducted in a language understood by the subjects and, where necessary, the contents of the information sheet are carefully explained.

> **NOTE**
>
> In order to submit the research for examination, or to publish it, it is imperative to gain prior approval. Only once ethics approval is granted, may data collection begin. Thus ethical clearance cannot be obtained for research that has already begun or been completed.

Prior to seeking ethics approval for your proposed research project, it would therefore be wise to address the following questions:

- Is the research to the benefit of those involved?
- Does the research cause any harm?
- Is the research fair with regard to the benefits and the distribution of risks and cost?
- Does the research uphold the dignity and autonomy of those involved?
- Have the participants given their consent?
- Is the selection of participants fair and scientific?
- Does the research have social or scientific value?
- Will the research be evaluated independently?

Research involving animal subjects

There are strict national and international norms concerning the ethical use of animals in teaching and research, and I use these guidelines here to identify the relevant issues. In South Africa, animal ethics committees are tasked with ensuring that scientific research and teaching activities involving animals comply with the relevant provisions of the South African National Standard SANS 10386: 2008 (*The Care and Use of Animals for Scientific Purposes*; www.biologicalsciences.uct.ac.za/sites/default/files/ image_tool/images/75/files/SANS10386.pdf) and institutional policies for animal use, incorporating the core ethical principles of:

- *Replacement* of the use of animals with alternative models where feasible.
- *Reduction* of the number of individual animals used.

◆ *Refinement* of experimental design, procedures, care and husbandry, to minimise or eliminate the impact on individual animals in terms of actual or potential pain, suffering, stress and lasting harm.

The role of animal ethics committees is to ensure that activities involving the use of animals undergo a prior, rigorous and scientifically informed ethical review process in evaluation of applications to:

◆ Ensure that animal experimentation takes place only where scientifically and ethically justifiable.

◆ Confirm that researchers/teachers are adequately qualified/trained to perform the research or activities involving animals, and that these activities are legal under South African law.

◆ Assess the *benefits* (scientific/educational quality and outcomes) of a proposed animal usage activity against the *costs* (stress/discomfort that target animals will suffer).

Failure of applicants to supply the required information in sufficient detail or to adequately motivate for the benefits of the proposed animal usage activity will inevitably result in delays in obtaining ethics clearance for projects.

Collection and processing of data

A useful source on the ethical use of data is Michael D. Mann's article, 'The ethics of collecting and processing data and publishing results of scientific research' (www.unmc. edu/ethics/data/data_int.htm).

The article begins with the question, 'Fraud or error?' Acknowledging that scientists do indeed make mistakes, Mann proceeds to show that whether one is dealing with fraud or an honest mistake, the result is the same: someone is led to *disbelieve* something that is actually *true* or to *believe* something that is actually *false*. Both are ethically wrong, undermining the most fundamental tenet of science, the entire edifice on which science is erected: trust. Every scientist must be trusted to do and say what is right.

Mann then proceeds to identify a number of areas in which this trust can be breached as the scientist approaches his or her data:

◆ Collecting data without appropriate controls.

◆ Omitting controls others may have pointed out.

◆ Using inappropriate sample sizes.

◆ Subjectively selecting what to observe.

◆ Failing to see events or seeing nonexistent ones.

- Failing to preserve data for a suitable length of time.

- Editing data and using it selectively.

- Making up data to fit a hypothesis.

- Using inappropriate statistical tests.

- Violating the assumptions of the statistical test.

- Performing multiple statistical tests.

- Probability pyramiding.

- Using computer software packages without questioning or examining results for accuracy.

- Failing to report contradictory observations.

- Changing the hypothesis for the paper to suit the research aim.

- Failing to report negative results.

In order to avoid these ethical pitfalls, Mann exhorts researchers to equip themselves properly for their research careers, beginning by applying scepticism to their own work. In addition, he recommends that they be well grounded in statistical tests, their assumptions and their proper applications.

Similar areas are covered in the *ASA Guidelines for Statistical Practice*, located at www.tcnj.edu/~asaethic/asagui.html. The International Statistical Institute (ISI) has its own Declaration of Professional Ethics, first formulated in 1985 and revised and adopted in 2010. See www.isi-web.org/about-isi/professional-ethics.

The supervisor and data analysis[4]

Is it is ethically permissible for the supervisor to play a role in the analysis of a student's data collected for empirical research, and, if so, to what extent? For many, the parameters are unclear, and accepted practice varies from discipline to discipline. Some institutions may have clear guidelines on this matter; in others the responsibility resides in faculties and/or departments.

It is helpful to identify the two major steps in data analysis:

1 Deciding which kind of analysis will be used.

2 Doing the analysis.

It is with the former that the student may seek advice from the supervisor or other colleagues—what strategies to use and what approach to follow. But the latter is the student's responsibility. Let us consider the linear progression in working with data:

---

4   Based on material originally provided by Kevin Thomas, UCT.

1   Collect data.

2   Become familiar with it.

3   Analyse it.

4   Interpret it.

Once data has been collected, it is after step 2 and before step 3 that the supervisor's advice may be sought, that is, not with the analysis itself. Once the analysis is run, the student should interpret the data and then ask the supervisor for comment. At this stage a typical comment might be: 'Why did you not provide an interpretation of that trend?'

While it is frequently necessary to employ the services of statisticians when working with data, it is clearly not permitted for the student to give collected data to a paid professional (or anyone else) to analyse and interpret. In some institutions even the possibility of statistical assistance is determined by departments themselves and hinges on perceptions regarding the parameters of what constitutes the student's own work.

The ethics of publishing

Intellectual property rights constitute a critical dimension of integrity in research, and are a source of untold problems, particularly in the supervision and examination of students' research. Most of the potential problems have to do with publishing, and here I shall discuss three related ethical issues: plagiarism, authorship and copyright. Ignorance in these areas in not confined to students: often staff members are unaware as well.

Plagiarism

Plagiarism has a simple definition: the act of representing as one's own original work the creative works of another, without appropriate acknowledgment of the author or source.[5]

Plagiarism is easy to define but not always easy to detect. It is also surprisingly easy to commit plagiarism, particularly in this digital age. Plagiarism is sometimes an unambiguous act of cheating, but more often it is unintentional, reflecting either negligence or incompetence:

> You are filling up pages on your screen with lots of good words and you forget that you collected those words from someone else … Most researchers who plagiarize inadvertently do so because they take notes carelessly.[6]

Among academics, efforts to spread research into several publications carries with it the risk of self-plagiarism, an issue receiving more attention now than it did in the past. People cite their own published work without referencing it. This is not acceptable

---

5   'Academic honesty and plagiarism'. www.academichonesty.unimelb.edu.au/plagiarism.html. Accessed 8 January 2015.

6   Booth, W.C., Colomb, G.G. & Williams, J.M. (2003). *The Craft of Research*, 2nd edition. Chicago, IL: University of Chicago Press, 201.

practice, although the issue is not always as clear-cut as some would suggest because, in order to get research 'out there' academics today are making use of a variety of media to 'publish' it.

The issue of plagiarism is dealt with further in Part 3 of this book in the context of student supervision.

The following guides may be useful:

◆ www.open.uct.ac.za/bitstream/item/.../09_citation_handbook_ccd.doc.

◆ www.medical.lib.uct.ac.za/sites/default/files/image_tool/images/42/ citation4medicsvancouver.pdf.

◆ www.academichonesty.unimelb.edu.au/plagiarism.html.

Many universities now have licences for plagiarism detection programs (for example, Turnitin) through which all student assignments are routinely run. Most academics are probably unaware that, increasingly, journal editors and book publishers are requiring that manuscripts submitted for publication be submitted to a similar test, designed specifically for material to be published (for example, iThenticate). These programs have two functions: to detect unreferenced material and to detect 'similarity index' in the material: depending on the *amount* of already published content reproduced and the *nature* of it, permission from original authors many need to be obtained.

Authorship[7]

Authorship is an important, but often neglected, consideration in the preparation of an academic publication. Because of the financial and reputational advantages of publishing, there can be bitter disputes over the assignation of credit, particularly if a number of people have been involved in the research or publication. Ideally the matter should be dealt with at the start of any joint project, and the appropriate disciplinary and institutional guidelines should be followed.

Traditionally, the main considerations have been:

◆ Whose names are to be included as authors?

◆ In what order will these be placed?

◆ Who will be designated as the main or corresponding author? The latter is the author who will bear final responsibility for the whole publication.

The first step is to define an 'author'. Normally an author is defined as someone who makes a significant or substantial contribution to the production of the publication. Guidelines specify that each author should have:

---

7   Prepared by Mignonne Breier. References: University of Cape Town. *Authorship Practices Policy.* PC 01/2011. www.uct.ac.za/about/policies/. Accessed 5 November 2013; 'Statements, permissions and signatures', *The Lancet.* www.thelancet.com/lancet-information-for-authors/statements-permissions-signatures. Accessed 5 November 2013.

- participated in formulating the research problem or analysing and interpreting the data, or have made other substantial scholarly effort, or a combination of these, and/or
- participated in writing the paper, and
- approved the final version for publication and be prepared to defend the publication against criticism.

In terms of this definition, you do *not* qualify to be credited as an author on the grounds that you are of high rank in a department or research team, obtained the funding for the research, supervised the research team or merely supported the writers in collegial ways; or if your role was only to collect or process data, for instance, in a questionnaire survey.

This last point is a hard rule to accept for young researchers who feel they have made a very important contribution to the publication and need a leg-up in their careers. They certainly need to be acknowledged but it is unwise for them to be credited as authors if data collection or processing is their main or only role. Being credited as the author of a publication is not just about reaping the glory of a piece of research. It is also about taking responsibility for the contents of the publication, with all the ideological, methodological, theoretical, legal and moral responsibilities this entails. Will you be able to defend the article or at least part of it, and do you accept its overall thrust? If you don't and can't defend it, you should not be credited as an author.

Authorship in the context of a supervisor–student relationship is a particularly important consideration. Again, it depends on the discipline and the relative independence of the student's work. In some disciplines it is common for supervisors to be second authors on all publications emanating from the student's dissertation. In other disciplines, this would not be appropriate unless the supervisor plays a significant role in the writing of the publication. It is certainly not appropriate in the case of a student whose work was largely independent of the supervisor (as in the case of many mature students). A Memorandum of Understanding (MOU) between the student and the supervisor should contain guidelines on authorship and these should be brought to the student's attention early in the supervision process.

In research teams, principal investigators need to be sensitive to the power relations at work and their intersection with race and gender. Bitter resentments can arise if junior researchers do not feel sufficiently acknowledged or if the permanently appointed academic gains mileage from the research conducted by a contract researcher, who has to find another job when the empirical research comes to an end. Sometimes this mileage is very literal, in the form of overseas conference travel opportunities.

To avoid authorship disputes, it is important to plan ahead. Make sure that your university or department or research team has an authorship policy, and discuss this with your co-researchers at the outset of the project. Junior researchers need to know the limitations of their role and senior investigators their responsibilities. As the project progresses, revisit your agreement from time to time. Has anyone's role in the project changed? Sometimes a researcher destined to be a main author leaves the project and a more junior researcher steps into the role. If the junior also contributes substantially to the publication they need to be accredited as an author. If their role remains at the level of data collection, they need to be mentioned in the list of acknowledgements—but not as an author. The final assessment of their role in the project and the writing of the publication might differ from the initial projection.

The next issue is the *order of names*. In some disciplines the convention is to list the names alphabetically, with an asterisk next to the name of the main or corresponding author. In others, the names are listed according to the importance of the role of the author. The first mentioned author is the one who takes overall responsibility and the following names are in decreasing order of contribution to the publication. (And here it is a good idea to give full, identifiable names, for instance, John Maximillian Brown rather than John Brown. Otherwise you will have great difficulty tracking your citations and developing an independent academic identity.)

A new, increasingly popular form of authorship is called the contributor–guarantor method. In this method, the contributions of individual authors are disclosed to readers and they are called contributors rather than authors. Guarantors take responsibility for the integrity of the entire work. Persons who have played an important role in the publication or research, but do not meet criteria for authorship, must be acknowledged in the Acknowledgements section of the publication and the nature of their contribution specified.

To sum up, good authorship practices depend on a few basic principles:

If you are a principal investigator

- Know the conventions of your discipline.
- Consult your university's policy on authorship, or develop your own if none exists.
- Discuss this policy with all the researchers in your project at the start of the research and again in the course of the project.
- If you want to publish in a journal, read the authorship requirements (as distinct from 'Guidelines for authors', which are usually concerned with issues of style, referencing, etc.) Some journals, including many in the humanities and social sciences, have no guidelines at all. Others, in the natural, health and engineering sciences, in particular, will have very stringent requirements. For example, *The Lancet* will require you to complete quite comprehensive forms

called Author Statements. Here you have to specify the role of each person listed as an author, and any conflicts of interest they may have. *The Lancet* also requires each author to sign that they have had access to all the data in the study 'and accept responsibility for its validity'.

If you are a postgraduate student or supervisor

◆ Include authorship guidelines in the Memorandum of Understanding and discuss these at the start of the supervision process and again in the course of the supervision.

◆ Be sufficiently flexible to accommodate students who work relatively independently, as well as those who need a great deal of guidance in their supervision and help with the writing of any publication that emanates from the dissertation.

Institutions should ensure that they have a general set of authorship guidelines in place and faculties and departments should adapt these in accordance with disciplinary conventions, provided that certain core principles are observed. There should also be mechanisms and procedures for the resolution of any disputes that might arise.

In general, good authorship practice rests on the principle of justice and good communication with your research colleagues. Be fair, transparent and reasonable, and discuss and reach agreement on authorship at the start of your research and in the course of it.

Intellectual property[8]

Intellectual property is a legal term referring to the 'intangible rights protecting the products of human intelligence and creation, such as copyrightable works, patented inventions, trademarks, and trade secrets'.[9] The roots of intellectual property lie in eighteenth-century English law, and the term covers a wide range of property created by musicians, authors, artists and inventors.

The challenge to researchers, whose work depends on consulting the work of others, is to understand the rules applying to intellectual property and to know how

---

8   Originally prepared by Charles Masango. References: Copeling, A.J.C. (1978). *Copyright and the Act of 1978*. Durban: Butterworth; Dean, O.H. (1987). *Handbook of South African Copyright Law*. Cape Town: Juta; Lahore, J. & Lancour, H. (eds). (1971). 'Copyright', *Encyclopaedia of Library and Information Science*. New York: Marcel Dekker, Inc.; Masango, C.A. (2009).'Understanding copyright in support of scholarship: Some possible challenges to scholars and academic librarians in the digital environment?' *International Journal of Information Management*, 29 (3), 232–236 and www.academia.edu/248697/Charles_A._Masango_Understanding_copyright_in_support_of_scholarship_Some_possible_challenges_to_scholars_and_academic_librarians_in_the_digi-tal_environment. Accessed 6 March 2015.

9   Entry on intellectual property, www.legal-dictionary.thefreedictionary.com/Intellectual+Property. Accessed 4 March 2015.

to acknowledge the use of such works in their own research. The aspect of intellectual property that is therefore our most immediate concern is *copyright*,[10] and hence it will be the focus of this section. Although original copyright law applied only to print material, today it covers—in addition to the works of creative expression mentioned above—the work of designers in various areas, programmers and webpage designers, that is, digital material.

In an effort to simplify the rules of copyright, we could say that the works of others we might wish to use fall into two broad categories: that which is covered by what is known as the '*fair-dealing exemption*' and that for which specific '*permission to reproduce*' (that is, refer to or use) is required. Both will receive attention, but for now there are certain general features of copyright that should be noted:

- ◆ Copyright does not protect the unpublished ideas and concepts underlying an expressive work. This exclusion constitutes a potentially explosive area in the scholarly world and has been the subject of many a bitter conflict. This is the reason why academics are urged to publish their ideas and findings in articles and books as soon as possible, or to express them and make them public in a tangible way, appropriate to the discipline.

- ◆ It is automatic and requires no registration.

- ◆ It is jurisdictional, depending on enactment in each country, while the Berne Convention represents an international standard of agreement. Some 41 African countries (approximately 70 per cent) are signatories of the Berne Convention.

- ◆ In most countries copyright protection of literary work lasts for the lifetime of the author plus 50 years. After this period the work is said to be in the public domain.[11]

'Fair-dealing exemption'

One can copy copyrighted information without infringing copyright because of the *fair-dealing exemption* (originating in the USA). This exemption refers to both *exception and limitation*: it makes an exception in allowing the use of copyrighted material without obtaining permission from copyright holders (subject, of course, to full acknowledgement) but this is allowed subject to certain limitations. Determining fair dealing is sometimes a balancing test rather than a clear-cut issue, for there are several issues to be weighed up:

---

10   Juta academic publishers have a comprehensive and useful guide, *Juta's Copyright Guidelines*, available at www.jutaacademic.co.za/media/filestore/2015/03/Juta_Copyright_Guidelines.pdf. Accessed 9 April 2015.

11   See Stanford University, 'Copyright and fair use' for explanation of 'public domain'. www.fairuse. stanford.edu/overview/public-domain/welcome/. Accessed 5 March 2015.

purpose of use, nature of the copyrighted material, size and significance of the portion used in relation to the whole, effect of use on the potential market and value of the work.

Fair dealing as relevant to academics allows for the following:

◆ Copying copyrighted material for certain purposes such as research, critique, teaching and under certain other circumstances that will not interfere with the legitimate rights of the copyright holders or be used for commercial purposes.

◆ One copy of one article from an issue of a journal and about 5 per cent of extracts, or one chapter from a published work.

◆ Multiple copying can be done legally with permission from the copyright holder.

There are times when efforts to obtain permission fail, usually because the copyright holder cannot, after a 'diligent search' be located. Such works are known as orphan works. Here a user must make a choice:

◆ Replace the material with alternative works.

◆ Alter the planned use of the copyrighted materials.

◆ Conduct a risk–benefit analysis, which means balancing the benefits of using that particular material against the risks that a copyright holder may discover its use and assert legal claims against you.[12]

The (fairly controversial) Orphan Works Act of 2008 (USA) provides for such circumstances in that the one who cites such work is not liable for compensation if the infringement was for a charitable, religious, scholarly or educational purpose. Although no African country has as yet promulgated this type of Act, it can, nevertheless, be used as a persuasive authority, even if not as not a binding principle. This is because the objective of various African countries' copyright Acts are against any obstacle that would inhibit scholars from creating, innovating and stimulating education.

The Orphan Works Act covers the single use of the material and the user should both disclaim any intention to infringe copyright and indicate the intention to acknowledge the copyright holder.

'Permission to reproduce'

Certain copyrighted works are not covered by the fair-dealing exemption and permission needs to be obtained for their use. Such works include poetry, music and other artistic works. Publishers are wary about seeking such permissions because it is a lengthy process and permissions are frequently refused.

---

12 Columbia University Libraries, Copyright Advisory Office, 'If you cannot find the owner'. www.copyright.columbia.edu/copyright/permissions/if-you-cannot-find-the-owner/. Accessed 5 March 2015.

In South Africa the Dramatic, Artistic and Literary Rights Organisation (DALRO)[13] serves a useful purpose for universities. DALRO administers various aspects of copyright,

making institutional licences available for the reproduction of extracts of copyright-protected works for internal use in that institution.

Digital information[14]

Computer technology emerged in the mid-1960s. Since then it has grown exponentially and is particularly useful to scholars in providing easy access to information. These days it is equally easy to misuse digital content, which is increasingly protected by multiple layers of intertwined legal and technological devices in the form of copyright law, licensing agreements, software and hardware management systems, and anti-circumvention laws.

Copyright protects digital content, access to which is governed most directly by *access licences*, a form of contract between an institution's library and a vendor. It is normally written by the vendor and is geared to the vendor's interests. It is important to note that in the digital environment, corporate rights holders no longer *sell* copies of literary works, but rather *provide access* in exchange for a *fee*.

Another layer of technical protection comes in the form of various kinds of *Digital Rights Management Systems (DRMSs)*, also known as Automated Rights Management (ARM). These systems function to:

- Prevent unauthorised copying of copyrighted digital content.
- Restrict copying if payment is not made.
- Regulate access to digital content.
- Identify digital content and those who own the digital licences.
- Ensure that the identification data are authentic.

Although DRMS by its own merit protects digital content, a further layer of protection operates in the copyright Acts of a number of countries, such as the USA, Australia and the United Kingdom. Here, the incorporation of an *anti-circumvention clause* has given yet more protection to digital content. This clause forbids access to a technologically protected work without the authority of the copyright holder and prevents the manufacture of and

---

13 DALRO is a South African organisation with international affiliation.

14 See Masango, C. (2007). 'Perceptions about copyright of digital content and its effects on scholarship: A South African perspective'. www.open.uct.ac.za/bitstream/item/9045/CHED_article_digitalcontentcopyright_Masamgo_2007.pdf?sequence=1. Accessed 6 March 2015; McCracken, R. (2004). 'Agreements, user licences and codes of practice', in C. Armstrong & L.W. Bebbington (eds). (2004). *Staying Legal: A guide to issues and practice affecting the library, information and publishing sectors*, 2nd edition. London: Facet Publishing, 122–139; Wyatt, A.M. (2005). 'Licences, the law, and libraries', *Journal of Library Administration*, 42 (3/4): 163–176.

trafficking in any digitally related entity that is covered by this clause.

Acknowledging digital sources

Accessing digital resources for teaching and research does not mean that the material now belongs to you—although it is easy to feel this way! Digital material must be acknowledged as diligently as hard-copy resources, and citations should include:

- as much detail of the publication itself as is available
- the URL (web address)
- the date on which the material was accessed.

This introduction to intellectual property lays no claim to be exhaustive, but is intended to raise awareness of some of the issues involved for academics and what provisions there are to deal with them appropriately.

Conclusion

Accessing and managing research information and being aware of provisions for both the safeguarding and use of intellectual property comprises a matrix in which actual knowledge production and dissemination takes place. To do this effectively, thinking ahead and detailed planning—the subject of Chapter 6—are essential.

CHAPTER 6

PLANNING YOUR RESEARCH

Developing as a researcher does not simply happen.[1] It requires the development of a research consciousness and vision as you become aware of the issues at stake and the most effective way of dealing with them. Yes, it may be possible to produce some brilliant ad hoc item of research, but the goal of producing sustained, quality research requires cultivating particular skills and careful, systematic planning. This applies to producing the research, as well as the framework within which it happens. In this section we consider the latter, developing the supportive framework that undergirds research productivity, which we might describe as *becoming research-savvy*.

Some key components in this process are to:

- Know what is required and available.
- Assume responsibility and take initiative.
- Manage time, anticipate needs and plan ahead.
- Cultivate the necessary skills.
- Develop a healthy sense of self in the role of researcher.

One of the enemies of research is passivity. A great ally of research is being alert and proactive. There are several reasons for this.

1   In contrast to other components of an academic job, like teaching and administrative responsibilities, there is no built-in system of accountability when it comes to research. It is sometimes only in your annual performance appraisal that attention is drawn to the fact that your research productivity has not been adequate.

2   When it comes to research there are seldom automatic structures and deadlines guiding the process. The initiative in setting these in place and determining pace frequently rests with the researcher, in other words, you. For example, in preparing an article for publication, unless you as author (or with your co-authors) work out a timeframe for completion and submission, the process can easily drift on and on. Many of us, given the other demands of our jobs, are prone to procrastination when it comes to issues related to research.

3   Except in relatively rare circumstances, the chances are that no one will be looking out for you—checking that you have time to do your research,

---

1   This chapter is based on ERP seminar material and sections from De Gruchy & Holness, *The Emerging Researcher.*

making you aware of funding opportunities, showing an interest in your progress, alerting you to an appropriate conference, ensuring that you know what the institution requires of you by way of research output. This means that it falls to you to be proactive—to take the initiative and accept responsibility for being informed and making things happen. Do not adopt a victim mentality if circumstances are less than favourable for research. It does not help.

Having made the point above rather starkly, let us continue by injecting some positive suggestions into the conversation. First and foremost, there is the issue of *research planning*.

Why have a plan?

What difference does it really make to plan your research? In addition to some of the points made above, there are several reasons—some obvious and others less so—why careful planning is necessary for research.

- The most basic reason is that if research is not planned it frequently does not happen. Other things crowd it out, like seeing students, attending staff meetings, marking scripts and fulfilling administrative responsibilities.

- It is a human tendency to push aside that which makes one feel uncomfortable, and for many new academics getting going with research leads to feelings of severe discomfort and even inadequacy.

- It is true that those working in research groups have a built-in support structure, but for those in disciplines in which traditionally one works alone, the prospect of research can be daunting. It is difficult to get out of the starting blocks.

- Planning is also important to make optimal use of time, space and other resources.

- Doing research and having research goals is one component of the whole academic and personal package, and it will happen effectively only if it is considered in relation to other things, for example, personal/domestic issues, teaching commitments, a term as HOD, and so on. Hence careful planning is important.

- Planning is necessary to avoid last-minute panic and the risk of missing out on deadlines and opportunities such as securing funding for a conference or meeting a submission date given by a journal editor. In other words, planning promotes a healthy rhythm and avoids disappointment and desperate ad hoc decisions and requests.

◆ Planning itself is a discipline and being disciplined in this way helps to encourage discipline down the line, in the details.

A useful exercise in preparation for drawing up a projected personal research plan is to reflect on the following questions:

◆ What obstacles are there for you to overcome in relation to your research?

◆ What habits could you develop (and others you could lose) to foster your research progress?

◆ What could help you to *optimise the time* you have for research?

How to plan effectively

The above exercise invariably raises interesting issues. This is particularly so when people are honest with themselves and identify personal foibles that have the potential to hinder progress with research. Identifying them might be the first step towards dealing with them constructively. A good (and common) example is the tendency to procrastinate. More than once, as we have gone around the room after an exercise to identify stumbling blocks, participants have introduced themselves thus: 'Hello. My name is Susan and I'm a procrastinator!'

But there are deeper, more problematic issues that surface too, ranging from perceived lack of departmental or institutional support to shortage of funds, inadequate skills, lack of self-confidence and lack of time. Inadequate proficiency in IT skills such as MS Word, Excel and bibliographic data management, adds to procrastination. An issue that frequently emerges is a sense of guilt for taking time for research—forgetting that research is not a nice-to-have extra, but a core component of an academic position. In what follows we try to extract some ways to address these challenges and hence to develop more effective research planning and productivity. In picking up on these points, at least two things stand out as fundamental to effective planning:

◆ Create a balance between being realistic and stretching yourself.

◆ Learn to manage time effectively.

Be realistic, but stretch yourself

Being realistic when it comes to research planning means setting reasonable goals in the context of other activities and your personal situation. This implies self-knowledge.

The maxim 'know yourself' dates, as far as we know, from Ancient Egypt and has journeyed with humankind through the Greek philosophers right up to the present, with parallels in most, if not all, cultures. It communicates a simple yet profound wisdom, relevant to research planning: be aware of personal strengths and weaknesses—build on the former and devise strategies to deal with the latter. Realistic planning cautions against being too ambitious, as this leads to discouragement and despondency when deadlines come and go and goals are not achieved. It impresses no one to promise a PhD proposal and two articles in the year in which a baby has entered your home! Being too ambitious in goal-setting sets you up for failure.

Having said this, it is equally important to stretch yourself when working out a research plan. 'Stretching' might mean taking steps to equip yourself better in a particular skill such as proposal writing. Or it might require you to be proactive in finding out how to source funding to get to a conference. It might mean committing yourself to a deadline for an article even though things will be tight. It will certainly lure you into the future with your research.

Learn to manage time effectively

The other element that lies at the heart of effective planning is to work well with time—on at least two levels:

- The first (which might be described as 'micro-planning') relates to time and space management on a day-to-day, short-term basis, in relation to research.
- The second (we call it 'macro-planning') involves identifying the elements that should go into a long-term plan and looking down the line—one, three, five or seven years.

Micro-planning: Time management, short-term planning and targets

1 Be creative with time and space.
2 Develop good habits.
3 Be organised and proactive.

A useful exercise is to estimate the relationship between your personal high-energy levels in a day or week and try as far as possible to use this time optimally in research planning. Once this has been established it becomes possible to consider the following:

- Aim, as far as possible, to do something research-related for at least 20 minutes every day.
- Try to negotiate with your HOD to have a research day or part day each week.
- Learn to use short periods of time—if you wait for big chunks you'll never do anything.
- Work in the space that suits you best, but also learn to work wherever you are— even if it is simply to jot down ideas in a notebook (keep a notebook next to your bed and in your bag at all times).
- Get into a rhythm that works for you—a lifestyle rhythm that includes research.

- Be systematic and disciplined, for example, open a 'Research information and support' file. Know how to lay your hands on things.
- Learn to work in such a way that you do not leave things to the last minute, for example, by entering deadlines (including self-imposed ones) in your diary and giving them the same status as other commitments.
- Keep a research log—to track and to serve as a personal 'research checklist'.
- Try to become part of a research support group or colloquium with some of your peers if you are in a discipline where this does not automatically happen.
- Set short-term targets (for example, submission date for an article or PhD proposal deadline).
- Know what resources are available to aid you in your research, for instance, library services.
- As far as possible, try to align your teaching and your research interests (not usually possible when you start out, but gradually work towards this).

Negotiate your teaching programme where relevant and possible—for example, try to concentrate teaching in one semester and have the other freer for research (this avoids the danger of compromise in either area).

What constitutes 'research output'?

Planning research presupposes that we understand what it is that we are striving for. What 'output' from our effort are we hoping to achieve?

Research output refers to:

- the products of research
- that have been peer reviewed and
- made available to the public.[2]

These 'products' or outputs, which are also considered to be the Key Performance Indicators (KPIs) of research, typically comprise the following:

- your own PhD (or Master's)
- peer-reviewed (preferably accredited) publications and other, non-textual, peer-reviewed output, for example, films, dramatic productions and exhibition curatorship; also patents and artefacts
- timely Master's and PhD supervisory throughput
- securing research grants

---

2   One could say 'put it in the public domain' but this term has specific associations with Intellectual Property issues so is avoided here to prevent confusion.

- *ad hominem* promotions
- NRF rating (in South Africa).

In view of current global trends, an additional indicator could be included:

- at a more experienced level, verifiable and fruitful engagement in interdisciplinary collaborative research.

Achieving these goals is associated inter alia with the following activities:

- conference participation and research visits
- sabbatical leave
- professional development
- accommodating personal issues.

Developing a macro-plan: 5–7 years

These elements, as well as any others relevant to your particular research situation, need to be structured into a medium to long-term research plan. Some people find it useful to work with a research-planning template, in which one axis lists the elements identified above and the other lists the years, possibly seven, beginning with the current year. What soon becomes evident is that the various elements are interlinked; none stands alone and all somehow play into one another.

Many new academics begin with two research priorities: to start publishing and to obtain a PhD. It is helpful to begin filling in the plan with relevant targets and working back from there, in other words, the submission date of your first article and your anticipated PhD graduation date. Very soon you will see what else is necessary along the way if these goals are to be achieved.

Assessing available time

The following template, as it stands, accommodates only research activities and reflects a medium to long-term period. Two things need to be said:

1 When working out the time available for research, it is critical to take account of teaching and other commitments. If you have a teaching-intensive first term or semester, followed by a lighter period, it makes sense to plan more research for the latter period, leaving the earlier time freer for teaching-related tasks.

2 The planning template can usefully be adjusted for planning a day, a week, a semester, a year or the period leading up to an event (such as a conference) to include each task to be accomplished in preparation for it.

Let us briefly consider each of the categories included in Table 6.1. (Comments are minimal because most issues are dealt with in detail elsewhere in this book.) *A similar table should be drawn up for the year ahead*, with the 12 months on the Y axis.

The year plan facilitates the breaking-down of broader research targets into steps and milestones, invaluable for measuring real progress. It may also be helpful to break individual components of the plan down into *steps leading up to an event*. For instance, a conference presentation would involve steps such as securing funding, submitting an abstract, registration and bookings, preparation of the paper, creating networking opportunities and post-conference publication.

Obtaining a PhD

In a marked change from the past, there is now enormous pressure on academics in all disciplines to obtain a PhD. One might argue the merits of this in certain disciplines, where a Master's was traditionally considered to be the terminal degree, but it is the reality facing new academics throughout South Africa and wherever international competitiveness is a factor. While it can be daunting at times, doing a PhD can also be a remarkably rewarding experience, with long-term benefits for the individual and the institution, and often society as well. Therefore:

- Do a PhD as soon as possible: don't procrastinate, but neither should you attempt it before you are ready.
- Try to work with an academic mentor who can assess your readiness for a PhD.
- Aim to make the process work for you, taking advantage of feedback from conference presentations and opportunities to publish as you go along.

When planning for your PhD, anticipate your graduation date, working back from there to slot milestones into your research plan. (Refer to Part 4 for further discussion.)

Securing funding

There is enormous variation in the research funding needs of individuals, differences often being discipline- and/or project-related. But every researcher will need to secure funding at some stage, be it a relatively modest amount to attend a conference or for much larger and ongoing expenses for equipment, fieldwork, graduate students, and so on. Regardless of your situation, there are certain principles to bear in mind:

- In conversation with a more experienced colleague try to work out a research budget—your anticipated needs over the next few years, for example, conferences, sabbaticals, fieldwork, equipment and student funding.
- Feed anticipated funding needs into your tabulated plan.
- Familiarise yourself with funding opportunities and take the initiative. Do not wait for others to find out for you.

Table 6.1: Research planning template

	A	B	C	D	E	F	G	H	I	J
2015										
2016										
2017										
2018										
2019										
2020										
2021										

A   PhD
B   Funding
C   Conferences and research visits
D   Publishing and peer-reviewed output
E   Postgraduate supervision
F   Sabbaticals
G   Professional development
H   Promotion
I   NRF rating
J   Personal issues

♦   Apply well in advance: for example, apply for conference funding about nine months ahead of the event, and be aware of application deadlines and time delay between submission, outcome and access to funds.

♦   Allow sufficient time to write a good proposal. This is critical.

Conferences and research visits

Attending and participating in conferences and undertaking formal visits with those who have expertise in your field can, if carefully planned and optimally used, substantially enhance your research career. Conferences offer scope for potential publications, feedback on work, updates on what is happening in the field, and, as with research visits, opportunities for networking and possible research collaboration. In terms of planning, bear in mind the following:

♦   Earmark appropriate conferences a year or more in advance and insert them into your plan. Similarly with research visits—begin negotiations at least a year in advance wherever possible.

♦   Explore funding opportunities and secure funding as soon as possible. In the case of conferences, do not wait until your abstract is accepted. This is too late.

◆ Depending on your personal and institutional situation, try for a conference every year, with at least one and preferably two international conferences built into a five-year plan.

As far as possible, aim to use travel opportunities for more than one purpose, for example, combine a conference and research visit in a single trip. (Refer to Chapter 7.)

Publications and other output

No matter what your discipline, as an academic you will be expected to produce regular, quality research output that is peer reviewed and made available to the public. For most people this means written publications; for some it will mean creative and other non-textual output. It is important to familiarise yourself with your faculty and institutional requirements to meet the criteria for being recognised as research-active, with appropriate goals included in your research plan.

◆ At lecturer level, aim for at least three journal articles or one monograph in three years, and include submission deadlines and progress targets in your tabulated plan.

◆ Have several articles at different stages simultaneously in process so that there is always one nearing completion to submit aannually.

Similarly, for those in the creative disciplines, set appropriate targets (for example, exhibition dates) and include these in the plan. (Refer to chapters 9 and 10.)

Postgraduate supervision

After taking up an academic position it will not be long before you are expected to supervise Master's and then PhD students. While the actual process of supervision belongs in your teaching portfolio, a graduated student is considered as a peer-reviewed research output for the supervisor (and, in South Africa, subsidy-earning for the university). Supervising also provides publication opportunities in the form of co-authorship with students. When considering supervision in the context of research planning, bear the following in mind:

◆ In disciplines where student funding is an issue, try early on to secure the funds that will enable you to take on a student.

◆ Avail yourself of opportunities for training in graduate supervision (part of professional development).

◆ Don't underestimate the time involved in supervision; be realistic in how many students you take on at any one time, and give attention to your possible absences, for example, sabbaticals.

◆ Be aware of a necessary tightening up on student throughput time. (Refer to chapters 12 to 14.)

Sabbaticals

Most institutions will have facilities for study and research (sabbatical) leave. Acquaint yourself with the policy and your eligibility, and identify an appropriate time for extended leave.

- Conceptualise a sabbatical project and output, for example, writing up your PhD thesis.
- Be sure to tie sabbatical leave in with your other research activities, taking it at an optimal time for your project.

Plan as far in advance as possible, particularly if you need to secure funding, and insert preparation milestones into your plan. (Refer to Chapter 7.)

Professional development

Many institutions provide a variety of opportunities for professional development, many of them designed to enhance your capacity as both a teacher and researcher. Unless individual academics assume responsibility for finding out what is available, these opportunities will pass by unnoticed.

- Appropriate professional development initiatives should be identified and built into a research plan, for instance, a research methods course, supervision training,
  research capacity-building seminars (writing for publication, grant-writing, bibliographic data management, etc.).
- Training in information management skills, usually offered by university library staff, is becoming critical and should be considered an integral part of professional development.

Note details of such opportunities in your research plan. (Refer to Chapter 5.)

Ad hominem promotions

Academics in universities that operate autonomously (that is, independent of the state) are able to take advantage of an internal promotions system, which covers the range of academic status from lecturer (sometimes junior lecturer) through to full professor. Each institution will have its own promotion criteria, available on university websites or from faculty offices. Aiming for *ad hominem* promotion can be tremendously motivating for academics. The beauty of academic promotion is that, provided the criteria are met (and relying on the integrity of the review process), no person need be excluded. It is not a case of *either* this person *or* that one for the position. From the perspective of planning, the following points should be noted:

- Familiarise yourself with faculty requirements and, on the basis of this, estimate when it might be feasible for you to apply for promotion.
- Enter a promotion application date into your research plan.
- Itemise what you need to achieve and set targets for each item.
- Because academic promotion takes into account all the core functions of the position, it is useful to construct a promotion timetable alongside the research plan, which accommodates other targets as well, for instance, teaching, supervision, social responsiveness, leadership and administration.

When the time comes, ask at least one, more senior colleague to review your application before submission.

NRF rating

Academics in South Africa are encouraged—and sometimes are put under pressure—to aim for rating through the National Research Foundation evaluation system (known colloquially as 'NRF rating'). This is a research benchmarking apparatus, and, although not unflawed, it incorporates an international peer-review process, which serves as an indicator of the quality of research being carried out in South Africa. It also provides certain benefits, both to the individual researcher and the institution with which she or he is affiliated. For those intending to apply for rating, the following points are relevant:

- Set this as a target in your research plan and work back from there, identifying what you need to achieve.
- Familiarise yourself early on with the different levels of rating and the associated criteria.
- Acquaint yourself now with the application form and begin practising your responses well in advance, for example, your research narrative.
- Prepare your CV appropriately, in line with the NRF template.

When the time comes to apply, *do not hurry your application*. A good application is often developed over a period of several months. (Refer to Chapter 2.)

Personal issues

The ideal for new academics when it comes to research is to sit down with a mentor to discuss, among others, the following issues:

- where you are now
- where you need to get to
- how you're going to get there and by when
- what problems you are encountering.

It is surprising how many people, eager to launch into their research careers, forget to take into account their personal circumstances when setting research goals. It is equally surprising how many people hold up their personal situations as a perennial explanation for lack of incentive and frank underachievement!

Be realistic about the constraints placed on you by personal circumstances. For example, don't plan an overseas sabbatical in a year when you have a child in matric; if you have limiting health issues, avoid committing to more research output than you will realistically cope with.

At the same time remember that, as with the marking of scripts and attending to administrative chores, so domestic issues will always be there. Don't hide behind these, but rather learn how to be creative within the parameters set by them.

An updated curriculum vitae (CV)[3]

An important postscript to this section is to urge you to *maintain an up-to-date CV*. We never know when we will be required to produce a CV, notably to substantiate an application. Do not be caught short, scrambling to enter data (for example, publications, graduated students, conference presentations, etc.) in time for a deadline. Your CV should be ready whenever you need it, to enable you to adapt it for specific purposes.

Curriculum vitae, literally translated from the Latin, means 'course of life'. A CV therefore documents your life's journey, providing an overview of what you have accomplished. As such, it is a key document, both as a means for others to evaluate your achievements and as a useful guide to personal assessment.

CVs can take various forms, depending on the purpose for which they are required. Assess the kind of CV that is required of you and tweak it accordingly, usually by:

- Omitting sections that are irrelevant or specifically excluded as a requirement.

- Expanding sections relevant to the immediate purpose of the CV, by providing more information. For example, in a funding application for a research visit, give details of any previous research visits and what the outcomes and outputs from them were.

Take careful note of any stipulations regarding your CV by the party for whom you are preparing it, for instance, 'do not provide biographical information or details of primary education'.

It is wise to keep an updated **General CV**, which would form the basis of CVs that you may need to design for other purposes. Other types of CV are:

- **Employment CV**, which should foreground previous experience or skills that might testify to your suitability for the new position.

---

3   Based on seminar material prepared by Gaëlle Ramon and Lyn Holness.

◆ **Shortened CV,** for example, as required by conference organisers, where the 'course of your life' would not help in assessing your credentials as a potential presenter.

◆ **Academic CV**, which is specially designed for academic purposes. This is the one you are most likely to need.

Contents of an academic CV

The following items should normally be listed in an academic CV. You may choose to begin or end with your most recent activities and achievements so long as you are consistent throughout.

◆ **Education.** Put an emphasis on tertiary education. Include degrees, diplomas and certificates; where and when they were obtained; if they were awarded with distinction of any sort; titles of dissertations.

◆ **Specialised training.** Include any specialised training that enhances your academic ability, for example, proficiency in several languages.

◆ **Professional involvement.** Include membership of professional associations.

◆ **Employment history prior to academia.** Include relevant details.

◆ **Academic positions.** Indicate the various positions you have held, where they were and for what period. This would include tutorships, fellowships, lecture-ships, departmental headships, current position, etc.

◆ **Administration.** List positions and responsibilities in your department, faculty or university more widely; membership of committees, etc.

◆ **Community involvement.** Social responsiveness is increasingly recognised as a core component of an academic portfolio, so activities that benefit the wider community (particularly those related to your research) should be listed.

◆ **Academic awards.** List items such as class medals, scholarships, post-doctoral fellowships, awards for teaching excellence, NRF rating, prizes.

◆ **Teaching experience.** Provide an overview of major courses you have taught at both undergraduate and graduate level. Detailed information is not usually necessary, but the general character of your teaching experience needs to be explicit.

◆ **Postgraduate supervision.** Provide details of current and graduate students.

◆ **Research record.** List the various projects in which you have been involved, indicating your roles, whether you fulfilled these roles, and the outcomes of the research.

◆ **Conference participation.** Provide a list of conferences in which you have participated, both local and international, with the following details: name of conference, dates, place, title of presentation, and whether this was for a seminar, plenary or poster session. *Remember, unpublished conference papers do not qualify as research output.*

◆ **Publications.** List publications according to category, providing all publishing details. Bear in mind the criteria for assessing scholarly publications and ensure that your categories reflect these:

- peer-reviewed journal articles, including review articles
- books: monographs, textbooks, single- or co-authored
- edited books: books you have edited or co-edited
- chapters in books
- guest editor of journals
- papers in conference proceedings: indicate clearly those with an ISBN/ISSN number
- book reviews: supplying all relevant details
- popular articles: non-peer-reviewed journals, magazines, newspapers, online articles, etc. *Do not underestimate the value of such publications.* With current rethinking about the meaning of 'research impact' and a focus on 'engaged scholarship' such publications are receiving greater recognition than in the past. This is in part due to funders' dissemination and impact requirements.

◆ **Electronic dissemination** of research. For example, blogging and tweeting, although not recognised for accreditation purposes, are gradually being acknowledged as a powerful means of making research public and achieving impact (albeit not yet in all disciplines).

◆ **Other forms of research output.** List, for example, exhibitions, works of art, patents and performances—in other words, all forms of output that are non-textual in nature. Provide as much detail as possible, such as names, descriptions, dates and places.

Identify a research focus

Planning one's research presupposes a research direction and specific projects or topics within that chosen area and field. Those researchers in disciplines in which it is normative to work in teams or research groups, and especially those who have developed an interest in the work of a particular unit within a discipline, will find it relatively easy to find direction and focus in their personal research. Some others, regardless of discipline, come through university studies with a clear idea of what they are interested in and will pursue it as a focus of their research. But this certainly does not apply to everyone. Many people struggle to identify a broad area of research within their discipline, let alone something more specific on which to focus. Here are a few points to consider:

- ◆ What are you passionate about?

- ◆ Try to identify gaps; this means knowing what is going on in the field.

- ◆ Talk to colleagues, especially senior colleagues.

- ◆ Find out about your department's research strategy. Some departments, particularly in applied disciplines, strive to become known as centres of excellence in research in a particular area. It is wise to look for a niche area here if possible.

- ◆ Where is the funding? At early-career level there may be fewer funding opportunities for what is called 'curiosity-driven' research, and more opportunities for research that is considered to have relevance to current issues. Nowadays funding is more likely to be found in collaborative rather than individual projects, so explore the possibility of working within a research collaboration.

- ◆ You need to start somewhere; possibly begin by writing an article from a dissertation you've written, or begin with small pilot project to test the waters.

- ◆ Sometimes, arriving at a focus comes initially through a process of elimination, by identifying what you are *not* interested in; for instance, you may have had enough of your thesis topic and need to move on.

- ◆ Availability of resources for particular types of research should be a key factor.

Once you have identified a focus for your research, your next goal should be to demonstrate coherence. In other words, down the line you should be able to look back and see how your research holds together. There should ideally be a thread woven through it, showing how your various projects cohere. Research should not be haphazard, jumping from one topic or area to another. Experienced academics may have more than one area of research interest and expertise, but when starting out it is important to develop your expertise in one area, with the long-term aim of eventually being known as *the* person in that area. We have seen (Chapter 2) that such coherence is particularly important for South African academics planning to apply for NRF rating. It does not mean that you *cannot* change; but if you do, do so mindfully.

One last word on the research focus: if you are struggling to decide on a direction for your research, do not panic! It may take time to become obvious, but sooner or later that direction will find you …

Conclusion

Planning is relevant to every aspect of one's academic portfolio, both on a day-to-day and a longer-term level. There are certain things that require extensive planning, and it is on these that we focus in Chapter 7.

OPTIMISING RESEARCH OPPORTUNITIES
SABBATICALS, CONFERENCES AND RESEARCH VISITS

There are certain components of an academic job that constitute opportunities that are not common in other professions. Sabbatical leave, attending national and international conferences, and research visits are among these. Each one provides opportunities for what in contemporary academic parlance is called 'staff and student mobility' which is important in an increasingly competitive, global higher education environment, where opportunities to position yourself in an international community of scholars are critical.

There are other reasons besides a research agenda to avail yourself of these opportunities, but it is the likely contribution to scholarship that comprises a central criterion in the granting of leave and funding for these activities. Because each requires careful planning, it is appropriate that we engage in a conversation around sabbaticals, conferences and research visits soon after reflecting on research planning more generally. I deal with each separately, although an ideal situation, of course, would be to combine all three in a single visit and/or period of time.

PERSPECTIVE

MOBILITY FOR EARLY-CAREER RESEARCHERS

The University of Cape Town has several mobility opportunities for academic staff offering study, training and research periods abroad, mainly in Europe, America and Asia. Some of these programmes are Erasmus-Mundus, Commonwealth Fellowship Plan, DAAD, British Council, Fulbright Scholarship and WUN. For early-career researchers they provide Master's and PhD candidates the opportunity to spend a research period in a research or academic institution abroad. These programmes are academically enriching as they allow local researchers to participate in the international research enterprise with confidence.

I was privileged in 2005 to be awarded a Commonwealth Fellowship to spend a year at Rothamsted Research in the United Kingdom, working on my PhD research. I had begun the process of undertaking a PhD in statistics in 2004. An Australian colleague referred me to Rothamsted Research, where I was fascinated by the prospect of working with the original developers of the statistical methodology needed for my PhD work. Prior to this I had done very little concrete work on my research topic, except for reading and understanding the vast amount of literature on the subject. So the fellowship award was timely.

My research work really took off when I was at Rothamsted Research. I now had access to both tools and ideas for my research, and over the year I spent there I made significant progress. I returned to South Africa a confident academic and eager to complete the research. A major challenge was co-ordinating the research work and ideas between my supervisors at the host institution and a local supervisor. My supervisors at Rothamsted Research were new to both me and my local supervisor. Ideally, for a PhD candidate to participate in a mobility programme, contact between the local supervisor and the researcher(s) at the host institution should already exist.

While overseas I had the opportunity to attend conferences, workshops and seminars which would have otherwise been unaffordable from Cape Town. At these gatherings I had the opportunity to network with international researchers in my field. This was empowering for me as an early-career researcher. Through this networking I managed to establish sustainable and worthwhile research collaborations. Over the years, I have engaged in research collaborations which have given me an international perspective and international exposure.

Freedom Gumedze

Sabbatical planning[1]

In the past many academics were able to regard sabbaticals as a right after serving a set period of time. This is no longer the case. Today, sabbaticals—now sometimes referred to as 'Research and Study Leave'—are no longer regarded as a right (as in the past) but a privilege imbued with responsibility. The new term itself signifies a shift from a sabbatical being regarded by many as a time for relaxation to one that must at the end provide evidence of scholarly productivity and of overall refuelling. In some institutions the opportunity to take such leave is contingent on so many other factors, not least financial ones, that it is rare. For those in institutions where sabbatical leave is possible, it is important to understand what it is designed for, and to plan for and use it optimally.

Institutions have their own sabbatical policies, which should be consulted, but generally requirements for research and study leave centre on a few main things:

- ◆ the applicant's employment, and particularly research, track record
- ◆ timing of the proposed leave in relation to departmental and faculty needs
- ◆ a well-prepared, comprehensive proposal demonstrating careful, realistic planning and the intention of producing clearly defined outcomes and a report at the end that tallies with the proposal.

---

1   See De Gruchy & Holness, *The Emerging Researcher*, 64–69. Other input in this section was provided by colleagues, frequently in workshop conversations.

What is sabbatical leave given for?

The term 'sabbatical' derives from the Hebrew and Christian scriptures, where it signifies a rest or break from regular activity. Sabbaticals in academia continue to refer to a temporary, uninterrupted break from routine, but it is a break in order to achieve some goal associated with scholarship. This could mean, for example, writing a book, completing a series of articles, developing a research proposal, undertaking research visits, doing fieldwork, preparing for and holding an exhibition, or upgrading professional skills. With slight variations between institutions, sabbatical leave is therefore usually granted for purposes of *approved scholarly or creative activity for research or, provided there is a scholarly dimension to it, for academic professional development, for example, improved teaching skills.*

Typically a sabbatical is for an extended period—up to a year and usually not less than three months—and is accumulated at a set rate for every year of employment, accruing each year at rates determined by individual institutions (refer to institutional websites for relevant policies). What I present here applies to the generic principles and purposes of sabbatical leave, and the focus will be on how to plan optimally in order to derive maximum benefit from it.

PERSPECTIVE

THE ADVANTAGES OF PLANNING: A RESEARCHER'S EXPERIENCE

(Prior to planning her sabbatical, this researcher attended a workshop on effective sabbaticals and set in place arrangements to visit an overseas institution during her leave.)

I found the sabbatical planning workshop incredibly useful, especially to be reminded of how long in advance one has to plan (given funding deadlines) for a one-year overseas stint. It also gave me a better idea of how to structure my timeline on what to do first.

I started planning for my six-month sabbatical in advance and structured it around the following:

* What I aimed to get done before going on sabbatical—complete data collection.
* What I would do during sabbatical—data analysis, meetings with my host in the United States, conference presentation, meetings with supervisor.
* What I aimed to get out of it (throughput—papers for publication).

Before going on sabbatical I identified key areas in the literature which I felt I would need to read during my time [in the USA] where I would have access to a wider selection of journals. I sent my host a plan of what I needed to do and how I thought I would benefit from consulting with her. I also met with my supervisor regularly to establish what I would need to focus on in terms of the chapter that I was writing.

> Because I had planned well, I was able to focus on my PhD and to make maximum use of the time I had. Since I had already identified all the areas on which I would need to focus, I could then start working on them as soon as I took my sabbatical.
>
> *Abongwe Bangeni* (following a successful sabbatical during her PhD research)

Preparation

Taking sabbatical leave is a major undertaking, and careful planning is required to make it productive and worthwhile. This applies particularly if one goes abroad. This presupposes an early start to planning—*at least* a year ahead. In conceptualising sabbatical leave there are a number of preliminary issues to consider, both technical and strategic.

- ◆ **Clarity about requirements.** Before you do anything else, become familiar with the requirements of the university and liaise also with your Human Resources Department on your eligibility status.

- ◆ **Personal situation.** Take your domestic situation into account when planning a sabbatical. If you have a partner and children and decide to go overseas, will your family accompany you? If so, you will have to raise additional funding, find suitable accommodation, arrange for schooling, take out additional health insurance, etc.

- ◆ **Deciding on the period of leave.** Periods of sabbatical leave are institutionally determined, sometimes with the option of three, six, nine or 12 months, depending on how much leave you have accrued. There are pros and cons for each length of time and these should be carefully considered. Much will depend on university policy, your department's needs, what you hope to do, where you are planning to spend your leave, and what period is considered optimal in your discipline. Remember to ascertain the approved starting dates for periods of sabbatical leave, as well as the situation with annual leave in relation to a sabbatical.

- ◆ **Departmental needs and requirements.** When applying for an extended leave of absence from the university, the needs of your department must be considered and this presupposes an early conversation with your HOD, sometimes up to two years ahead. Your HOD has the responsibility to ensure that the teaching programme of the department can be sustained adequately in your absence. But he or she also has to ensure that the needs and expectations of all members of staff are considered, meaning that careful departmental planning is necessary. For this reason, sabbatical leave cannot always be taken when you become eligible for it, or when you would like to take it.

- ◆ **Supervision responsibilities.** If you are supervising Master's or PhD students, ensure that your planned leave does not adversely affect them. In fact, leaves of absence such as sabbaticals are one of the reasons why some departments and institutions insist on either team supervision or co-supervision. You are respon-sible for informing your students timeously, making alternative arrangements for supervision if this is appropriate, and generally ensuring that what you have agreed to in the Memorandum of Understanding is honoured (see Chapter 12). Electronic communication makes distance supervision feasible today in a way that was not previously possible, so that being away is not necessarily an insur-mountable problem.

♦ **Formal application.** Become familiar with your university's application process, particularly how far in advance you need to apply. However, it is advis-able to apply formally as far in advance as possible.

♦ **Sabbatical proposal.** The onus is on you to convince the university that you merit a sabbatical and are able to raise the funds necessary for it. Therefore prepare your proposal with care, making sure that what you plan to do can be achieved within the period of the sabbatical, and that it relates to the resources available at the place where you will take it. Clearly indicate your anticipated outcomes and outputs (articles, a book, art installation, development of a tool, etc.) together with timeframes. Provide as much detail as you can, including, if possible, journals being targeted, the publisher of your book, venue and dates for an exhibition or performance, etc. (see suggested proposal template below).

♦ **Prior work.** Sabbatical leave is sometimes taken to complete a major project, and this presupposes that you have already done a great deal of work on it. At other times, a sabbatical may be taken to launch a project, but even then preparatory work should have been done to make this possible, and this should be reflected in your proposal. You cannot spend the first week of your sabbatical asking: 'What am I going to do?' and 'Where will I find that?'

SUGGESTION FOR A SABBATICAL PROPOSAL TEMPLATE

While there is often no template for a sabbatical proposal, there are nevertheless certain things it should contain. Having consulted several university websites and found a high degree of consistency in what makes a successful sabbatical proposal, I offer the following suggestions.

Guidelines

* It need not be a lengthy document. However, it must contain *sufficient infor-mation for the reviewers to evaluate the merit of the proposal* and the benefit it will have for the staff member and the institution (your HOD, the Dean and the Deputy Vice-Chancellor for Research).

* *It must be clear and concise*—do not be too wordy; make it easy to assess.

* *Motivate* well, providing clear *goals*.

- *Be as specific as you can* with things like names of individuals and institutions, actual dates (of, for example, conferences, short courses, research visits), journal details, etc.
- Supply as much *supporting documentation* regarding your proposed activities as possible, for example, letters of invitation and ethical clearance documents. (Even if it is not required by your faculty, it is wise to have the documentation available.)
- If possible, use this as an opportunity to demonstrate *coherence in your research*, in other words, show how your sabbatical project ties in with your general research focus.
- *Plan to work hard, but also be realistic* in what you intend to achieve during your sabbatical.
- Bear in mind that the *proposal* and your *final report* should tally. Construct the proposal to facilitate this.
- Take note of *how far in advance* of the sabbatical period the proposal must be submitted at your institution (much earlier if possible, to facilitate planning).

The proposal
- Requested *period of leave* (include motivation for this particular time).
- *Narrative summary* (150–200 words) of your project and what you intend to do in your sabbatical—in other words, what are you actually asking the university to give you paid leave of absence for?
- Provide details of *pre-planning*. This would include things like:
  - Approaches made to an overseas institution for office and/or bench space and use of other facilities; offers to give lectures and requests to participate in seminars; requests for meetings with prominent scholars and other colleagues in your field, etc.
  - Conferences, colloquia or workshops you plan to attend, and attach supporting documentation to your application.
  - Research already done in preparation for sabbatical, for example, data you may have collected.
  - Arrangements you have made with a collaborator.
  - Arrangements you have made for your postgraduate students during your anticipated absence.
  - Proof of purchase of a laptop to enable you to work away from home.
  - Funding you have raised for sabbatical support.
- *Timeline of pre-, actual and post-sabbatical activities*. This should be *tabulated* and *specific*, and include *anticipated outputs with dates*.

- *Anticipated outcomes*, for example, professional growth (such as short courses attended) and the likely impact on teaching and research.

- Anticipated *outputs* (in addition to their mention in tabulated plan), for example, completion of a PhD or articles in peer-reviewed journals.

- *Assurance* that a detailed report will follow immediately on your return.

Additional documents to be submitted:

- an updated CV

- a sabbatical budget (in cases where encashment of leave or a study travel grant is being applied for)

- any supporting documents to confirm sabbatical plans.

Choosing the right time and place

- **When to take it.** Whether you plan sabbatical leave for the beginning, middle or end of a project depends on the nature of your research and when it would be most appropriate. It could be to write a proposal, consult with collaborators, do data collection, or 'write up' a thesis or complete a book.

- **Choosing the appropriate place.** Where do you go on sabbatical? Some academics find it useful to stay at home; others find it is necessary to go to another university, regionally or overseas. Many factors play a role in making this decision. But the main one should be related to your research needs. What resources do you need for your research at this time and where will they be available? These resources may be archival; they may be related to people in your discipline who could provide stimulus and inspiration for your work; you may need to collect data in a particular place; or you may need the resources of a particular laboratory.

- **Travelling abroad requires advance planning.** Whereas arranging a sabbatical at home may be comparatively straightforward, travelling abroad requires a great deal of advance planning. Not only do you need to decide on the best location, raise the funding, etc., but you also need to be in negotiation with the department/institution at which you wish to be based. Although having developed peer contacts and making personal contact with them will be of great help, you cannot simply arrive and expect to be warmly welcomed! You host institution will have to make the necessary preparations. For instance, you will need access to the library or laboratory space and other resources; bench costs will have to be negotiated, where applicable; you will need to obtain permission to participate in seminars and make arrangements to engage with academics in your field. In one of our sabbatical seminars, a participant, speaking from bitter experience, reminded the group of the importance of arranging physical access to the university itself. This person arrived to start her first day at her host institution and discovered that she had no way of entering the premises!

- ◆ **Conference participation.** Attending appropriate conferences during your sabbatical is a major plus if you are overseas and within easy reach of such events. Explore possibilities of attendance and participation in advance of your sabbatical, and make the necessary plans to attend and present at those that are relevant to your research.

- ◆ **Strategic encounters.** Travelling during your sabbatical will provide opportunities to consult with colleagues, some of whom may be leaders in your field. Your choice of time and place for the sabbatical should be influenced by accessibility to such people, with whom you should set plans in place ahead of the actual visit.

- ◆ **A time of renewal.** Not all your time on sabbatical will be (nor should it be) given to research. Remember, the original meaning of a sabbatical is a time of renewal and refreshment. Sabbaticals are opportunities for recharging your academic and personal batteries, so it is useful to know in advance about opportunities to broaden your cultural horizons and enjoy a different environment. Do not lose sight of this during your sabbatical, so that when you return you are, in fact, ready for the tasks that face you.

Funding research and study leave

Funding is critical. Take the initiative well in advance to find what resources are available to you through the university and elsewhere. Be careful to establish exactly what the respective funds can be used for. Some major financial considerations are:

- ◆ travel funding (air and ground; getting there and being there)
- ◆ accommodation and subsistence
- ◆ equipment costs
- ◆ bench costs (for laboratory usage)
- ◆ family expenses (for example, schooling)
- ◆ insurance, especially health insurance
- ◆ conference expenses
- ◆ purchasing books, stationery, photocopying, etc.

When applying for funds make sure that you note the various *deadlines for submitting applications.* Your sabbatical could be jeopardised if you fail to meet these deadlines.

Follow up

Inevitably there will be many tasks awaiting you on your return, perhaps a heavier teaching load and additional administrative responsibilities. But your sabbatical responsibilities do not end when you return to the university. There are two major things that relate directly to your sabbatical research that need to be attended to:

- **Your sabbatical report.** This is not only an account of what you have accomplished on your sabbatical, but it also plays an important role in determining whether or not you get sabbatical leave next time around. So prepare your report with care. One way to ensure that this does not become a burden after you return, and that it adequately reflects what you did on sabbatical, is to keep a *log* or *journal* while on leave. If you keep this up to date, indicating what you did—people you consulted, seminars and conferences you attended, books you read, seminars you may have given, and writing you managed to accomplish—compiling your report will be that much easier and it can be submitted soon after you return. Our institution has no template for a sabbatical report, but the critical thing is that the proposal and report should tally. In other words, report against what you indicated in your proposal that you would do, providing as much detail as possible.

- **Outcomes and outputs.** In your proposal you indicated anticipated outcomes and outputs of your sabbatical. Progress on each of these should be reported, and if you have not accomplished what you set out to do, explain why not. Do not ignore this. The time has now come to ensure delivery! Enough said.

Conference participation[2]

Going to conferences and presenting papers is integral to academic life and this can be immensely beneficial in a number of ways. But most of the time no one actually prepares us for this—how to select a conference, how to prepare for it, how to present and how to derive maximum benefit from participating and from simply being there. The aim of this section is to open up the issues involved in participating in a conference.

Why present at conferences?

- To put work into the public domain before someone else does.
- Conferences provide an ideal social space to discuss your work, and this means taking advantage of networking opportunities presented by them.
- To test ideas and obtain feedback/peer review on your work.
- To acquaint yourself with what is happening at the cutting edge in your field.

---

2   This section draws on the combined experience of John Cooper, John W. de Gruchy, Jane English, Lyn Holness, Charles Masango, Gaëlle Ramon and Les Underhill.

- ◆ To take a first step to a publication or PhD proposal.
- ◆ To position yourself on the national and international research radar screen.

In some disciplines it is customary for a supervisor to enable her or his Master's and PhD students to attend and present at conferences by covering the related costs. Part of our institution's new research strategy is to afford *every* PhD student the opportunity to attend an international conference in order to present and obtain feedback on their work and to be exposed to the global scholarly community. However one looks at it, this is an enormous privilege and students should be encouraged to approach the opportunity with diligence, and to prepare presentations to the best of their ability.

Planning for a conference

In planning for a conference the primary question ought to be: *How is this going to benefit my research?* To help in identifying an appropriate conference, a number of issues need to be considered.

- ◆ **Selecting a conference**
    - Ask colleagues in your field with conference experience for advice.
    - Are there society/association conferences that would be relevant for you?
    - Is there an annual conference in your discipline or area of research?
    - Do a Google search and check the results with colleagues.
    - Build up a list of potential conferences for the future (this facilitates advance planning).
    - Try to plan trips for other purposes (for example, research visits) to coincide with the conference.
    - The secret is to identify an *appropriate* conference—not the one in the most enticing location!
    - There are certain conferences that, by design, feature in the programme the leaders in the field who are there to present updates on the latest developments. These conferences are especially relevant to new academics if the research field is a relatively narrow one or if there is only a small local representation of it.
- ◆ **Type of conference**

    There are different types of conferences, and it is important to select one that is most relevant to you at this particular stage of your research career:
    - those on a single theme within a focus area of a discipline (often small conferences)
    - those grounded in a particular discipline/sub-discipline/society

- generalist ('omnibus') conferences with a wide range of interest sections (sometimes thousands of participants).

◆ **People likely to be there**

For many academics the greater value of a conference lies not in presenting a paper but in networking with colleagues, some of whom may be leaders in the field, from other institutions and other parts of the country or world. Conferences provide opportunities to:

- Consult with the expert on an issue critical to the study in which you are engaged.
- Engage with someone who has expressed interest in a collaborative project.
- Identify potential external examiners of your students' theses.
- Meet journal editors and potential book publishers.
- Meet new people working in your field.

◆ **Timing of the conference in relation to**:

- funding cycles—apply for funding about nine months in advance
- what you're working on and the stage you're at (for example, in a PhD) teaching and other commitments.

Behind the scenes: Conference organisation

Conferences do not materialise out of the blue. Conference organisers put a great deal of time into planning them, and they work hard behind the scenes to run them. Put yourself in their position and ask *what would be helpful to you*. Here are some suggestions:

◆ **Time-related**

- Keep rigidly to deadlines.
- Contact the conference organiser early and submit your abstract timeously. Slots get filled up.
- Should you have a place on the programme and need for some reason to withdraw, inform the organisers immediately.
- Arrive at the conference with all that you need for your presentation.

◆ **Management-related**

- Supply exactly what is required (for example, length of abstract, appropriately presented CV).
- Presentation committees aim to fill the programme with papers that are excellent and not merely adequate, so your abstract needs to convince the organising team of the merits of your paper.

- Make sure your proposed paper slots comfortably into one of the categories or sections on the programme.
- Read electronic communications relating to the conference meticulously, and so avoid unnecessary queries to the organisers.

What to present

◆ A rule of thumb for conferences is that you *give a paper when you have something to say*. Having something to say derives from different sources and this will determine the type of paper presented:

- work in progress (for example, a PhD proposal)
- work about to be submitted for publication
- results from a particular stage and/or facet of the project
- single or co-presentation.

◆ Select a topic very carefully:

- bearing in mind which specialists in the field might be there
- familiarising yourself with the current debate in the area
- being aware of what has been published
- identifying something unique but relevant, the key being to have a unique angle.

◆ Make sure that the research you are presenting is developed enough to permit fruitful discussion.

Sometimes it is good to submit more than one proposal if you have several potential papers to present.

Title of the paper

Titles are important. They have the potential to attract both programme organisers and potential attendees of your session should you get on to the programme, or to evoke a 'give that one a miss' response. The secret is to arrive at a combination of features when it comes to the title of your paper:

◆ It should be descriptive of content, containing just sufficient in the way of indicators to what the paper will be about.

◆ The title itself should be reasonably short, possibly with a colon followed by a more descriptive subtitle.

◆ It should be something that will grab attention without being gimmicky, and will attract the attention of the organisers and people to your session.

Proposal/abstract

The aim of the proposal is to provide the committee with enough information:

- To understand what the paper is about.
- To be convinced that it will be of interest.
- To assure them that you are aware of current developments in your field.
- To assure them that you will put in the necessary preparation.

A good abstract:

- Explains what the topic is.
- Provides rationale for the topic.
- Indicates the scope of the paper.
- Explains what the audience will gain from the presentation.
- Should be concise and to the point, that is, exercise economy of words, adhering to the length of abstract required by the organisers (if there are no guidelines it should be approximately 200–250 words).

Preparing the paper

There are a number of useful guidelines to preparing a good conference paper:

- The key is to prepare well in advance. Begin several months ahead of the conference.
- Bear in mind that unless you are a keynote or plenary speaker, you are likely to have 20–30 minutes *in total*—that is, for the presentation and discussion. Make sure of your time allocation in advance and prepare accordingly.
- Many people find it useful to write a full paper and adapt it for the conference presentation, that is, to identify 'talking points' for the conference. There are some conferences that require submission of full papers prior to the conference (to facilitate a pre-conference peer-review process with publication in mind). When adapting the paper, remember the following:
  - Do not try to present the full paper and risk running out of time and not reaching the main point!
  - Prepare a presentation that will cover your paper in the allocated time (often 15 minutes for presentation). For those speaking to notes rather than making visual presentations, a useful guide to preparation is that it takes roughly three minutes to present an A4 page of about 400 words.
  - Highlight the main points you want to make and build your presentation around these.

- If reading your presentation is unavoidable, prepare something with an audience in mind. You are not writing for a journal at this point!

  - Use direct speech.

  - Read in a natural, conversational tone.

  - Use short sentences.

  - Use a less complex structure than something written for publication.

  - Look at the audience as much as possible. This helps to maintain a conversational tone.

- In many disciplines PowerPoint presentations are presumed. Remember the following:

  - To be effective, slides should not be cluttered with information, whether graphics or text.

  - They should contain the main points referred to above.

  - They should be clear and easy on the eye.
  - Visual material should not detract from the oral presentation. You are there to deliver a paper, after all.

  - Present approximately one slide per minute. Your audience is there to listen to you. They can read the paper later.

  - Whether you are using PowerPoint or any other audio-visual material, find out if these need to be submitted in advance of your session.

  - Make sure that you are up to date with the current debate/literature/findings and make this clear in your paper. This immediately enhances your credibility with the audience.

- As to the content of the paper itself:

  - Put it in context so that it makes sense to the audience. For example, if you are an ornithologist in the southern hemisphere speaking about migratory habits of birds, you will need to remind northerners of seasonal differences.

  - Develop a focused argument without too much detail. For new presenters this requires practice. You cannot afford to waste time and words on unnecessary detail. Remember, you will be talking to people from within your field, who therefore do not need everything explained.

  - Draw out conclusions that demonstrate the relevance and reach of your work.

  - Have all references at hand, possibly in a closing slide with unreadably small text—to remind the audience that the references do exist.

◆ Practise out loud before the conference, timing yourself and asking family, friends or colleagues to listen and offer critique. Consider presenting to yourself in the mirror if you have no other audience.

MAKE SURE OF THE FOLLOWING IN ADVANCE

Date and time of your presentation.

Venue—where it is and how long it will take you to get there; go to the room in advance.

Electronic equipment available and functioning. If possible, *load your presentation* in advance and check that it is projecting and any features (such as animations and video clips) are working.

Presenting the paper

◆ Arrive early.

◆ Identify and make yourself known to the person chairing the session if you have not done so already.

◆ Check with a colleague that your voice is projecting properly.

◆ Be enthusiastic—the audience will pay closer attention and be more responsive.

◆ Depending on the platform layout and size of the audience, it is better to stand rather than to sit.

◆ Speak to your paper if possible, do not read it.

◆ Speak *to* your audience, *not at* them.

◆ Speak simply but not simplistically.

◆ Speak slowly, loudly and clearly, and project, but keep a conversational tone.

  • Remember that there will be those in the audience who are listening in a language other than their own. Anticipate this, respectfully parenthesising explanations for specific disciplinary terms, if necessary.

  • If you are presenting in a second language, the same presentation rules apply: slow, loud, clear.

◆ Explain abbreviations the first time you use them.

◆ Dealing with nervousness: take a drink of water to avoid a dry throat and tell the audience: 'This is my first talk to an international audience and I'm a bit nervous, but I am excited about my work and hope you will be too.'

◆ Have note cards as well as slides so you are not tempted to put too much information on the slides.

- Never learn any of your speech by heart. You are not an actor.

- Remember, you are an academic. Your audience wants content. They do not expect to be entertained.

- Be succinct and to the point. Avoid 'trailing off' your sentences and your paper. End positively, thanking the audience for their attendance.

- *Do not* go over the allotted time.

SOME POINTERS TO COMMUNICATING WITH CONFIDENCE[3]

Develop a **positive attitude** to your presentation to overcome lack of confidence (for example, remind yourself that you have prepared well).

Relax and breathe deeply before starting in order to overcome your anxiety; consciously relax your body.

Look up, **make direct eye contact** with the audience and use animated facial expressions.

Be conscious of body language or non-verbal cues (for instance, avoid repetitive gestures like fiddling with a pen; don't be completely static; use gestures spontaneously).

Use space well (for example, stand as close to your audience as possible to create a warmer atmosphere and give yourself more authority).

Speak slowly and clearly, with appropriate pauses.

Dealing with feedback

- Listen carefully and jot down each point as the person speaks. This serves three purposes:

  1 A prompt for your response to the issues raised.

  2 A reminder of issues raised by your paper when you come to rework it for publication.

  3 It creates time for you to be formulating an answer.

- Not all feedback will be constructive. Don't be fazed or become defensive.

- Take special note of any literature you may have missed in your preparation.

- If someone raises a useful point or a question you are not able to answer, offer to connect with them afterwards to discuss the matter further (this is an indirect way of networking too).

- Relax—there is little time for discussion during the presentation programme!

---

3   See English, J. (ed.). (2012). 'Presentation skills', in *Professional Communication: Deliver effective written, spoken and visual messages*. Cape Town: Juta, 151–178.

Networking and your academic future (these go hand-in-hand)

Networking, as we saw in Chapter 1, is a hallmark of academic life. Conferences provide a good opportunity for this. To maximise on these networking opportunities, it is wise to be strategic:

- If possible, find out ahead of time who of note will be at the conference and, where possible and appropriate, make contact beforehand and arrange to meet at the conference.

- Rehearse a 'way in' to a meaningful exchange with someone with whom you really want to engage. For example, familiarise yourself with their latest publications so that you are able to refer to these (remember, academic pride is alive and well in the upper echelons, and people like nothing better than to hear their work referred to and cited).

- Allow time at the conference to meet new people, remembering that sometimes the most useful conversations happen 'in the margins'—over lunch or coffee, or even serendipitously in the elevator/lift.

- Do not miss important sessions. Conferences help to position you in your discipline, both nationally and internationally.

- Record the essence of significant conversations you have had each day, making careful note of things to follow up on.

- Follow up on contacts as soon as you get home—even if it is simply to say how good it was to meet them.

> **NOTE**
>
> You may discover, on contemplating your participation in an upcoming conference, that there is to be a section focused exclusively on your research field. Find out in advance who is co-ordinating that section and who else will be presenting. Do a Google Scholar search on each of these people to find out if there are commonalities between your research and theirs, and if there seems to be scope for any sort of future collaboration. You could then establish contact prior to the conference, or at least arrive at it able to initiate meaningful conversations.

Poster presentations

Sometimes abstracts are accepted for posters rather than paper presentations. These should be prepared with care, bearing in mind that they have potential both to attract people to your work and to provide excellent networking opportunities, often allowing for conversations that would not be possible in a seminar context. What follows are some generic guidelines for poster presentations:

- Check guidelines provided by conference organisers. (Do this for each respective conference.)

- Prepare your poster completely before arriving at the conference and do not underestimate the time required to prepare it—design, print and lamination.

- Components of the poster should be clearly visible from one metre away so that people walking past can see it. Check the print size carefully beforehand, in consultation with others.[4]

- Check the poster for the following with colleagues, family and friends: clarity, readability and visual appeal.

- Be concise—avoid providing too much information.

- Be creative—your poster needs to stand out, attracting viewers (like bees to bright flowers!).

- Figures and tables look better in colour than in black and white.

- Do not cram your poster. Provide additional information on a handout, taking upwards of 50 copies with you. At the top of each handout the following information should be visible:
  - title
  - authorship (indicating first author, where applicable)
  - e-mail address (of first author, where applicable)
  - university affiliation
  - name of conference, year and location.

- Always wear your name badge.

- For poster sessions:
  - Be on time.
  - Do not leave your poster.
  - Be prepared to engage.

- Go to the conference prepared with the following:
  - tape, thumbtacks, etc. in case these are not provided
  - flash-drive containing your handout material
  - additional paper in case you run out of handouts
  - calling cards if you have them.

---

4   English, *Professional Communication,* 208-210.

Research visits

Much that is relevant to research visits has been covered in the foregoing discussion on general research planning, sabbaticals and conferences, since such visits can frequently be conducted in the context of either sabbaticals or conferences. But there are times when it is necessary (or optimal) to arrange a research visit on its own, and this requires particular preparation.

Reasons for a research visit

There are several circumstances that may justify a research visit. Whatever the circumstances of the visit, preparation is necessary. You may need to:

◆ Attend a workshop.

◆ Spend time in a laboratory.

◆ Meet with collaborators.

◆ Consult with a supervisor.

◆ Visit libraries and archives.

◆ Visit a centre of excellence in your field.

Preparing for a research visit

◆ *Secure funding* in advance. Obtaining funding will usually require the following:

  • A proposal for the visit, indicating background, aims and outputs.

  • Evidence of acceptance for a course or workshop where applicable.

  • A letter of invitation from the person you wish to visit, indicating institutional affiliation and relevance to your research.

  • A budget for the trip.

◆ Simultaneously make other *practical arrangements*:

  • Liaise with those you wish to consult.

  • Reserve a place on courses and workshops.

  • Arrange laboratory facilities or entrance to libraries and archives.

  • See to travel and accommodation arrangements.

The value of research visits

While research visits have always featured in academia, they are becoming critical in a globalised research environment where international partnerships are increasingly necessary to secure substantial funding, and where networking and establishing oneself among a community of scholars is paramount. For early-career academics this might seem daunting, and becoming part of a global community does not happen overnight. In fact, it takes years of groundwork to establish a local identity first and then incrementally develop wider credentials, as your work becomes known.

A second reason for research visits is much closer to the experience of emerging researchers: accessing resources (people, structures and places) that are necessary to ensure your development as a researcher. They comprise preliminary steps in exploring the national and international research platform.

Documenting and reporting on research visits

As with sabbatical leave and conference attendance, keeping a log of what you do, who you meet and what progress you make towards your stated goals for the visit is imperative. This will inform the report you will be required to submit on your return.

Conclusion

None of the activities discussed in this chapter, and indeed no research, can be undertaken without adequate funding. Skills in raising funds are not a birthright. They need to be learned and honed. This is the topic of Chapter 8.

SECURING AND MANAGING RESEARCH GRANTS

Introductory comments

Research in some disciplines requires a great deal of funding, while in others funding requirements are minimal. At some stage, however, every academic will require research funding, whether it be a modest amount to attend a conference or a budget for financing the various elements and stages of a large project. Raising research funds and managing grants are not inherent abilities. As with other research-related activities, they are skills that need to be learnt, and this takes time and practice. Unsuccessful grant applications can usually be traced back to one of two issues: inappropriate selection of the grant itself or an inadequately prepared proposal.

I begin by addressing the issues around actually securing funds, including the elements of a proposal, after which I provide some guidelines for the management of grants once they have been secured.

Principles of successful grant-writing

Each research grant is unique and will have specific criteria stipulated by the funding agency. But there are a number of generic principles that apply to all successful grant-writing. When considering these principles, be aware that the significance of some of the points raised will vary according to the nature and scope of the funding need. You should, therefore, modify your proposal according to the requirements of the criteria of the particular grant.

Know what is available and identify an appropriate funding agency

There are at least four possible ways to find out what funding might be available for your particular research needs, and it is incumbent on the individual researcher to take the initiative, be informed about what is available and do as much as possible to identify an appropriate funding agency.

1 Make sure that you know what is available at *your university* and, along with this, ensure that your name is on any research information mailing list at your institution.

2 Conduct *Internet searches* for funding opportunities in your particular field. One does not require advanced computer skills to do this. A simple Google search using keywords is a good place to begin.

3   Consult *funding databases* such as Research Professional Africa, which provides details of grants in every discipline for which researchers on the African continent are eligible. (This point presupposes institutional involvement because licences or subscriptions are required.)

4   *Consult colleagues.* The importance of this cannot be overstated. Sharing information in academia is part of what we mean by collegiality, and the experience of seasoned academics is invaluable.

Once a potential funder has been identified, the task of carefully studying the grant criteria and processes begins. At this stage two things are of critical importance:

1   *Determine whether your project fits the priorities or areas of interest of the funders and whether you are able to meet all the requirements.* That is, make sure that there is a good fit between your project and what the funding body actually funds. This requires a careful study of the funder's interests the type of projects they have funded in the past. Remember, though, that funders' priorities sometimes change, so it cannot be taken for granted that a similar project will be funded in future. At best, previously funded projects can serve as a guide.

2   Ascertain whether you are *able to provide the deliverables stipulated by the funder.* For example, a requirement may be that the project should play a capacity-building role and that at least two PhD students should be team members, each working on an aspect of the project. If you are unable to recruit such students or provide appropriate supervision for them, there is little point in applying for the grant.

This means that the *current call* for applications is what is relevant. It is sometimes possible to tweak a project just a little to fit a funder's criteria, but do not push this too far: funders are sharp-eyed and see through such things! After all, there is a lot at stake for them.

When seeking funding you should be familiar with *funding cycles* and plan as far in advance as possible. Proposals take time to process, partly because of the review process, and results will not be available to applicants before the due date.

Demonstrate meticulous planning

Having read your proposal, the funder should be in no doubt that you have meticulously thought through and planned for every aspect of the project. The onus is on you to demonstrate that nothing will be left to chance and that you are paying attention to detail. This helps to reassure funders that their money is in good hands and that the project will be carried through to successful completion. If you allow room for doubt, your project is unlikely to impress the potential funder.

Why should the funder care about your project?

In all fundraising the onus is on the applicant to market the project to potential funders. This suggests that the function of a proposal is both to *inform and convince* the funder about the value of the project, and a carefully crafted proposal should aim to do precisely this. The emphasis should be on *aspects of the project that the funder will like best*, using their guidelines for clues. In addition, the proposal should address the following:

- the feasibility of the project
- the robustness and relevance of the project in relation to current debate in the field
- the reasons why you are an appropriate person to undertake this project (which, of course, leads into the preparation of your CV).

With regard to *feasibility,* funders will consider first and foremost your own track record and level of experience in relation to the project for which funding is required. In other words, they will take into account the risk factor involved in entrusting you to manage their funds in the successful execution of the project. There should, therefore, be a correlation between your credentials and the funding request. Other factors considered by a funder will be the project timeframe, the anticipated outputs and the budget, which will be weighed up in relation to the proposed research activities and the usual size of grants awarded by the particular funding body.

The funder will then give consideration *to your project in relation to current debate and other research* being undertaken in the field. It is up to you to demonstrate your familiarity with the field generally and with other work currently being done in the area. This means engagement with both current literature and other developments in the field, as well as knowledge of seminal texts and/or developments. Your project should then be located in this broader context and your particular contribution identified. To further convince funders, you will need to indicate what background work you have already done in preparation for the project.

The *scientific merit and robustness of the proposed research* is a related consideration in determining a funder's interest in financing your project. It is up to you to convince them of this. In order to do this, you will need to convince funders, inter alia, that the methods you plan to use in conducting the research are appropriate and that you are competent in applying them.

An inevitable question follows: *what makes you the appropriate person for this project?* Why are you more suitable than someone else? At this point there comes a shift from marketing the project to marketing yourself, and for this the preparation of your CV is critical. A point worth remembering when preparing a grant proposal is that it will be sent to reviewers and reviewers who have little time to spare. Take care not to irritate the reviewer with an ill-prepared application, and remember that a reviewer does not want to plough through unnecessary detail to find what is relevant.

The *careful preparation of your CV* can go a fair distance in persuading a reviewer that you and your project are well matched and that it is worth funding. Conversely, a poorly presented CV can plant doubts in the funder's mind about your suitability for a grant. Here, then, are some pointers for the appropriate presentation of your CV for the purpose of securing research funding:

- ◆ Some funders (in South Africa, the National Research Foundation is an example) require that CVs be presented in a particular format. Be mindful of this when studying grant guidelines and take care to adhere to the funder's directives.

- ◆ Tweak your CV to foreground aspects that will be relevant to funders, giving more attention to areas in which they have a particular interest. You may have conducted research or taught in several areas, but only in one that is a priority for the funder. As much detail as possible should be provided to underscore your activity in this particular area. This serves the dual purpose of aligning yourself with the funder's priorities and indicating your suitability to conduct the research.

- ◆ Do not supply irrelevant information, for example, biographical data and personal contact details *unless specifically requested to do so.* By the same token, do not omit information that is relevant to the criteria for funding. If the eligibility criteria include gender, age and nationality, for example, these should be included.

Ethics clearance for your project

A concern of funders will be that you have given appropriate attention to *ethical issues* related to your project, and that, where necessary, you have obtained both institutional and any other ethical clearance required for it to proceed. Verification of such clearance should be submitted with your funding application.

In order to meet this requirement, you need to familiarise yourself with your institution's research ethics procedures. If you are unsure whether ethics clearance is required for this research, make sure that you consult those with experience in the area and who will be able to guide you. Remember, ethics approval is never granted retrospectively, and funders are aware of this.

Writing for reviewers

As already indicated, reviewers have very little time to spend on each application, so you should ensure that they are able to grasp your project at a first quick reading. This has implications for how you write your proposal. Remember that the review panel may well comprise a mix of backgrounds and include specialists in your area, specialists in other areas and generalists such as the programme manager or a representative of the body or group that stands to benefit from the research.

Try therefore to ascertain whether the reviewers will be

- from your area of specialisation
- from the broader field in your area of research
- from outside of your area or even discipline
- from outside of academia
- a mixture of the above.

If there is to be any sort of mix, the proposal itself must cater for all. It should be carefully crafted, with some parts demonstrating expert knowledge (including knowledge of the terminology and status quo in the field) and other parts written for the generalist/lay-person. The former is important to demonstrate your competence in the field, while the latter's importance lies in ensuring that the proposal is comprehensible to all reviewers (this is also sometimes a test of the down-to-earth relevance of the project).

Allow time: do not hurry the application

Many proposals fail because inadequate time has been allocated to their preparation. A common mistake is to underestimate the time it takes to prepare a good proposal, and this applies especially to the novice grant-writer. A hurried application soon becomes obvious to reviewers. Therefore:

- Be clear on the submission deadline.
- Begin your application well in advance so that you have time to prepare it slowly and with care.

Remember, some funding applications have an *internal* (institutional) as well as an *external* (funder) deadline.

Presentation

The success or failure of a grant proposal can hinge on its visual and structural presentation and the impression this creates on the reviewers. This fact should not be underestimated. Funding agencies receive many applications and the onus is on you to make yours catch the eye of the reviewer. In light of this, there are certain presentation guidelines that could enhance your chance of success in the acceptance of your proposal. It should be neat, easy on the eye and easily readable. Take special note of the following:

- Unless you are absolutely sure that those reviewing your application are from your immediate field of research or area of specialisation, write for the edu-cated, intelligent layperson.

- Avoid obscure language and convoluted descriptions.
- Use short sentences, each making one clear point.
- Be grammatically correct.
- Do a spell-check.
- Should you be writing in a second or third language, ask a colleague for whom it is a first language to check what you have written and advise accordingly.
- Regardless of language issues, give your application to at least one colleague to read. Sometimes a reader who is *not* in your field is valuable; he or she will tend to read more objectively.
- Proofread *everything*. Then proofread again.

Follow the funder's instructions meticulously

Bearing in mind all that has been said so far, the following is critical: the starting point of any funding application should be to *sit with the funder's guidelines, with a highlighter in hand, and go slowly and systematically through the application, marking the salient points*. There is no substitute for this. To spell it out in more detail:

- Read through the application requirements carefully before filling in anything.
- Make a note of documentation that needs to be submitted with the application, ticking each one off as you secure it.
- Supply *all* the information requested, in the *format* in which it is requested.

Remember that if you are required to submit your application electronically, you will be unable to submit it without completing all the steps.

Preparing a budget

Try to get some idea of the size of the grants awarded by the funder.

- Check their websites for lists of grants awarded, especially to researchers in your own institution or others working in your field.
- If possible, engage with someone who has received funding from this particular agency as to how they developed their budget, being aware of how easy it is to overlook costs likely to be incurred by the project. Once the application is submitted it is not easy to request a budget change if you suddenly think of an overlooked cost.
- In determining an appropriate budget there is a fine balance between covering all your costs and appearing greedy. In competitive bids, you can be beaten by proposals of equal merit that are deemed to be more realistic and economical than yours.

◆ Be aware that you might not be able to get all the funding you need from one funder. On the other hand, be upfront about funding that you have raised elsewhere for particular line items in your budget. One of the unforgivable offences in academia is 'double-dipping', that is, to accept funding for the same budget item/s from more than one source. Therefore take care to indicate clearly what aspects of the project are financed through a different funding agency. The need for transparency is one reason for this. Demonstrating to your potential funder that you have, indeed, given thought to all the project's funding requirements and taken appropriate initiative is another.

◆ Read the guidelines carefully and limit your budget to costs that the particular funder will cover. These may include: equipment and running costs, travel and accommodation for field trips, payment of research assistants (usually at a specified hourly rate), bursaries for postgraduate students and conference travel.

◆ Avoid requesting items that are specifically excluded by funders, as indicated in the guidelines. For example, many funders do not pay salaries. This is not a problem for an academic whose basic salary is covered by the university. Usually there is funding for a research assistant on an hourly basis, but it becomes an issue if you are trying to raise money for a research unit and for researchers who are not on the university payroll. Research units that have to raise funds for contract staff or overheads need to search for *core* funding.

The proposal should justify each item in your budget so that there is a match between objectives and budget items. The budget should not present surprises. If you want to go to a conference, explain in the body of your proposal why this is necessary; if you need money for fieldwork, provide details of it in the proposal, carefully explaining how this fits into the project as a whole.

Understanding terminology

Terms such as 'goals', 'aims', 'objectives', 'outcomes' and 'outputs' are expected and they need to be used to demonstrate that the project has been thoroughly considered and planned. But these terms are very often misunderstood and misused, not least in project proposals. It is important to understand what the terms refer to and how they are appropriately used in describing aspects of a project. Different sources may define these terms slightly differently, but their function is to provide a means to 1) demonstrate that the project has been meticulously planned and 2) methodically articulate the elements of the project. Table 8.1 is useful in clarifying the terms and showing their application.[1]

---

1   Supplied by Jane English.

Table 8.1: Project terminology and its uses

TERM	DESCRIPTION	EXAMPLE
Goals	What you aim to achieve; your first prize; may be just beyond reach, but shows vision	To uplift women and so contribute to improving humanity
Aims	Your single overarching desire	To secure a new avenue in which women may be employed
Objectives	The breakdown of achievements you intend to have made by the end of the project	To analyse the plastics industry for areas in which only men are employed currently but which would be suitable for women
Outcomes	The real data that the project will produce	An analysis of the male-dominated jobs, their specifications and features that would make them appropriate to the employment of women
Outputs	The publications and activities that will develop out of the research and place it in society	Academic papers; publications in the plastics literature and industry; application to a company to place women in certain jobs; workshops for management

Aims/goals

Aims and goals are sometimes seen as synonymous or at least closely related. They refer to *the overall purpose of the study*, the general, long-term vision and broad desires for the project, that is, what you hope to achieve. They should relate directly to the study's objectives. The aims of a project emphasise *what* is to be accomplished in the long term rather than *how* it will be accomplished, and they should reflect the aspirations and expectations of the research topic.

Many funders are interested in *capacity development*, particularly when it addresses issues of equity and redress. This should be considered when identifying goals and corresponding objectives, even if they are ancillary to the main project. For example, a goal could be research capacity development for two PhD students.

Objectives

The objectives of a project are generated by aims but they are more specific, verifiable and measurable. They refer to results achieved within a specific timeframe and accomplished with available resources. A project often has a general objective (what is to be achieved in general terms), which is broken down into specific objectives of smaller, logically connecting parts. Objectives serve both as a basis for evaluation of a project and an ongoing measure of what has been achieved as you revisit them along the way.

In seeking for clarity in identifying objectives it is useful to employ the 'SMART' technique:

- **Specific:** Be clear about what will be achieved.
- **Measurable:** Quantify results and measure when they have been achieved.
- **Achievable:** Ensure they *can* be achieved.
- **Realistic:** Ensure they can be attained with available project resources.
- **Timed:** Ensure they can be attained within a specified timescale.

When selecting aims and objectives for your project, take account of both the *priorities* and *exclusions* of the funder. Make sure that you understand the funder's vision—take note of their mission statement and acquaint yourself with the descriptions of their themes. With regard to the capacity-building example provided under Aims/goals, a corresponding objective would be the graduation of two PhD students.

Know your funder's ideology, and don't ask for money if you don't support that ideology!

Outcomes

Outcomes refer to the concrete, observable and measurable changes your project will bring, and their likely impact. Examples are the training of staff for increased effectiveness, impact in the community, role in policy-making, etc. Outcomes are indicators of success. This suggests that throughout the project you should reflect on the outcomes you envisage and the progress made up to that point.

Outputs

Outputs are ways in which the products of research are disseminated and made available to the wider public. The term refers to deliverables such as peer-reviewed journal articles and books; creative works like musical compositions, exhibitions and artefacts; patents; graduation of research students (Master's and PhD students); tools or toolkits; blogs, etc. Some outputs, namely, the knowledge and experience gained from the project, are less clearly tangible, but can be shared in tangible form. An example here would be the project report, which could then be shared with the community.

Title page

This should be a single page forming the front cover of the proposal. Unless the funder's guidelines specify differently, the title page should include the following:

- date
- project title

- location/s of the project
- name of the institution
- name of the principle investigator
- any other relevant single line information.

Abstract

It is important to note that the abstract should be *written last* but it will be *considered first* by reviewers, being positioned on a page of its own immediately following the title page. Having said this, it is sometimes useful to prepare a *draft abstract* right at the beginning. This could keep you on track when developing the proposal itself, and can be refined at the end. The final form of the abstract should be produced once you have completed a draft proposal. The decision to fund your project may hinge on the impression created by your abstract.

An abstract for any piece of research should address five main issues:

1   What are you going to do (context, problem and research question)?
2   Why is it important (rationale and motivation)?
3   How are you going to do it (methods and research design)?
4   What difference will it make (contribution to knowledge and other outcomes)?
5   How will you evaluate it (measure its success)?

Abstracts are usually 250–300 words in length, or as specified by the funders. They should be sharp and to the point, exercising word economy but at the same time covering all aspects of the project. The aim of the abstract is to *draw the funder's attention* to the project and in order to do this effectively, some funders require two abstracts: one for specialists in the field and one for non-specialists.

The following is a useful outline for an abstract, teasing out the questions identified above into the various elements of the project. The approximate length suggested for each one gives an indication of proportion in relation to the whole abstract:

- Summary of the *background and problem* (2–3 sentences).
- Statement of the *purpose* of the research (1 sentence).
- Statement of the *importance* of the research (1 sentence).
- Identify the *research question* (1 sentence).
- Indicate the *feasibility* of the project (1–2 sentences).
- Brief description of *theoretical framework* (2–3 sentences).
- Brief description of *relevant data* (2–3 sentences).
- *Targeted group*, if relevant (1 sentence).

◆ *Hypothesis* (2–3 sentences)—what is your 'hunch'? This is a statement of belief which your research will prove or disprove.

◆ *Methods* (1–2 sentences).

◆ Description of the *contribution to the field of knowledge* that the research will make, and the *transferability of outcomes*, where applicable (2–3 sentences).

◆ Brief description of *evaluation methods* and *expected results* (2–3 sentences).

Reviewers' recommendations

Once the reviewers' reports are submitted, a decision will be taken as to whether or not your project will be funded, depending on which of the following recommendations each reviewer makes:

◆ Strongly recommended for funding with no revisions.

◆ Recommended for funding with minor revisions.

◆ Reformulate and resubmit after substantive revisions.

◆ Not recommended for funding—poor or inappropriate application.

Should you be required to make revisions, do so immediately, meticulously attending to each point raised by the reviewer. Then resubmit the application according to the funder's instructions as soon as possible.

Institutional protocols

Each institution will have protocols associated with external funding applications. In most cases the applicant does not apply directly to the funding agent, but through the relevant institutional body. This is not designed to complicate the process of securing funding. It has in part to do with quality control and accountability, and in part with the mutual protection of institution, applicant and funder.

Notes on the proposal

Not all funding agencies provide an application template and they depend on the applicant to put together an appropriate proposal. Start by reading the whole application form carefully. If there is no form provided, study the call and guidelines for applications. Make a note of things like priorities of the funders, application deadlines and required documentation to accompany your application. Then *write a draft containing your ideas.*

Proposal outline

◆ Title page

◆ Abstract

◆ Summary (3–4 sentences, which may be used as an introduction)

◆ Project description

- Methodology
- Research design
- Aims, objectives, outcomes and outputs
- Budget
- Team members (indicate qualifications and exact role of each)
- Timeframe
- Evaluation strategies (if required by the funder).

Proposal review guide

The following questions[2] might be helpful in evaluating the quality of your own proposal.

- Is the problem statement well defined and novel?
- Is the conceptual/theoretical framework appropriately developed?
- Does the research lend itself to multidisciplinary/interdisciplinary approaches? If yes, is this aspect appropriately developed in the proposal?
- Are the research questions appropriate to address the research problem?
- Are the research objectives clearly defined and do they align to the conceptual framework?
- Is the proposed methodology appropriate to address the objectives? Does the proposal illustrate that the required expertise is available or how the expertise will be obtained to apply the methodology appropriately?
- Is the overall requested budget realistic to achieve the objectives?
- How well does the proposed research align to the university's and national research strategies?
- Are the ethical considerations appropriately addressed in the proposal?

Principles of grants and project management[3]

The complexity of grant and project management depends on the size of the grant and the scope of the project. If you are the Principal Investigator (PI) in a collaborative project involving a substantial sum of money, several colleagues, students and external partners, there will be more management required than for a modest grant for a PhD project or to enable you to get to a conference. Similarly, details of grant management will depend on the specific stipulations of the funder (which for many South African academics is the

2   Excerpt from the South African National Research Foundation guide.
3   This section draws on several articles including the following: Selby-Harrington, M.L., Donat, P.L. & Hubbard, H.D. (1993). 'Guidance for managing a research grant'. www.ahrq.gov/profes-sionals/clinicians-providers/resources/nursing/funding/grants/grant-management.html. Accessed 18 November 2013. This information was originally published in *Nursing Research*, 42 (1), January/February 1993; 'Managing projects'. London: Research Office, Imperial College. www3.imperial.ac.uk/researchsupport/managingprojects/managingbudgets. Accessed 26 November 2013.

National Research Foundation) and on institutional processes. But the principles of good management remain the same regardless, and can be easily applied.

All funders have reporting requirements, frequently involving annual progress reports as well as a final report. The quality of your reporting, providing evidence of good management, may well determine whether you will be considered for future funding. There are four main areas, with inevitable overlap, requiring management:

1   Managing work.
2   Managing people.
3   Managing time.
4   Managing money.

What follows are generic guidelines for managing a grant and, by implication, the project itself that is being funded.[4] Each of the points incorporates elements of one or more of the four areas identified above.

- ◆   **Responsibilities of the principal investigator (PI)**
  The principle investigator, in whose name the proposal is submitted, is the person with overall responsibility for the project and for managing the grant. This includes technical and financial management of the award, the management of the project within the terms and conditions of funding, adherence to reporting requirements and timely communication of significant project changes.

- ◆   **Reporting and accountability**
  In all successful grant management, what is actually done—that is, project execution, including the end products—must tally with the proposal. A related principle is that grant-holders should familiarise themselves with the requirements of the funder, particularly insofar as reporting is concerned. Prepare reports meticulously; do not hurry them; adhere to the required format; and submit them on time. Remember that your chances of securing future grants may well depend on the quality of your reporting. To facilitate both reporting and accountability, it is wise to keep a log in which you document progress, difficulties, delays, and so on.

- ◆   **Institutional and agency support**
  One secret to managing a grant is never to guess what to do when you are unsure. Rather, seek advice. Colleagues with experience in grants management can be invaluable in helping you to avoid mistakes. But there are two people

---

4   There are several software packages available for project management, such as Microsoft Project, but these come at a price.

who are critical in supporting you: the institutional delegated authority (usually someone in the research or contracts office) and, if it is an external grant, the agency's Programme Officer (PO). Both are concerned with the administration of the grant and are, therefore, familiar with the policies and requirements of the funder. Contact with both parties should be established early on and retained throughout the life of the grant. Remember: if in doubt, ask.

◆ **Waiting period and grant implementation**
Once an award is made, you should be in a position to implement it right away. This presupposes effective use of the waiting period between the award and actual availability of the funds, with the necessary groundwork being done: reviewers' recommendations for proposal adjustments made; permissions sought and granted; questionnaires prepared; team members and/or collaborators briefed; arrangements in place for interviewing, space and equipment organised, etc.—all depending on the nature of the project.

◆ **Time management**
Time management is closely related to project objectives, and therefore deals with tangible, measurable entities such as tasks and timeframes, including milestones to measure progress.

The *Gantt chart*—a type of bar chart used extensively by those managing large projects (both within and outside of academia)—is a tool that can usefully be adapted for smaller-scale projects. Developed by Henry Gantt, an engineer, in the early 1900s, a Gantt chart focuses on the project's time schedule in relation to its various activities and those performing them. It breaks the project down into smaller parts, and one of its uses is to show the time and dependency relationship between various tasks and those performing them. In other words, it shows what needs to be completed before a subsequent task can be performed. Such charts are also useful for measuring the time actually taken for each task and the project as a whole in relation to the time originally estimated, suggesting how adjustments could be made.

Many Gantt charts are highly sophisticated, and for those interested in creating them, a Google search will prove informative. There are several software packages available at a price, but it is also possible to create a Gantt chart using Excel. For most emerging researchers it is the *principles* of such an exercise that are important, particularly to show if a project is on track. A chart by its very nature is clear and concise, and information can be taken in at a glance. Apart from its role as a tool in time and personnel management, this type of chart provides fingertip information for reporting purposes. It is also useful for personal time management and accountability when there are no other collaborators in the project.

In a nutshell, time management should address three questions arising from the proposal:

- What needs to be done?
- Who will do it?
- By when will it be done?

◆ Financial management

It is one thing to be awarded a grant and quite another to learn how to spend the money! Step one is to find out from both your funding agency (via the PO) and your university research finance office what the rules and procedures are. If this is the first funding you have received, the initial step would be to request that a personal research account be opened in your name.

Grants are awarded against an approved set of budget items, all of which are directly related to the project. It is usually not permissible to use funds for items that do not appear in the budget or to transfer funds between budget headings. The latter, a reallocation (virement) of funds, is sometimes possibly with permission from the funder.

Example: A budget line item may be for conference funding—to present a paper at a specific conference, on specific dates. It sometimes happens that an abstract is not accepted or another funding need becomes more urgent. In cases like this the grant-holder may apply to the grants manager to reallocate funds either to a different conference or another budget item.

◆ Personnel management

For some PIs, supervising other team members is the most difficult part of managing a grant. Here are some pointers:

- It is critical that each team member has a clear brief as to her/his role in the project and that this be aligned with the contents of the proposal.
- Regular meetings should be set up for progress reporting, measured against previously agreed targets. It is wise to run them formally, with the agenda sent out in advance, and minutes taken.
- Team members should be briefed on efficient interaction and communication with stakeholders, funders and institutional personnel.
- A conflict management strategy should be in place.

◆ Authorship issues

To avoid misunderstandings about authorship of reports, publications and presentations arising from the grant, an authorship policy should be developed and documented, possibly in an MOU, at the outset. This is particularly important regarding the role and expectations of student research assistants. Regardless of agreed authorship policy, it is the PI who is accountable to the funding agency for the dissemination of information generated by the grant.

◆ **Communication**

Effective communication is critical to the success of any operation involving more than one person. In managing a grant in accordance with the project plan, effective and ongoing communication between all the players is paramount, to ensure delivery in terms of funder requirements and the project plan. In view of this, the PI should, from the start, set measures in place to ensure good communication. Keeping the institutional contact person and funder's PO appropriately apprised of progress is integral to communication responsibilities.

◆ **Reporting**

Meticulously meeting funders' reporting requirements is critical to grants management. Supply exactly what is asked for and submit all reports on time. Should you be in doubt about any aspect of reporting, consult your institutional representative or the Programme Office. Future funding is largely contingent on efficient reporting.

◆ **Continuation and future grants**

Some grants come with the opportunity for renewal at the end of the funding period. Where this is the case, timely preparations should be made for a renewal application, with submission dates for such an application being ascertained in advance from the funder. With some funders it is easier to secure a second grant following directly from a successful project rather than to allow a time lapse between them and then start afresh. Both continuations and future grants will be directly dependent on how the existing grant has been managed.

Conclusion to this chapter and Part 2

Because research is inevitably and in some measure dependent on funding, it is imperative that every academic develop skills in raising and managing research grants. The material of this chapter is designed to introduce early-career researchers to the terrain of grants and to provide building blocks for the development of skills in this important area.

Throughout Part 2 we have considered a range of issues and opportunities that undergird successful research and that require the development of particular skills. The ultimate aim of all research is to get it 'out there', which requires its packaging and presentation in ways that make it accessible to a target audience. This may be broadly described as placing research in the public sphere, and the term 'outputs'—usually in the form of publications—is the vehicle of this public-making, the theme of Part 3.

PART 3

GETTING RESEARCH INTO THE PUBLIC SPHERE

GETTING RESEARCH INTO THE PUBLIC SPHERE

In the past, the heading given above might simply have been 'Publishing your research'. Much of the conversation in the next three chapters will indeed be about publishing in the conventional sense—peer-reviewed articles and edited or authored books. But the research landscape is changing. Previous norms are being challenged:

- Both funders and the public are looking for the social impact of research.
- Increased awareness of inadequacies in how we measure the value of research is slowly being acknowledged.
- Different channels of communication of research are becoming mainstream, for example, open access publishing and social media.

This means that different, frequently bypassed, perspectives on the making public of our research require attention, in addition to what many disciplines consider normative.

For the majority of academics conventional publishing will be the primary form that their research output assumes. For some, patents will also constitute an output. But there are other forms of peer-reviewed research output to be acknowledged and accorded their rightful place. Such outputs include creative works (curated exhibitions, musical compositions, dramatic productions, choreographed dance, architectural design, etc.), legal judgments and developments in clinical practice. In some contexts the writing of books is also undervalued as a research output.

There are a number of reasons for this bias, two of which stand out. The first is that, despite mileage gained by the humanities in recent decades, the assessment of scholarly work continues to be strongly skewed towards the sciences.[1] Most scientific research output occurs in the form of scholarly journal articles, and other forms of output are measured against this as the standard. The other major reason (related to the first) in South Africa has to do with the government subsidy system, which rewards institutions directly for publications that meet certain accreditation criteria, privileging textual output and, notably, journal articles. Enormous pressure is therefore placed on academics to publish journal articles, which qualify for subsidy, in preference to other forms of output. Institutions have their own internal faculty research evaluation criteria, used inter alia for promotion assessment. Similarly, the South African National Research Foundation

---

1   That is, the traditional science model. With the increase of interdisciplinary research and the relativising of the scientific enterprise, largely through discoveries in quantum physics, the traditional positivist model of scientific research is no longer quite as secure as it once was.

(NRF), in evaluating research, employs disciplinary panels, each with its own set of criteria. But the subsidy issue, which is influenced by the monopolies controlling the academic publishing world, continues to be a powerful force in South African academe.

In the assessment of scholarly research output there are two driving factors: publication and peer review. The word 'publish' has a Middle English origin and is derived from the Latin *publicare*, which means to 'make public'.[2] Publishing is closely associated with written (textual) work in common understanding, although good dictionaries provide alternative, nuanced meanings as well.[3] Understood in the extended sense, the alternative types of output mentioned earlier meet the criteria of what it means to publish. The challenge comes with peer review of the work. What constitutes academic peer review of a musical composition or a sculpture, or a clinical procedure or building design? How does one manage the logistics, given that sometimes the public-making is not permanent, as in a performance? What is actually being evaluated? Scholars from these disciplines usually have a clear idea of what it constitutes, but, despite this, certainly in South Africa, consensus on the issue has yet to be reached, not least with the Department of Higher Education and Training. This makes it extremely challenging for early-career academics working in disciplines in which the default form of output does not meet accepted criteria.

Another factor to be considered is assessment of the impact of research. Again, we encounter a skewing towards a traditional model of citation count, impact factor and, more recently, the h-index, all of which will be considered in due course. But, notably because of opportunities for dissemination of research through the electronic and other media, alternative ways of measuring research impact are being developed and are gaining ground. The 2013 San Francisco Declaration, noted in Chapter 2, signifies a milestone in this regard, although its effect will take time to be felt.

We can offer no solutions here. The point of raising the issue of different types of research output and assessment is to make clear that, while much of what follows focuses on publishing in the conventional sense, the reality and the value of other forms of output should be equally recognised, and for now we live with the challenge of how to assess their worth and have this recognised.

For the present our focus remains on textual publishing in its various forms. This is the subject of the following three chapters.

---

2   This creates a challenge for those doing commissioned, and, especially secret, research, where the researcher does not own the data and is, therefore, not free to publish.

3   For example, the entry for 'publication' in the (2002) *South African Concise Oxford Dictionary*. Oxford: Oxford University Press, 944.

CHAPTER 9

SCHOLARLY PUBLISHING
FROM MOTIVATION TO PUBLICATION

As an academic you will be familiar with the pressure to publish—preferably in a scholarly journal. We have noted that this might not be the appropriate route for some people's research, but for the majority it will be. The aim of this chapter is to provide necessary background information and then to follow the progress of an article from submission to publication.

What are the functions of scholarly publishing?[1]

The reasons why academics publish their research are to:

- Register the intellectual priority of an idea, concept or research findings.
- Certify the quality of research and the validity of findings.
- Disseminate new research to potential users.
- Preserve the scholarly record for future use.
- Gain scholarly recognition of their work.
- Locate a researcher in the local and international research community.
- Provide stepping stones on which others might build.
- Meet the need for funds. In the South African context, publications approved by the Department of Higher Education and Training (DHET) are subsidy-earning, and institutions depend on this subsidy to meet research costs.
- Achieve a sense of personal fulfillment.

Published research that is approved by the DHET (in keeping with international standards of research evaluation) meets the following criteria:

- It comprises original research obtained through systematic investigation in order to gain new knowledge and understanding.
- Peer evaluation of research is a fundamental requisite of all approved publications and is the mechanism for ensuring and enhancing quality.[2]

It should be remembered that there are many journals that meet these criteria but which are not accredited or subsidy-earning. Among these are some journals that are highly

1   This chapter draws on seminar presentations by Mary Nassimbeni and on De Gruchy & Holness, *The Emerging Researcher*, Part 2.

2   See www.researchoffice.uct.ac.za/publication_count/overview/. Accessed 3 March 2015.

regarded within particular disciplines, and where the readership comprises those for whom the material is relevant and potentially beneficial, both to the discipline and the researcher. It is therefore important, particularly for young academics trying to become known in their areas of research to publish here as well.

From an individual's point of view, publishing is important to communicate ideas and findings, and to establish a research niche (hopefully to become known eventually as the authority in a particular field). From the university's perspective, publication is a major marker of institutional productivity and, because of peer review, of the quality of that productivity.

What should I publish?

There are two types of material out of which publications are born:

1   Transforming something that has already been written for another purpose, for example, a lecture or series of lectures, a thesis, a conference paper, a report or a popular article.

2   Starting from scratch, based on new research.

Sometimes the two are blended in order to accommodate new material that has appeared since the original work was completed. Reworked material to be submitted for publication must be able to stand alone, bearing in mind that familiarity with the original work cannot be presumed on the part of the reader, so the current work needs to be located in its context.

Let us tease this out further by considering in more detail the options for publishing, acknowledging that in order to qualify as a scholarly publication a strict peer-review process is involved:

- ◆   **Your thesis.** There are four ways in which publications may arise out of a thesis.

  1   Publishing it as a monograph, which will require a thorough reworking of the thesis (see Chapter 10).

  2   Publishing results as they become available while you are engaged in the study. This is normative in some disciplines, notably the sciences.

  3   Reworking sections/chapters of your thesis as separate articles once you have completed it.

  4   In some PhD programmes the thesis arises out of the publications. In this case a number of published articles dealing with aspects of a particular question or problem are woven into a thesis.

- ◆   **Journal articles.** In many disciplines journal articles are the usual channels for communicating the results of research.

◆ **Review articles.** These normally comprise critical comparison of a number of significant books or articles that have recently been published on cognate themes. They are substantially different from book reviews, and, depending on their scope and quality, are recognised as full articles.

◆ **Books.** In some disciplines, publishing a scholarly book is the ultimate goal.

◆ **Chapters in books.** Academics are often invited to contribute chapters to edited books. In order for the book and your chapter to gain accreditation, make sure that the selection and publishing includes approved peer-review mechanisms and that your institutional affiliation is clear.

◆ **Editing books and journals, for instance, as guest editor.** This is a useful academic exercise, albeit a time-consuming one. Before agreeing to take on the task, make sure the publication meets peer-review and other quality assurance criteria, for example, do not agree to guest edit for a journal known to have a suspect editorial policy. Editorials are not considered to be articles, so be sure to have a chapter or article of your own in the book or journal issue.

◆ **Conference proceedings.** Publishing in conference proceedings is common and encouraged in many disciplines. Yet not all researchers are aware that conference proceedings do not automatically achieve accreditation. There are two ways in which articles in conference proceedings may be accredited, and both hinge on peer review:

1 Some conferences require submission of completed papers for pre-conference peer review. On the basis of this, only certain papers are selected for presentation at the conference and subsequent publication.

2 Other conferences invite post-conference submission of papers to be peer reviewed and considered for publication. This also means that only selected papers are published.

In both cases the proceedings require an ISBN number and verification of the peer-review process. Conference proceedings that do not automatically carry accreditation are those comprising a non-peer-reviewed collection of all the papers presented.

◆ **Research reports.** Research reports *as such* are not accredited as scholarly publications. It may sometimes be possible to transform a commissioned report into a journal article, which would then follow the same process as other journal articles. In order to do this, permission must be obtained from the party for whom the report was prepared.

◆ **Popular articles and social media.** These do not carry scholarly credit in the conventional sense, but are important for disseminating research findings to a wider public. With the growing imperative to make research available and accessible to the public, reporting research in popular and informal ways is gaining importance. This should not be a substitute for scholarly publishing, but should complement it.

Publishing in journals

In the past there was only one option for journal publishing: *print journals*. In recent years, *online journal* publishing has made great strides, an advantage being quicker publications. Another development in recent years is the opportunity afforded by *open access publishing*. Open access, for reasons that we hope to make clear, is gaining much ground as its significance, particularly in terms of impact, is being recognised.

All of this compounds the challenge faced by many early-career academics as to how to select an appropriate journal in which to publish. Although there are times when one might 'get lucky', for example, a special edition of a journal on the very topic on which you are working, for the most part getting published requires a combination of planning, strategy, focus, time, skill and commitment. The following points are important:

- **Networking.** This is one of the values of attending conferences. Networking leads to research co-operation, to an awareness of what's happening at the cutting edge in your field, and to introductions to journal editors.
- **Become acquainted with editors and publishers:**
  - Make contact with editors.
  - Be invited on to book reviewing panels.
  - Be invited on to an editorial board.
  - Offer to guest-edit an issue.
- **Carefully target appropriate journals:**
  - Consult a few recent issues to see what is currently being published and if you could contribute to the debate.
  - Be proactive in ascertaining if a journal is planning a special edition on a particular theme into which your work might slot.
  - Does the journal publish research in your field?
  - Does it reach your intended audience?
- **Consult 'Instructions to authors'** (usually found inside the back cover of print journals as well as on websites).
  - Become familiar with house style, length, submission process, referencing style, etc.
  - Adhere meticulously to all instructions.

◆ **Print, online, open access:**

- What is the usual time delay between acceptance and publication?

- Online material appears sooner than print versions.

- If it is open access, what costs will be involved for you as author?

◆ **'Specialist' or 'omnibus'?**

- Specialist journals are often those that have appeared in the last 30 years and are more specialised, have more focused markets and a smaller circulation.

- Omnibus journals are often the longest living, aim to cover an entire discipline and have larger markets.

◆ **Local or international?**

- Top international journals with a high impact factor (see later discussion) are first prize. It is more difficult to publish here, and the waiting time is usually longer, but it is ultimately worthwhile. Remember, for those of us working in the Global South, and particularly Africa, there is an added challenge to make our articles relevant to an international audience if we hope to get them accepted.

- Local journals are important as well, to support local societies and the national research enterprise by raising the standard of these journals. However, be aware of the inherent danger in some local publishing, even in accredited journals. Certain disciplines have 'easy' journals, where the acceptance rate is so high that one can almost guarantee a publication. Some local journals have severely compromised editorial policies, with board members and most authors coming from single institutions.

- For early-career researchers it is important to *start publishing*—to boost confidence—so starting local might be a good place to begin, particularly for those publishing alone without the backing of a high-profile co-author.

◆ **What to avoid:**

- A delay in starting to write. Most successful writers across the disciplines would give this advice: start writing as soon as you can. You learn to write by writing.

- Writing without an audience in mind. Remember, you are writing for specialist peers.

- Writing without having identified a journal upfront. Many people do this, and sometimes it is unavoidable, but it is not advisable.

- Lack of confidence in your knowledge and opinions. Make sure you are up to date with what is happening in your discipline, and that what you say is well founded and accurate.

- Data presentation that is not reader-friendly.

- Neglecting the appropriate format for your article, determined by disciplinary conventions (for example, IMRAD in science) and journal style.

- Poor writing style and small inconsistencies and errors.

- Submitting penultimate drafts.

PERSPECTIVE

PERSONAL PUBLISHING STRATEGIES

Before I discuss strategies in choosing a journal for manuscript submission, I must point out that any publication in a refereed journal is an achievement. What is important is for the authors to maximise the number of readers who are not only interested in the subject matter but also will find the work useful to build on, either in industry work or in further academic work. This means that sometimes lower-ranked journals might be a better option in terms of maximising the number of readers and for the impact of the article.

I put a lot of thought into where to submit manuscripts. At this stage of my career, I am in favour of submitting to those journals that are international, on the ISI list and highly ranked in my discipline—both for readership and personal prestige. Good journals also tend to provide great feedback even when they reject your paper.

I tend to rate my papers and choose journals in terms of innovativeness, sophistication and complexity. By innovativeness, I mean whether my paper will add incremental newness to the literature and whether it is a question posed previously or a relevant question posed by this manuscript for the first time. By sophistication, I mean whether I have posed the problem and/or the solution in a strategic way. Most of my work has some mathematics to it and complexity refers to the solution process that requires high mathematical thinking. These definitions are purely illustrative and not absolute but I believe they are useful and can be translated into any field.

Another strategy in selecting journals is to consider the general conversation in my research field and within the journal itself. I spend considerable time scouring through journal lists to find an appropriate journal. A special edition of a journal is particularly useful, although there are positives and negatives to consider. Sometimes editors do not receive enough good manuscripts and this compromises the quality of the edition. On the other hand, editors of special editions are appointed for their speciality and achievements. As a result, they have a wide network of specialised reviewers, providing excellent feedback—even though there is, therefore, a greater chance of rejection.

To increase my chance of acceptance I find the following strategies useful:

- Once I've found an appropriate journal, I ensure that the language of my manuscript fits in directly with the style of the journal.

- I use the letter to the editor to point out important facts about the paper: for instance, that my work carries previous conversations in the journal further.

- For an overseas journal, demonstrating the article's relevance to the international conversation on the topic (in my case, emerging markets) is important.

Kanshustan Rajaratham

The peer-review process

We dealt in Chapter 1 with the place of peer review in academia. We now focus on a particular process of peer review at work: the evaluation of articles submitted for publication.

Optimising your chances

- Understand the publication process.
- Be aware of your audience.
- Select the right publication and understand its language and style.
- Compose an eye-catching title (but not a gimmicky one).
- Write a good abstract.
- Follow directions given in the 'Guide to authors'.
- Keep your cover letter simple.
- Keep both the editor and reviewers in mind, making their tasks as easy as possible.

Peer review

Peer review has two functions when it comes to publishing: quality control and enhancement, that is, to distinguish between good and bad research and to inform the author how best to make improvements.

- The first operates by selection/rejection.
- The second operates through constructive criticism.

THE PEER-REVIEW PROCESS IN A NUTSHELL

- The editor receives your manuscript with a covering letter. It will either be rejected out of hand or sent out for review. Editors, therefore, are the gate-keepers in publishing.
- If not rejected, the article is sent to reviewers.
- Reviewers' verdict: 'Accept with minor/major amendments' or 'reject'.
- Feedback given to author.
- Amendments are made.
- Publisher supplies proofs.
- Article is published.

Reviewers ask two basic questions:

1 Was the research conducted well?

2 Was it reported well?

There are four possible judgements:

1 Immediately publishable.

2 Publishable with amendments

3 Possible publication: revision and reassessment.

4 Not publishable.

Criteria

- Importance of research question.
- Originality of work.
- Strengths and weaknesses of
  - purpose
  - conceptualisation
  - methodology
  - interpretation of results/findings.
- Writing style.
- Presentation of results/findings.
- Ethical concerns.
- Relevance to readers.

Reviewers' comments

The following could be among the reviewer responses:

- Request a clarification of concepts.
- Require stronger defence of arguments.

- Suggest different statistical analyses.
- Recommend structural changes.
- Require correction of facts/figures
- Point out overlooked literature.
- Suggest stylistic changes.

Each point should be addressed before resubmission of the article, with a covering letter explaining exactly what you did. Should you disagree with the reviewer on any point, explain why. One strategy is to cut and paste each reviewer's comments into a document and then to reply to each one, explaining what you have done to address their concerns, and if not, why.

PERSPECTIVE

DEALING WITH REVIEWERS'/REFEREES' COMMENTS

Some suggestions about how you could get the best out of the feedback without being overwhelmed by it:

Start by reading through the editor's and referees' comments—with as open a mind as possible. (I find it helpful to print out the referees' reports and use different coloured markers for this exercise.) Mark each point of praise with the first colour marker so that you start with a clear picture of what they consider to be the paper's strengths. Now, using a second colour marker, highlight all the critical comments that you agree with or that make sense to you (even those that require a huge amount of work to address).

Using a third colour, mark all the comments that you reject, or that you think are valid, but which you do not want to deal with (possibly because to do so would take your article in a different direction).

Take your second colour markings as a basis for rereading the paper and noting the changes that could be made quite easily to meet the referees' criticisms.

Make a list of what you would need to do to meet the more demanding points that were raised. For example, reading and analysing the articles they recommend. Another example: deciding on which of the several 'issues' or 'themes' you raise in the article should be chosen as the main theme around which you will develop your central argument, and which themes can be mentioned, but then bracketed as being 'beyond the scope of the present paper'.

It is seldom possible to recraft an article to satisfy all the referees' comments (which, in any case, sometimes pull in different directions). As an author, you are entitled to decide which comments make most sense and then act on your decision. Of course, if you reject too many of the comments, that amounts to a decision to send the article elsewhere.

At the end of the day you have to ask yourself two related questions:

1 Do you want the article to go into this particular journal?

2 Do you have the interest and energy needed to meet some of their more important criteria?

Shirley Pendelbury

Working with proofs[3]

♦ **Read your proofs at least twice:**

First, *read them against your original manuscript* to check: that all parts of the manuscript have been included; for accuracy; for proper spelling, punctuation, separation of paragraphs, order of headings and citation of references, figures and tables; spelling and punctuation that may have been altered by the copy editor to match the journal style.

Second, *read them for sense,* for example, does the article hold together after the reviewer's changes were implemented?

♦ Queries from the copy editor or typesetter will be included with your proofs. Deal with each of these as appropriate.

♦ Limit changes to the correction of errors. Corrections at this stage are expensive and new errors may be introduced.

---

3   See Taylor & Francis, Author Services, 'Working with proofs'. www.journalauthors.tandf.co.uk/ production/checkingproofs.asp. Accessed 3 March 2015.

Table 9.1: (Usual) components of an article[4]

SECTION	PURPOSE
Title	Describes content clearly
Authors	Ensures recognition
Abstract	Summary on what was done
Keywords	Useful for abstracting and indexing
Introduction	Explains the problem, sets the scene
Literature review	Locates the study in a theoretical framework
Methods	Describes how data were collected
Results	Describes what was discovered
Discussion	Discusses implications of findings
References/bibliography	Acknowledges sources of ideas, facts
Acknowledgements	Recognition of those who helped (for instance, financing the project; accessing sources)

Disciplinary perspectives

Publishing differs across the disciplines:

- In some disciplines it is more straightforward (but not necessarily easier) than in others.

- There is more scope for and expectation of creativity in some disciplines than in others, for example, in writing style.

- In some there are also more options for publishing.

Arguably, at the two extremes we have scientific publishing and publishing in law.

1. Publishing in science: IMRAD formula

Scientific publishing is mainly by way of journal articles and letters. The outline for an article is fairly standard. Because scientists tend to work in teams, with inexperienced researchers under the mentorship of senior colleagues, the 'IMRAD' formula is well known. The formula is also commonly used in the social and behavioural sciences, and is aligned with the model that applies to all academic writing: *Introduction, Body, Conclusion (IBC)*. This applies even in the humanities, where matters of nuance, style and communication carry greater weight than in the various sciences.

The IMRAD formula is spelt out as:

- **Introduction.** This should be written last and include discussion of the following: hypothesis; background to and justification for your study via the results

---

4   See Elsevier. (2015). 'How to write a scientific paper: A general guide', for *Oral Surgery, Oral Medicine, Oral Pathology and Oral Radiology*. www.oooojournal.net/article/S1079-2104(05)00320-3/fulltext#sec3. Accessed 3 March 2015.

from other studies; a list of objectives—how you plan to organise your paper and what you plan to accomplish.

♦ **Method.** The 'recipe' for how the data was found, and how the material and equipment was used. A well-written Methods section is basic in science in order to allow other researchers to repeat experiments and obtain the same conclusions.

♦ **Results.** What did you find? Data is displayed via tables, figures and graphs.

And

♦ **Discussion.** This section, together with your results, will establish your credibility as a scientist.

2. Getting legal research into the public domain[5]

Many early-career law academics struggle to know how to launch themselves into the publishing world. A discrete law perspective is included here because of the substantial differences in things like publishing options, source material, authority, timing, etc. in comparison to other disciplines. However, *many of the principles described are common to publishing across the spectrum of disciplines* and therefore have relevance for other readers as well.

Types and stages of research output

Legal research can take several forms, but the most common are: a case note, an article, online commentary, a book review and a submission to a professional body.

♦ **A case note**[6] is a useful way to begin for an inexperienced researcher. It is a critical analysis (not just a description) about a recent judgment or perhaps a comparison between two judgments. It usually begins with an introduction, which identifies the area of law involved, the significance of the case and its central legal issue. The idea is to hook in the readers, alerting them to a change to the law, or to a clarification or incorrect interpretation of the law. The introduction provides a reason why a reader must continue reading. You may like to be provocative by saying what you intend to argue, for instance, that the case was wrongly decided, that it constitutes good precedent or provides needed clarity.

It then usually makes sense to begin with a summary of the law before the case so that the reader can understand the significance of the case. This section may involve reference to the common law or part of a statute and the leading cases. It could be that the case you intend discussing is the first to interpret a

---

5   Prepared by Alan Rycroft.
6   www.issafrica.org/uploads/SACQ_GuidelinesCaseNotesFeb14.pdf, accessed 3 March 2015. These unpublished guidelines for case notes were drafted for students by Professor Alan Rycroft and entitled 'The essential features of a case note'.

statute, in which case your introduction may explain what you understand by the purpose/mischief behind the statute.

You will then need to explain the facts of the case. This section requires you to walk a tightrope. This is a summary, clearly reported, avoiding words like respondent/applicant/appellant, which could cause the reader to lose track of who is who. Rather opt for descriptors like buyer/seller/ employer/lessor, etc. Unnecessary facts and dates should be pruned. Significant conflicting evidence should be briefly noted. In this section you are reporting, not judging or evaluating, and this is not a long section. Ask yourself whether a detail has any bearing on the case at all. If not, cut it. (Although sometimes a graphic detail makes the case memorable, like a dead snail in a ginger-beer bottle, as in *Donoghue v Stevenson*.) Try to tell the story in an engaging way.

The next stage is to present the court's decision. The theoretical key to the common law system of precedent is the distinction between the *ratio decidendi* and *obiter dicta* in a case. Your task is to isolate that portion of the judgment, which contains the *ratio*. But as someone said, 'An *obiter dictum* in one case may become *ratio decidendi* in the next.' Similarly, a minority judgment may find approval in a subsequent case. So alongside the *ratio* you may want to refer to a hypothetic consideration raised in *obiter* or to the minority judgment.

At this point you will be ready to explain the significance of the case, amplifying the promise made in your introduction. Here your critical voice must come through as you move from the descriptive factual account to an analytical and evaluative stage. Key questions to answer are: Was the court's decision appropriate? Does this decision change/conform with existing law? Was the reasoning consistent with previous reasoning in similar cases? Is it likely that the decision will significantly influence existing law? Did the court adequately justify its reasoning? Was its interpretation of the law appropriate? Was the reasoning logical/consistent? Did the court consider all/omit some issues and arguments? And, if there was omission, does this weaken the merit of the decision? What are the policy implications of the decision? Are there alternative approaches, which could lead to more appropriate public policy in this area? If your finding is that the decision creates legal precedent or, conversely, upholds legal precedent, what does this mean? What are the implications for the legal and public policy contexts in which this decision sits?

Do not assume that judges get it right; it is helpful to remember that they have chosen one approach and that the other party fought the case believing in another approach. You should feel free, if you can justify it with sound reasons, to be politely critical of the judge. Do not be intimidated by the thought that you are exposing yourself in print—the worst that can happen is that someone else will join the debate, which will do wonders for your national profile!

Finally, choose a title that is descriptive of the content. While it is amusing to read humorous titles, if you want to attract a wide readership the title will be the single most significant way for readers to find it. As NRF rating measures 'impact', you might like to increase your chances of being cited elsewhere with a title that is accurate as to its content.

- **An article** is distinguished from a case note in that it is a broader or deeper treatment of an area of law or policy. While a case note may be limited to a commentary on a new case, an article is expected to advance an argument and make a fuller contribution. While different law journals have distinctive approaches, most ask their reviewers to comment on whether:
  - the quality of the research is acceptable
  - the contribution adds to the current knowledge within the field
  - the author's goals are clearly stated and whether the contribution follows through by achieving these goals consistently and cogently
  - the author's assumptions are acceptable and theoretically justified.

Answering these questions will help in assessing whether you are meeting the standards expected of an article.

Finding the inspiration for an article is difficult. Here are some questions that might trigger your decision: has there been a cluster of recent cases around a single legal issue? Has a recent decision altered the law? Is the difference in approach between the court *a quo* and the appeal court worth commenting on? Is there a draft Bill? (See 'caveat' below.) Is there a 'dangerous' or controversial idea you want to float? Have you browsed law journals from abroad to check for emerging legal issues? What from your teaching syllabus strikes you as unclear or an underdeveloped area of law?

There are some caveats (warnings) that you should take into account: How long will it take to write? How long will it take to get published? Will events overtake you and make your article dated/redundant? Have you checked to see if the topic has been covered in law journals? Have you checked with the editor to see if s/he has received an article on that topic?

- **An online commentary.** More and more legal research takes the form of online commentary such as blogs. This research is valuable because it disseminates knowledge rapidly and widely, and can be hugely influential (see for example, Professor Pierre de Vos's blog, 'Constitutionally Speaking'). But because online publication is seldom peer reviewed, this kind of research will not receive institutional recognition, although its impact is probably far wider than that of conventional legal publishing.

♦ **A book review** is a critical evaluation of a recently published book. Like a case note, this is a useful way to begin a research career because it exposes you to how books are structured and the standards required in getting a book published.

♦ **A submission to a professional body** can take a variety of forms: a submission to the South African Law Commission, or to a parliamentary committee, or to a professional or commercial body. On occasions, a professional body commissions this research. Unless you can convert the submission into an article, this research may not reach many readers. If it is commissioned research you may not have the freedom to disseminate it. Like online commentary, this kind of research may show social engagement (and build a professional reputation) but will probably not result in institutional recognition.

Engaging with theory and structuring an argument (these principles apply to all disciplines)

As indicated above, an author's assumptions must be acceptable and theoretically justified. This means that there is an expectation that a writer will locate the topic in a theoretical framework (for example, if you want to write about a case that holds a company criminally liable for culpable homicide, you will have to engage in both criminal law theory of causation and culpability and company law theory of corporate personality).

An article is not just a descriptive story: it is an argument. The writer makes it clear to the reader that s/he is using the research with the express purpose of 1) confirming or 2) challenging/questioning the prevailing wisdom or law or practice. This can be done by expressly including words such as, 'This article will argue that ...' in the introduction, alerting the reader early on to what the argument is going to be.

In constructing the argument, you may find that a judgment does not make sense or creates unease in your mind. If this happens, diagnose whether your unease is in the area of values, logic, principle or policy.

♦ **Values.** Check the normative sources of values, such as the Bill of Rights, UN Conventions, ILO Recommendations, etc.

♦ **Logic.** Slips in logic usually happen because a decision is reached that is unsupported by any evidence, based on speculation, entirely disconnected from the evidence, or supported by evidence that is insufficiently reasonable to justify the decision.

♦ **Principle.** If you think that a judge or writer has wrongly described an underlying principle, you will need to find other authorities that support your alternative formulation of the principle, or explain why the principle should be remodelled.

◆ **Policy.** Knowing that policy is an 'unruly horse', where do you look for authority as to what is public policy? Legislation? The SA Law Commission? Empirical research of attitudes?

Dissemination and impact

There is a range of journals, from those that accept articles on any topic (for example, *South African Law Journal*) to those with a specialist niche (for instance, *Industrial Law Journal*). Once you have identified the most appropriate journal, check the house style of the journal to which you intend submitting. Some journals allow footnotes for case notes. Others do not. It will save time if, from the beginning, you shape your case note or article in the correct style. Most journals have online guides to their house style.

Conclusion

This chapter has provided a brief introduction to publishing principles and options, with an emphasis on journal publishing—aspects of which will receive further attention in due course. In anticipation of this, we turn our attention in Chapter 10 to publishing a book.

SCHOLARLY PUBLISHING
WRITING A BOOK

If a scholar wants to continue his or her education, then the thing to do is to write as well as read books.[1]

Basics about books

The provocative statement above may be disputed by some, but it certainly draws our attention to the place of books in academia. In some disciplines the writing of books is highly esteemed. In fact, in the humanities the publication of a monograph is considered to be the supreme research output, and at higher levels it is sometimes a condition for promotion. Similarly in law, books are highly valued. In other disciplines the writing of research-based books is rare, the focus being on journal articles. It is true that there is more certainty about publishing a journal article than a book. There are a number of reasons for this, the most immediate (and most significant for the new academic) being the assurance of an acceptable publication if the journal is listed (accredited). Another reason, notably with online journals, is that publications appear much more quickly than with books. But there is a distinct place for books, as we shall see. The secret is to be savvy about them.

Different types of books are published in a university context and each has its place. *Textbooks*, for example, are critical for teaching and learning purposes in all disciplines and require constant revision as situations change and as fresh and more appropriate ways of communicating information to students become available. As a rule, textbooks do not contain new knowledge. Rather, they represent a reconfiguring of existing knowledge for a particular purpose. An enormous amount of creativity goes into producing good textbooks, and the writing of these is accredited to an academic's teaching portfolio.

Accreditation of books

For our current purposes we focus on what are described as *scholarly books*, that is, those that make a fresh contribution to knowledge, adding to the current debate in the field. In South Africa the Department of Higher Education and Training (DHET) has strict criteria for the accreditation of books as subsidy-earning research output. These criteria are rigid but useful in identifying the features of true scholarly books, summarised as follows:

---

1   Rose, R. (2010). 'Writing a book is good for you', *European Political Science*, 9: 417–419. www.palgrave-journals.com/eps/journal/v9/n3/full/eps201018a.html. Accessed 27 August 2013.

- ❖ The purpose of the book must be to disseminate original research and new developments within specific disciplines, sub-disciplines or fields of study.
- ❖ The book should provide evidence of peer review in the publishing process, either in the book itself or in an affidavit from the publisher with details of the review process.
- ❖ Institutional affiliation should be clearly stated.
- ❖ The book must have an ISBN number.
- ❖ The length of the book should be at least 60 pages, excluding covers, references, bibliography and appendices (based on the UNESCO definition of a book).
- ❖ The primary target audience for the book must be specialists in the relevant field.

A dissertation/thesis or part thereof that is reworked and published as a monograph (or book chapters and/or articles) must go through its *own peer-review process* in order to qualify as a separate research output. Examination of the thesis does not count as peer review of the reworked material. We will return to this because the publishing potential of and from theses often goes untapped.

Books that do not qualify as research output are the following:

- ❖ dissertations and theses (without reworking and subsequent peer review)
- ❖ textbooks and study guides
- ❖ inaugural speeches
- ❖ reports forming part of contract research (this is a contested issue)
- ❖ works of fiction
- ❖ documentation of case studies
- ❖ book reviews
- ❖ subsequent editions, unless new research is included
- ❖ dictionaries and encyclopaedias
- ❖ autobiographies.

As a way into a discussion of book writing we consider the differences between scholarly articles and books.

What is the relationship between a scholarly article and a book?

A point sometimes overlooked is that, in terms of value, it is not a case of either/or between journal articles and books. Individually they both have value, even though their value differs in certain respects. Many academics successfully develop their research profiles through a combination of journal and book publishing, and it is possible to use a series of already published articles as the basis for a carefully crafted book. Journal articles, notes Richard Rose,[2] can be a good way to probe aspects of a subject as part of a process of gaining understanding, but it can take years of intensive probing of those articles to grasp what the main issue is. Rose himself produced a major monograph drawing on two decades of articles, showing that writing journal articles and books can be complementary activities.[3]

Table 10.1: Features of books and journal articles[4]

BOOKS	JOURNAL ARTICLES
In-depth examination of a broad topic	In-depth, but on a specific, narrow topic
Wider scope	Sharply delimited scope
Longer lag between event or development and publication. This has an impact on the scope of the product, allowing for: - more complete information - deeper analysis - broader historical perspective - more contextual, both within and outside of discipline - more cumulative coverage of topic	Important for reporting fast-paced, competitive or time-sensitive research - captures the 'spirit of the moment'
Wider readership (primarily specialists and peers, but also professionals and educated laity)	Narrow readership (specialists, peers)
Longer timeframe (often several years) with a more protracted publishing process	Shorter timeframe with a more streamlined publishing process
	Provide forum for ongoing debate

Books, then, are of a *different genre* to journal articles—a completely different exercise—in the features identified above and also in length, style and language, aim and publishing process.

---

2   University of Aberdeen and Director of the Centre for the Study of Public Policy, University of Strathclyde, Scotland. See Rose, 'Writing a book is good for you', 3.

3   Unfortunately current international bibliometric systems are biased in the direction of journal publishing. A satisfactory way of establishing the impact of books has yet to be devised. Bibliometric statistics therefore tend to exclude book authors from their calculations.

4   A useful webpage, on which this table is based, is located at www.library.uvic.ca/instruction/research/bookvjour.html. Accessed 27 August 2013.

There are a number of situations where the writing of a book is indicated, notably the following:

- To make the results of research available to a *wider audience*.
- To bring together *different aspects of your work*.
- *A thesis that lends itself to publication as a whole* rather than being divided into self-standing articles.
- A burning desire to explore a topic in depth: *passion*.

How does one determine the scope of a book?

- Publisher's word count.
- Less is more likely to succeed.
- Thread running through—identify it up front; test all the way.
- Prepare an abstract and see what emerges.

SOME GUIDELINES FOR WRITING A BOOK AND DETERMINING ITS SCOPE

Most of the following points have been adapted from a guide to developing research questions.[5] They apply equally well as guides for writing a book:

1 *Know the area*—be familiar with what is happening at the cutting edge in your field.
2 *Widen the base of your experience*, for example, across disciplines—this will enrich your thought processes and your writing.
3 Use techniques to *enhance creativity*, for example, read good literature.
4 *Be open*—don't allow earlier decisions on method or technique to decide the questions being asked (this is important, especially where there is dependence on computerised statistical analysis packages).
5 *Cut it down to size*—don't try to cover everything or tackle a set of questions that is too wide or diffuse.
6 *'Workshop' your ideas*—with peers and possibly postgraduate students.
7 *Be alert to recent developments*—especially when converting a thesis.

From dissertation to book

Reasons for publishing a dissertation as a book:

- Some theses are not easily broken into discrete publishable parts.
- Because of the topic, it would have greater impact if published as an intact study, that is, as a book.

---

5   Robson, C. (2002). *Real World Research*, 2nd edition. Oxford: Blackwell Publishing, 56–58.

♦ When certain themes can be lifted out and developed into a book-sized study of their own.

Publishers are reluctant to publish theses. They are not marketable. So a thorough reworking and a convincing proposal are critical. Do not submit an untransformed thesis manuscript to a publisher. *The recipe for a dissertation is not the formula for a book.*

In transforming a thesis into a book, remember the following:

♦ *A reduction in size will be necessary.* A publisher is unlikely to accept a manuscript of much more than 60 000 words.

♦ *You are moving out of one genre and into another.*

Thesis = primarily a work of scholarship and argumentation
Book = primarily a work of communication.

♦ *You are writing for a different audience*—from three examiners who *must* read it to readers who *choose* to read it.

• Do some homework on who is likely to read your work and make it accessible to them.
• You are not proving anything to examiners in a book.
• This means that some of the technical detail (for example, an overlong literature review or methodological intricacies) may need to be omitted. (*But*—strike a balance: your book needs credibility!)

♦ *A book requires some creativity* while a thesis demonstrates technical competence:

• Reshape the material to enhance potential readership and sales. Lighten it; give it 'voice'; entice the reader.
• Consider its usability for graduate students and professionals.
• Consider elements that could be *added* to the book, for example, possibly extend the analysis to include a wider context and so enhance its relevance.

♦ Dissertations that 'wrestle with their origins' and are contentious are *not necessarily more publishable as a book* than one that 'picks no academic quarrels'.[6]

♦ Some dissertations fall into the trap of making claims that are 'too grand for the evidence mustered by the author'.[7] *This won't fly with a publisher.*

♦ Ask yourself: *what has happened in the interim since I wrote my thesis?* New literature on the subject? New developments in the field? Altered situations requiring more fieldwork or experimentation?

---

6   Germano, W. (2005). *From Dissertation to Book*, Chicago, IL: University of Chicago Press, 20, 21.
7   Germano, *From Dissertation to Book*, 18.

Generic elements of a book proposal

A writer keeps one eye on the script and one on the audience. A publisher keeps half an eye on the audience and the other one and a half on the marketing of the product.[8]

Each publishing house has its own proposal requirements and usually these are available on the web. But most of the requirements are generic, and the object of a proposal is to convince a publisher that your project is so good that it is worth their while to invest in its publication; in other words, market your idea. A good book proposal, whether the study is original or derived from a thesis, should contain the following:

- An accompanying letter, addressing the commissioning editor by name rather than simply 'Dear Madam'.
- Title and sub-title of the book.
- Synopsis/overview of the book plus rationale, that is, a narrative description of the book's themes, arguments (expressed concisely and clearly), goals, place in literature, scope and special features that make it unique.
    - Why are you the right author for this particular book?
    - What difference will your book make?
    - Why?
- Target readership and your role in promoting/marketing the book. Who will buy your book and why? Indicate anticipated primary, secondary and subsidiary readership (for example, peers and specialists in the field, postgraduate students, interested and educated 'laypeople').
- Author biography—your professional history and current position; publication history; some publishers like a sample of what you've previously published. In the case of a multi-authored book, provide details of each author/contributor and the specific role that each will play (for example, X will write chapters 4–6).
- Anticipated length, that is, word count (be careful to check first on the sort of length the publisher likes to work with for similar books); indicate length of preface, acknowledgements, bibliography, appendices, etc. separately.
- Anticipated timeframe—when will the manuscript be ready?
- Competition—show that you are aware of what else has been published in the field, citing similar titles. How will your book add to what is already out there? Publishers need to know that you are aware of who you are competing with.
- Preliminary table of contents—with brief description of each chapter.

---

8   Haarhoff, D. (1998). *The Writer's Voice: A workbook for writers in Africa*. Johannesburg: Zebra Press, 280.

◆ Indicate inclusion of graphic (non-textual) material (graphs, maps, photographs, charts, tables, etc.).

◆ Sample chapters, if required (depends on publisher; possibly first chapter plus one or two other key chapters). *Do not send the whole manuscript.*

◆ It is helpful to indicate endorsement of the project by a recognised authority in the field, especially someone known to the publisher.

THE PUBLISHING PROCESS IN A NUTSHELL

Approach the publisher with a *proposal*.

Some publishers send the proposal out for preliminary review, and on the basis of this, indicate their '*intention to publish*', subject to satisfactory review of the whole manuscript.

If the proposal is accepted, the publisher will inform you and usually appoint a *project manager* with whom you will deal from now on.

The project manager will liaise with you about *deadlines* for the manuscript.

Once the manuscript is submitted, it will be sent out for *peer review*.

If reports are satisfactory, you will be informed about *recommended changes*.

Once the changes have been made, the manuscript is sent back to the project manager, who will give it to an *editor*.

You will receive the *editor's comments* and should go through them very carefully. If you disagree with anything, say so.

Implement those you agree with and *seek advice if you are not sure.*

This process may be repeated. *At the editing stage there is considerable scope for any changes that you wish to make.*

Once the corrections have been made the manuscript is sent to the *typesetter*. *From now on only minimal changes can be made and they should not disturb the page layout.*

The next time you see the manuscript will be at *first proof stage*. Read it through carefully for typos, spelling mistakes, grammatical errors, etc. If you make other changes at this stage you may have to pay for these (these are known as 'author's corrections').

You may be asked to look at *second and third proofs*, although this seems to vary between publishers. By now you should be satisfied with the manuscript.

Sourcing a publisher

- ◆ *Regular commercial publisher*. This is first prize in many ways, but commercial stock has to move so it is likely that your book could soon be remaindered or put out of print.

- ◆ *Academic or university press*. These are more likely to publish academic books, especially if you are a relatively unknown author; they often require subventions; the smaller ones are generally not the best at advertising and distribution.

- ◆ A publisher with an *interest in the field* and a history of publishing in it.

- ◆ For academic purposes (subsidy) make sure that the publishing house has an established and verifiable *pre-publication review process*.

- ◆ Use *international conferences* as an opportunity to meet with potential publishers—make yourself known.

- ◆ Take a copy of your proposal to conferences; try to arrange an interview.

Working with a publisher

Once you have sourced a publisher for your book, you begin a journey that needs to be managed carefully. Stepping out of line at any point—especially proving to be unreliable—will certainly jeopardise your chances of publishing with them again. Working with a book publisher is in some respects the same as working with a journal editor. There are principles that apply to the whole publishing process. Because of the size and scope of a book in comparison to an article, there are obviously differences as well.

The following principles should be uncompromisingly adhered to:

- ◆ Once a book has been accepted by a publisher, one person will be appointed to manage the project.
    - • It is this person with whom you should maintain good communication.
    - • Do not approach anyone else, for example, with queries.
- ◆ Prove yourself to be a reliable client.
    - • This is demonstrated most clearly in strict adherence to negotiated deadlines for each stage of the project, as well as final submission.
- ◆ Should you for any reason be unable to meet a deadline, discuss this as soon as possible with the project manager.
- ◆ Do exactly what is required, reading the publisher's guidelines for authors carefully, noting things like referencing style, etc.
- ◆ Address reviewers' comments and suggestions meticulously, even if there are those you choose not to implement. In such cases, explain your reasons.
- ◆ Address recommended editorial changes in the same way.

Reviewers (the pre-acceptance review process)

Writing a book is an intensely personal thing. You spend hour after hour nurturing it, turning raw words into something you can be proud of. You've done your best to convey your message, and to make a book that's both accurate and entertaining. It's gorgeous.

It's really quite a shame that you have to show it to other people.

But you do.

And those other people don't realize how much work you've put in, and how subtly you've plotted it, and how many ideas you've researched. They just want to tell you what's wrong. That's their job—they're reviewers.

Dave Thomas[9]

Remember:

- There are different types of reviewers. Most are supportive and helpful, but on the extreme are the ignorant, the arrogant and the pedantic—but it is important to learn from each of them.

- Address each point raised by the reviewer, ticking them off as you go.

- If you don't agree with a recommendation, explain why. Do not simply ignore it.

Negotiating a contract

Once a manuscript has been accepted for publication, that is, after the peer-review process, the publisher will negotiate a contract with you. In academic publishing, details of the contract are not as critical as they would be for a top novelist who can expect to get rich on royalties! Most publishers' contracts follow the same format and include similar details. Nevertheless, a contract is the mutual seal of commitment between author and publisher. It is a legal document that can be drawn on should there be a breach on either side. It is therefore wise to ask a colleague with book publishing experience to review the contract with you before you sign it.

The editorial process

To what extent is a writer bound to accept editor's changes? Manuscript editors come in towards the end of the process, after the reviewers' reports have been dealt with and the manuscript resubmitted. Their editing is usually confined to minor stylistic issues, punctuation, spelling, typos, referencing, etc. An editor is there to enhance the presentation and readability of your book, so take all suggestions seriously.

---

9   Thomas, D. (2007). 'Reviewers, and how not to kill them', in *Writing a Book*, Part 7, www.pragdave.pragprog.com/pragdave/writing_a_book/index.html. Accessed 22 April 2015.

Launching and marketing

Although publishers undertake to advertise and distribute their authors' books, they depend on the authors to provide them with information. Usually they request data about possible journals for reviews of the book, and the names of well-known academics who might recommend the book or use it in their courses. They will also be interested in knowing about events at which you will be speaking or lecturing. But you will have to do a great deal to make your book known through arranging book launches (which publishers will sometimes fund) and giving copies to colleagues who would be willing to read the book and perhaps recommend it. Publishers appreciate it when their authors play a proactive role in this regard.

Conclusion

Whether we publish in journals, books, conference proceedings or reports, ultimately it is the impact of the work that counts. This, as we have seen, is becoming a contested area. The aim of Chapter 11 is to break open the idea of research impact, explaining conventions and identifying trends.

CHAPTER 11
RESEARCH IMPACT

Research impact is an expression commonly used in academia and its meaning is evolving fast. Once understood almost exclusively in bibliometric terms, the meaning of research impact has expanded dramatically to include the tangible benefits that research brings to society as well. We have seen that funding agencies are increasingly requiring details of anticipated impact, for example, in the social sphere or policy-making, as a condition of their grants. This extended meaning of research impact has been built into many institutions' revised research strategies, calling for research to be available and accessible to stakeholders and to have a tangible impact. It is also something increasingly linked to social responsiveness as a core academic function. In this chapter we consider a range of perspectives on research impact, from the traditional (science model) to those reflecting contemporary research challenges and opportunities.

Understanding impact factor and h-index, with pointers for choosing a journal[1]

One of the core academic functions is to produce new knowledge and disseminate it. For those publishing in journals, the choice of journal therefore becomes important—in the interests of both the researcher and the advancement of the discipline or field. But before choosing a journal, several factors should be considered in making new research available to the targeted audience.

In the various sciences, terms such as 'impact factor', 'Citation Index®' and 'h-index' in relation to journals are familiar. This is historically less so in other disciplines. But even here the increasing sophistication of bibliometric systems, together with bibliometric links with the research status of both universities and individuals, suggests that all academics need to be familiar with this terminology and its publishing implications.

Impact factor (IF) is defined as 'a measure of the frequency with which the "average article" in a journal has been cited in a particular year or period'.

The IF of a journal is calculated annually, using records from the two previous years. Hence, the journal's IF for 2012 will be as follows:

$$IF\ 2012 = \frac{number\ of\ citations\ in\ 2010\ and\ 2011}{number\ of\ articles\ published\ in\ 2010\ and\ 2011}$$

---

1   Prepared by Luigi Nassimbeni and Gaëlle Ramon.

Example: Journal A published a total of 20 articles during 2010 and 2011. Articles from these two years were cited 19 and 25 times, respectively, in 2012. Based on the formula, Journal A's IF for 2012 would be:

$$\text{IF } 2012 = \frac{19 + 25}{40} = \frac{44}{20} = 2.2$$

The IF for a journal has come to mean a lot more than its simple definition. It has come to imply quality of research and reflects directly on the authors and on the institutions they represent. Consequently, publishing in high IF journals is often synonymous with high-level work that has the potential for significant impact in the field. High IF journals are also associated with high visibility and this exposure can result, potentially, in even higher citation rates.

It is important to note that citation rates and IFs are discipline-related, owing to the varying citation practices in the research community, and in some cases to the size of the community. Therefore one cannot compare the citations and IFs of one discipline with those of another. In addition, one can expect a higher IF and more citations for review journals, so the type of journal within a particular discipline affects IF as well.

Using the Journal Citation Reports from the ISI Web of Knowledge (July 2013) for specific disciplines:

◆ **Chemistry**, highest IF 2012 = 21.75 for *Nature Chemistry*.

◆ **Environmental Studies**, highest IF 2012 = 14.47 for *Nature Climate Change*.

◆ **History**, highest IF 2012 = 0.80 for *Comparative Studies in Society and History*.

◆ **Management**, highest IF 2012 = 6.70 for *Journal of Management*

◆ **Mathematics**, highest IF 2012 = 3.57 for *Journal of the American Mathematical Society*.

◆ **Medicine** (General and Internal), highest IF 2012 = 51.65 for *New England Journal of Medicine*.

Each of these journals is regarded as the flagship of the discipline, and the respective IFs cannot be measured against IFs in any other discipline. Comparison is valid only between journals in the same discipline. This means that articles in *Comparative Studies in Society and History* (IF 0.80) are no less worthy than those in the *New England Journal of Medicine* (IF 51.65).

As a direct result of the publication of their work, individual academics in text-based disciplines develop and establish *publication profiles*. Their profiles and the impact their research has on the discipline can be measured by the citing of their articles by others. One of the measures commonly used to measure the impact of individual researchers or research groups is the *h-index*. This measure—which, like impact factor, relies on citations—also has a discipline-related significance rather than an absolute value and favours academics who have been practising for a number of years.

H-index is defined as the number of published articles by an author (h) with citation numbers of those articles equal to or greater than h. For example, a researcher with an h-index of 12 has, among all her or his published articles, 12 articles with 12 or more citations each.

Researchers can obtain their h-index using various interfaces such as the ISI Web of Knowledge, Google Scholar or Elsevier's Scopus—but because different sources are used to extract the citations, the final results may vary. H-index is often quoted in applications for academic jobs or when applying for grants from statutory bodies such as the South African NRF. Therefore, when referring to these metrics, it is important to include the date of generation and the database from which it was generated.

Although the h-index has certain advantages, it also has a number of weaknesses, mostly shared by IF. Among these are the following:

- It does not distinguish between the contribution of individual authors in a multi-authored paper, and takes no account of author placement.

- It ignores the context in which the papers are cited, for example, whether used to support an argument integral to the article or whether it is cited simply to flesh out an introduction.

- It does not distinguish between negative and positive citations.

As we have seen, the 2012 San Francisco Declaration challenges the adequacy of these bibliometric systems as the sole measures of research excellence. It does not recommend replacing or discounting them, but contends that alternative measures are required to measure the value of certain types of research output that are not measurable in the conventional bibliometric sense.

Having acknowledged this, researchers at South African institutions are, nevertheless, encouraged, if possible, to select journals accredited by the DHET, that is, those listed by:

- the Institute of Scientific Information (ISI)

- the International Bibliography of the Social Sciences (IBSS)

- the DHET as approved South African journals.

Regardless of the impact factor of the journal, each article will earn a full subsidy unit for the university, provided that all the authors are from the same university. In the case of multi-authored papers, where more than one South African institution is represented, the subsidy is divided pro rata to contributions between the institutions. This means that if an article has three authors, with two from institution A and one from institution B, the subsidy will be divided as follows:

- ◆ Two thirds (66.66 per cent) will go to institution A
- ◆ One third (33.33 per cent) will go to institution B

In the case of contributions from collaborators not at South African institutions, that portion of the subsidy is forfeited. Hence, if three authors are from South African institutions and one from overseas, the forfeited amount is 25 per cent.

To aid the recording of research outputs and claiming the subsidy-earning units, universities make use of databases in which all research outputs need to be entered (for example, IRMA; InfoEd Global). It is the duty of each researcher to ensure that his or her publications are logged into the system every year.

Some researchers are tempted to boost their research output in order to benefit from the subsidy policy.

- ◆ There are cases where quality of articles is compromised in favour of quantity, placing the reputation of both individual and institution in jeopardy.
- ◆ Quality should always be favoured over quantity.
- ◆ Mature researchers will focus on publishing one very good article in a good journal rather than many in lower-rated journals, an effective strategy when it comes to evaluation of the researcher's profile, notably in the sciences.

Tensions might arise with regard to publishing in local journals, and certain factors should be borne in mind:

- ◆ They may have lower IFs, but researchers may want to support their local societies—and hence the national research endeavour—by publishing in them.
- ◆ They often provide opportunity to engage in debate with colleagues working in the same field—something much more difficult for fledgling academics in high-profile international journals.
- ◆ Although local publishing could result in lower-visibility publications, a mitigating factor is that the journal could possibly be abstracted by international databases.
- ◆ Exercise caution and discretion in selecting local (in our case, South African) journals. Many of them (but certainly not all), although accredited, have severely compromised editorial policies and peer-review processes. This undermines their reputation, and if you use them too frequently, it will compromise your reputation as well. Ask advice from senior colleagues familiar with the publishing landscape.

◆ For early-career academics it is important to *get published* and it is not always wise to aim too high in terms of the journal right at the beginning of your career, especially if you are publishing alone. Another useful purpose is served by taking advantage of publishing, as a new researcher, in less stringent journals: you will get more writing practice as more of your articles are accepted!

Open access publishing[2]

Above all else, academics want their work to be read. Success lies in citations by other scholars, and by your work having an impact both within the academy and in society at large. This necessitates other scholars and potential readers beyond the university having access to your scholarly output. At the same time, research funders want to see their investments pay off. These imperatives come together and are enabled by digital technologies, which make access to online content easy.

It is this realisation that gave rise to the Budapest Declaration in 2001, which stated:

An old tradition and a new technology have converged to make possible an unprecedented public good. The old tradition is the willingness of scientists and scholars to publish the fruits of their research in scholarly journals *without payment, for the sake of inquiry and knowledge. The new technology is the internet ...*[3]

It is this meeting that defined *open access* in a way that continues to be used today. Open access became a mainstream issue in 2012, which marks the year that research funders in many countries put in place policies that made open access publishing a condition of grants being given, for instance, the National Institutes of Health (NIH) in the US. It is a global movement and it is growing rapidly in importance for the scholarly community.

By 'open access' of literature we mean:

◆ It is freely available on the public Internet.

◆ Any user is permitted to read, download, copy, distribute, print, search or link to the full texts of these articles, crawl them for indexing, pass them as data to software, or use them for any other lawful purpose, without financial, legal or technical barriers, other than those inseparable from gaining access to the Internet itself.

The only constraint on reproduction and distribution, and the only role for copyright in this domain, should be to give authors control over the integrity of their work and the right to be properly acknowledged and cited.

Open access is part of a constellation of 'opens' in academia, including open data, open educational resources (teaching resources), open science (especially to do with

---

2   Prepared by Laura Czerniewicz.
3   Opening sentences of the Budapest Open Access Initiative, 14 February 2002. www.budapestopenaccessinitiative.org/read. Accessed 3 March 2015.

replicability) and open research. While open access generally refers to journal articles, it can also refer to other outputs such as working papers, reports, monographs and book collections.

There are several reasons to opt for open access publishing. Among these are the following:

- It has been shown in numerous studies across different disciplines to increase citations.
- It demonstrates a commitment to public access, transparency and its value for development.

Open access to journal articles can take place through what is known as the *green route* or the *gold route*.

- The *gold route* refers to publishing in open access journals, that is, those journals whose business models are designed to be open access.
  - These journals do not charge subscriptions but finance their operations in various ways including, most famously, through article processing charges (APCs).
  - Many subscription journals offer authors an open access option. This has been criticised for being 'double-dipping' as publishers earn from both readers and writers, and some APC funds do not allow for this.
- The *green route* refers to self-archiving of a version of the article, in an institutional repository or on a personal website.
  - Publishers have different agreements about when and how this can be done, ranging from pre-peer-reviewed proofs through to final proofs.
  - Researchers can find the details of what they are able to do on Sherpa Romeo, a website of publishers' agreements for different journals.

In other parts of the world, APCs may be covered by specific government allocations. This does not exist in South Africa and there are no policy requirements for open access. Despite this, many South African scholars go the open access route either because they have to (through grant requirements) or because they choose to for all the benefits that open access brings.

For emerging researchers with limited funding, as for those in poorly resourced institutions, the cost to the author for open access publication (where costs are effectively transferred from user [subscription holder] to author) is a challenge. However, as the importance of open access is acknowledged, notably because of its potential for impact, some institutions are making provision to assist with these costs, which are often way in excess of print journal page costs.

Additional information about open access[4]

◆ Open access (OA) literature is digital, online, free of charge and free of most copyright and licensing restrictions.

◆ OA removes *price barriers* (subscriptions, licensing fees, pay-per-view fees) and *permission barriers* (most copyright and licensing restrictions). The Public Library of Science (PLoS) defines it as 'free availability and unrestricted use'.

◆ There are at the time of writing more than 4 000 fully OA peer-reviewed journals, with two new titles published per day.

◆ There are 1 500 OA repositories, with a new repository added every day.

◆ Scientific Commons—30 million OA items. www.scientificcommons.org/

◆ Directory of OA Journals. www.doaj.org/.

Improving visibility of your work: Institutional repositories

Among the benefits of OA publishing is that citation rates are increased by 36–200 per cent. Archiving your work in an institutional repository is an excellent way to make it accessible and to increase citations. Not all universities have such repositories, but the value of these is being increasingly appreciated.

Dissemination and impact: rising to new and old challenges[5]

Reconnecting science and society has a deeper purpose than developing the next marketable technology. It is about the kind of society we want to create, a society in which there is optimism, confidence, and purpose. Scientists need to know why they are doing science, and society needs to know why it supports them.

Neil Turok[6]

University research strategies and the securing of funding are increasingly contingent on satisfactory answers to two questions:

1 In what way is the research innovative?

2 Is it strategically planned for positive impact on policy-makers, socio-economic aspects of the lives of target populations, the physical environment, etc?

In other words, how will the research benefit the world? What impact will it have?

For research to have impact it must be accessible to stakeholders, and for this to happen effective dissemination strategies are crucial. As the mutual approach of research

---

4   See Suber, P. (2004). 'A very brief introduction to open access'. www.legacy.earlham.edu/~peters/fos/brief.htm. Accessed 3 March 2015.

5   See 'Impact and dissemination of research findings', www.erm.ecs.soton.ac.uk/theme8/impact_and_dissemination_of_the_research_findings.html. Accessed 26 March 2013.

6   Turok, N. (2012). *From Quantum to Cosmos: The universe within*. London: Faber and Faber, 49, 50.

and the real world gains momentum, interesting shifts are observable. First, traditional understandings of 'dissemination of research' are being shaken to the core. Second, 'impact' is being redefined—from being restricted to scholarly citations to now including its total effect 'out there'.

These two shifts come together in contemporary modes of communicating research and its outcomes to a broader community of stakeholders:

- presentations: at scholarly and professional conferences and meetings

- publications: scholarly, professional and popular

- the media: radio, TV, newspapers and pamphlets

- audio-visual devices: CD and DVD

- less likely audiences: schools, NGOs and community forums

- social media: tweeting, blogs, Facebook, etc.

It is the impact of the last of these, social media, that is the most profound, and which is the focus of altmetrics, the creation and study of new metrics based on the social web for analysing and informing scholarship.

ALTMETRICS

'These new forms reflect and transmit scholarly impact: that dog-eared (but uncited) article that used to live on a shelf now lives in Mendeley, CiteULike, or Zotero—where we can see and count it. That hallway conversation about a recent finding has moved to blogs and social networks—now, we can listen in. The local genomics dataset has moved to an online repository—now, we can track it. This diverse group of activities forms a composite trace of impact far richer than any available before. We call the elements of this trace altmetrics.'[7]

The experience of Melissa Terras, a professor at University College London (UCL), illustrates the effectiveness of the social web and altmetrics. At one point Terras made a decision to blog and tweet about her published research papers and the stories behind them. Her citation rate immediately soared: 'What became clear … was the correlation between talking about my research online and the spike in downloads of papers from the institutional repository.'[8]

We saw earlier how the San Francisco Declaration is challenging the adequacy of narrow bibliometric assessments of research impact and value; although the document originated within the scientific community it may in time have relevance for other

---

7   See Priem, J. et al. (2010). 'Altmetrics: A manifesto'. www.altmetrics.org/manifesto/. Accessed 26 January 2015.

8   Terras, M. (2012). 'The impact of social media on the dissemination of research: Results of an experiment', *Journal of Digital Humanities*, 1 (3), Summer. Available at www.journalofdigital-humanities.org/1-3/the-impact-of-social-media-on-the-dissemination-of-research-by-melissa-terras/. Accessed 25 March 2013.

disciplines as well. The situation in law provides a powerful illustration of current inadequacies. Perhaps the most prized response to a publication in law is citation by a judge in a court judgment. This is because where the law is not clear, a judge looks to 'secondary sources' (such as textbooks and articles) to provide a basis or justification for her/his judgment. For the writer of the textbook or article, this is the ultimate compliment and recognition because academic research then plays a direct role in the formulation of the law, as articulated by the judge (other disciplines have have their own parallel norms for measuring real impact within their disciplines).

Such acknowledgment of an academic contribution is not, however, reflected in any index because judgments, despite being in the public domain, highly influential and widely studied, are not regarded as 'publications'.[9]

Conclusion to this chapter and Part 3

The agenda of this chapter is not to be contentious or divisive. Rather, by introducing these various perspectives, it aims both to inform emerging researchers about existing research impact measures and to illustrate needs and trends towards a broader understanding of impact in response to contemporary challenges in the research environment. This is not to suggest a lessened value for existing research impact measures, but the need to accommodate and acknowledge the worth of other measures as well.

There is a sense in which one's impact as an academic is also reflected in the supervision of the research of others, notably postgraduate students. Supervision is an integral dimension of the academic portfolio, and is the focus of Part 4, the final section of this book.

---

9   Law comments by Alan Rycroft.

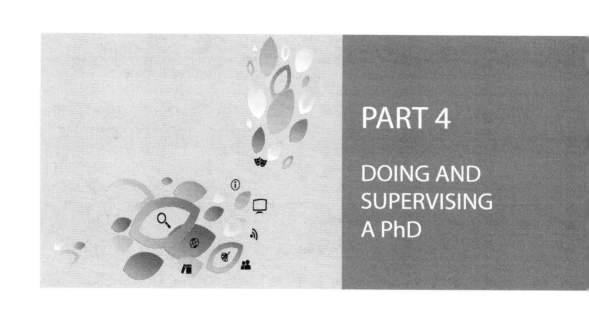

PART 4

DOING AND
SUPERVISING
A PhD

PART 4

DOING AND SUPERVISING A PhD

One of the interesting features of our regular supervision workshops over the past 10 years is that on any one occasion usually about half of the participants (who are drawn mainly but not exclusively from the cohort of early-career academics) are simultaneously both students and supervisors. In most of these cases, they are engaged with their own PhDs while supervising Masters' students. This has created an interesting and useful dynamic, and according to post-workshop evaluations has considerably enhanced the value of the workshop itself. The reason for this is obvious. Both perspectives are constantly discussed and held in tension in the conversation. For the student, the supervisor is ever-present with her or his challenges; for the supervisor, the student's point of view cannot be overlooked. The conversation is thus kept at a practical, hands-on level. The unambiguous aim of these workshops is to provide tools for best supervisory practice, the end result of which is to enable the student to produce and graduate with the best dissertation of which she or he is capable within a reasonable time period.

It is with this in mind that I have opted to combine discussion of the PhD process with graduate supervision in Part 4. While the main focus is on PhDs, the same principles apply to the writing and supervision of Master's dissertations as well. The difference is one of scope, not quality.

Most academics have stories about their own experiences of being supervised—some good and some bad. Guidance of a good supervisor and mentor is usually reflected in an individual's mentoring and supervision of others. Good practice helps perpetuate good practice. But sadly some people have received very little supervision and mentoring themselves, or that which is simply bad. The result is that some graduate supervisors perpetuate bad practice, the example set for them by their own supervisors.

Graduate supervision is situated at the interface of teaching and research. At many universities the actual supervision process is accredited to the supervisor's teaching profile, while a graduated Master's or doctoral student is classified as research output for the supervisor, and, of course, also for the student. Supervision has to do with the development in the student of research and related skills, while a successful outcome of the process marks the production of a peer-reviewed piece of research. From both a teaching and research perspective, therefore, training in supervision is essential for the development of best practice among early-career researchers, and for successful research experiences for students.

Many new academics are thrown almost immediately into the role of supervising, and most feel inadequate to the task. For this reason, supervision training is part of the process of researcher development, aimed at growing the cohort of well-trained supervisors in higher education institutions. From a sub-Saharan perspective, quality graduate supervision, which implies quality graduates, is critical if we are to compete internationally with any measure of success. This refers not only to academic competence. Because the effects of such research ultimately reach the public sphere—through the transferability of knowledge—what happens in promoting graduate study at universities can have a longer-term effect on society and national development as well.

Acknowledging differences in detail in the supervision and graduate study processes in the various institutions, it is nevertheless possible from what follows to extract principles and adapt them to different contexts.

In approaching thesis production and its supervision, we must remember that while there are many generic issues, there are also some differences between the sciences and humanities (both understood here in their broadest sense):

◆ The role of conceptualisation and theory in the respective streams.

◆ In the sciences, thesis production is necessarily more linear than in some other disciplines, where a thesis might develop organically in the early and middle stages.

◆ This has an impact on thesis structure and the weight given to different sections.

◆ The extent of financial support required by some students (mainly in laboratory-based disciplines where graduate study is usually full-time) in contrast to some other disciplines.

These and other divergences will become apparent as we proceed, and perspectives from both streams will be included. There are also differences between disciplines within the same stream—methodological ones, for example. But irrespective of differences, in all cases the process of doing a higher degree (Master's or PhD) and supervising it ought to be grounded in a Memorandum of Understanding (MOU) or similarly described agreement between the supervisor and the student, which serves as a point of reference for the whole process. Most such MOUs will cover similar ground, confirming the issues common to all graduate study and its supervision. Our conversation will be grounded in the MOU.

In South Africa part of the national higher education strategy is to drastically increase the number of PhD graduates, but supervision capacity is lacking. For this reason new models of supervision, marking a shift from the one-student/one-supervisor model, are being mooted. As an excursus to Part 4, I include an introduction tothe proposed models. The thrust towards the training and graduation of quality PhDs is also evident in new programmes, which link PhD students from Africa with other institutions in both South Africa and abroad.

Among the recommendations of a study by the Academy of Science of South Africa (ASSAf) is that a diversity of doctoral programmes should be encouraged since a one-size-fits-all model is no longer adequate.[1] Such diversity would include professional doctorates and PhD by publications. However, at present most early-career academics will be responsible for supervision in the traditional model and this is, therefore, our focus in the chapters that follow.

This section comprises three chapters:

Chapter 12: Embarking on a PhD: Supervisor and student perspectives

Chapter 13: Writing a thesis: The preparatory stages

Chapter 14: The writing process: Submission and examination

---

1   *The PhD Study*, Consensus Report, 2010, 112.

EMBARKING ON A PhD
SUPERVISOR AND STUDENT PERSPECTIVES

For an academic staff member, obtaining a PhD is no longer a matter of choice. A PhD (or equivalent) is now widely recognised as essential for academic advancement. In some disciplines this is a relatively new development, one that is important to bring research both in South Africa and in the wider African context into line with trends and standards in the global research environment. Many early-career researchers already have their PhDs when appointed to academic positions, but this is not always the case, and frequently the challenges in achieving this goal are daunting. Academic staff members have to pursue their doctoral studies amid the other components of an academic job, and they may have personal responsibilities and challenges that other PhD students do not have to face.

Whether for a student or staff member, doing a PhD is not for the faint-hearted, but at the same time it can be a remarkably rewarding experience, one that for many people retains lifelong status as a high point of their personal achievement. Similarly, successfully supervising one's first PhD is recognised as a significant achievement. But both students and supervisors should retain a balance, remembering that a PhD is not one's magnum opus and will not provide the final word on any topic. Do it, do it as well as possible, but do not prolong the process unnecessarily.

The nature of a Master's and PhD

The difference between a Master's degree and a PhD is important.

The **Master's** process is training in research, characterised as follows:

- It demonstrates ability to do research in a particular field or discipline.
- It employs appropriate methods.
- A Master's dissertation is sometimes described as a major exercise in methodology.
- Most institutions offer a variety of Master's degrees, depending on faculty and department. The degree may be by dissertation only or by a combination of coursework (or the equivalent) and a short dissertation. In some cases professional Master's degrees are now being offered.

A **PhD** demonstrates:

- An ability not only to do research, but also to make a contribution to knowledge in doing so.

◆ That you have become a fully professional researcher, someone worthy of being listened to as an equal in your field.[1] This lofty status is based on a number of presuppositions that a potential PhD candidate would do well to note:

- You have something to say that your peers want to hear, and you know where you can make a useful contribution.

- Your command of what is happening in your field enables you to evaluate what others are doing.

- You are able to re-evaluate your own work and that of others in the light of current developments.

- You conform to the ethical requirements of your discipline and any profession associated with it.

- You have mastery of the appropriate techniques for research in your field, for example, research methods, use of apparatus, etc.

- You are able to communicate the results of your research effectively in the academic and professional spheres.

- All of the above are carried out in an international context, acknowledging that your peer group is worldwide.[2]

TERMINOLOGY

The words 'dissertation' and 'thesis' are often used interchangeably, as they will be in what follows. In some universities, 'dissertation' refers to the outcome of Master's research, and 'thesis' to that of doctoral research.

The meaning of supervision

To supervise in this context means to oversee the process of writing and the successful completion of a graduate thesis. To oversee, in turn, means the following:

◆ To advise in the management of a project.

◆ To expertly guide through the process.

◆ To ensure that scientific/scholarly quality is maintained.

◆ To provide a pastoral role where necessary, directing the student for appropriate support.

---

1   Note that in some disciplines doing a PhD was, until relatively recently, the exception rather than the rule. For various reasons things are different today, but the reality is that there are many current academics without PhDs whose research status is not in question because they have consistently and cumulatively proved themselves in other forms of research output.

2   Based on Phillips, E.M. & Pugh, D.S. (2003). *How to Get a PhD: A handbook for students and their supervisors,* 3rd edition. Maidenhead: Open University Press, 21.

Beginning the process (1): The supervisor's perspective

Some of our supervision workshops begin with a series of role-plays. Each comprises an interaction between a potential student and a potential supervisor, with conversations reflecting the respective scenarios. The aim of the role-plays is to highlight, for both potential supervisor and student, issues that require careful consideration at the outset.

The scenario range includes the following:

◆ A student with no experience in interdisciplinary research naïvely wishing to embark on an interdisciplinary study at PhD level.

◆ A student being pressurised by family to pursue graduate studies despite her limited ability and contrary to her personal wishes.

◆ An academic under pressure to take on his first PhD student but being asked to supervise in an area in which he has no expertise.

◆ A supervisor being asked to salvage a Master's project after an abortive supervision relationship and the resignation of the colleague who was supervising it.

◆ A student whose previous studies have been completed at another institution and who now wishes to register for a graduate study at your institution.

These role-plays raise a number of critical issues and point to some useful strategies. Some of these are less relevant to certain disciplines and situations than others. In the sciences, where research is often undertaken in teams or groups, it is likely that a student has proved his or her ability when embarking on a PhD. The challenge here might be to secure funding in order to secure the student. But the humanities student who has worked alone and completed all previous studies elsewhere, and who now wishes to do a PhD at your institution, poses a different challenge.

Allowing for these differences, there are two broad areas of concern to be taken into account before embarking on a supervision relationship:

1   Assessing the student's ability and readiness to do graduate studies.

2   Assessing your suitability and capacity to supervise *this* student working on *this* particular topic.

In making an assessment, the following may be helpful:

◆ Evoke responses from the student that will indicate his or her grasp of the field and the topic, implications of the proposed study, experience with a particular method, degree of commitment and awareness of what is involved.

◆ Where you doubt the student's writing ability, request a piece of written work that reflects the areas about which you, as supervisor, would be concerned, for example, the ability to communicate ideas in writing and clarity of thought.

- ◆ With students in all fields of research coming from other institutions, both within and beyond national borders, make preliminary enquiries before taking them on, if possible before the first meeting. Academic transcripts and enquiries via a previous HOD are useful.

- ◆ Have a sense of the funding implications of the project and other needs of the student before agreeing to supervise. Do the student and project meet the criteria of the possible funder?

- ◆ Ascertain whether the student has a feasible research topic/project, or is open to suggestions about alternatives; whether the research field relates to your own expertise and interests; and whether there are the necessary resources in the department and university for the topic to be researched.

- ◆ Will the student require any training pertinent to the study, for example, in a particular research method or in the use of equipment?

- ◆ What is your sense of compatibility? Is this a student with whom you could work over the next 3–5 years (in the case of a PhD)?

- ◆ Will the student require high maintenance or be able to work to a large degree on his or her own?

- ◆ In making your assessment you should keep in mind your own availability, weighing up things like:
  - your other academic commitments
  - the number of students you should supervise at this stage of your career
  - plans to take sabbatical leave in the near future.

- ◆ Do not give the impression that you will accept a student until you are sure that this is the right thing to do.

- ◆ Would it be appropriate to refuse to supervise?

Whatever you decide, you must be fair to students, refraining from giving false impressions or creating expectations. If they have the potential but you do not think you can supervise them, confirm this and encourage them to find an alternative supervisor. If you do not think that they have the potential or capacity, inform them in a way that does not belittle them.

In this case you may be able to suggest some alternative way forward in terms of their interests and hopes. A supervisor should ascertain what is driving a student, remembering that some students experience family and community pressures to achieve high academic goals.

SUPERVISION ...

'Doing this job is a labor of love, involving what Eric Erikson calls "generativity", the capacity to nurture the next generation.'

Joan Bolker[3]

Beginning the process (2): The student's perspective

Setting out in graduate study does not happen in the same way for every student.

- For some it will be the logical progression from a successful undergraduate experience to more focused advanced study.

- Others will be grasped by an idea they feel compelled to pursue.

- Still others are keen to take advantage of studying further under the mentorship of a particular scholar, possibly a leader in the field.

- There are those who embark on Master's and particularly PhD study reluctantly, perhaps under professional or family pressure.

Readiness for a PhD

Some universities have a provisional registration facility, which is helpful for several reasons:

- It allows for formal supervision while developing a PhD proposal.

- For some it is a spur to making decisions and getting going, overcoming a natural tendency to procrastinate in embarking on such a daunting path.

- In formalising the decision to do a PhD, it sets in place deadlines for doing so: identifying a topic, writing a proposal/protocol, securing funding and, where necessary, obtaining ethics clearance.

But early registration is qualified advice. It is important to have a grasp of the issues at stake before you begin. The following points are among those that you should keep in mind before registration.

- **Appropriateness of the topic/project.** Because of the potential investment of the time and energy involved, the process should derive the maximum benefit possible.

  - A topic may flow out of participation in a research team working on a larger project, a group working in a particular laboratory, or the interests of the supervisor.

  - In less clear-cut situations, an important question in selecting a topic is this: are you familiar with other research being done or that has been completed

---

3   Bolker, J. (1998). *Writing Your Dissertation in Fifteen Minutes a Day: A guide to starting, revising and finishing your doctoral thesis.* New York: Henry Holt, 159.

in the field, and can you find a gap—bearing in mind that a PhD requires you to make a fresh contribution to knowledge?

- Your own interests and passion should be a factor, as well as the importance of the topic in terms of where the discipline is headed.
- It is unwise to choose a topic for which there is no one with sufficient expertise to supervise.
- In some departments and institutions there may also be pressures encouraging research in a certain direction, not infrequently because of external factors.
- The priorities of funders will play a large role in determining the topic to be researched.
- Although this is sometimes a controversial issue, the value of basic research should not be underestimated.

- **Availability of resources.** Needs will differ according to discipline but the following issues should be considered:
  - Does the library contain the necessary literature or have access to literary and electronic resources that you might need?
  - Will you require a particular piece of equipment for your project, and are the funds available to acquire this if necessary?
  - Is there sufficient local expertise in the area of your research to make your study feasible?
  - Is it in an area that is likely to attract funders?

- **Choice of the right supervisor.** It is important to identify someone with the necessary academic ability and with whom you can work.
  - If you are a staff member, you will probably do your PhD in the department in which you are located; in other words, you will have a colleague as your supervisor. This introduces another set of dynamics, which need to be taken into account and carefully managed.
  - Sometimes the choice is between an expert in the field and someone known to be a good supervisor. The two do not necessarily coincide.
  - Other issues to consider are the likely absences of the potential supervisor, her or his track record in timely student throughput, effectiveness in providing feedback on written work, etc.

All of this leads into the next section: the *Memorandum of Understanding (MOU)* between student and supervisor.

A NOTE ON THE EXPERTISE OF A SUPERVISOR ...

In many cases (although not all) experienced supervisors are successfully able to supervise students who are not working directly within their field of expertise. Of course, supervisors need to be competent within the broad discipline in which the student is working, but sometimes what is needed is not an advanced knowledge of the subject as much as the ability to supervise competently. After all, a doctoral student, in particular, should soon be in advance of his or her supervisors in terms of the specific topic of research, even if this is not the case to begin with. Better a very good supervisor who has a competent knowledge of the broader field, than a brilliant specialist in the specific field who is unable to supervise or communicate clearly with students ...

John W. de Gruchy[4]

The Memorandum of Understanding (MOU) between supervisor and student

Relationships, responsibilities and roles

Doing or supervising a Master's or PhD can be fraught with problems, most of which originate in misunderstood and/or miscommunicated expectations. For this reason, many universities (following models adopted in business) now routinely require a Memorandum of Understanding (MOU) or something similar, which outlines in appropriate detail what the student and supervisor can reasonably expect of each other. This is discussed and signed by both parties and then endorsed by a higher authority. The MOU is then revisited annually to evaluate progress. The importance of this document (initially resisted by many supervisors and regarded lightly by some HODs, but now taken more seriously) in averting potential conflict cannot be overemphasised. (See Appendix A for a generic MOU template.)

> *Most supervision problems are predictable and preventable.*

> *Many horror stories have their origin in the supervisory relationship rather than in the research topic or the external examiner.*[5]

Purpose of the MOU[6]

The relationship between supervisor and student is critical in achieving a successful graduated dissertation or thesis. It is closely tied to mutual expectations, and involves an ongoing interplay between intellectual, technical, strategic, institutional and personal

---

4   De Gruchy & Holness, *The Emerging Researcher,* 115.
5   Refer to Rugg, G. & Petre, M. (2004). *The Unwritten Rules of PhD Research.* Maidenhead: Open University Press, 32. See Ch. 4, 'Supervision: Or, PhDs, marriage and desert islands', 32–45.
6   Drawing on *The Emerging Researcher,* 116.

factors. An MOU is intended to help establish a good working relationship between supervisor and student, essentially addressing two questions:

1   What can a student reasonably expect from the supervisor?
2   What can a supervisor reasonably expect from the student?

It provides a formalised standard baseline designed to:

◆   Pre-empt misunderstanding.
◆   Clarify expectations.
◆   Encourage mutual responsibility/accountability.
◆   Ensure that practical issues are taken care of.
◆   Establish a partnership and avoid power play.
◆   Provide a reference point against which to measure progress and to consult should problems arise.

It may be possible, depending on institutional rules, for faculties to adapt the MOU in order to meet their particular needs and requirements, and it may be further adapted by departments and individual supervisors for the same reason. But it is critical that it be discussed, agreed to and signed early in the supervision relationship and renegotiated annually. For the document to be helpful it needs to be taken seriously by both supervisor and student, and this presupposes departmental support as well. Whether or not an MOU or an equivalent is mandatory at your institution, it is recommended as a very useful tool for exploring and regulating both the supervision relationship and the process of thesis production.

Many universities on the African continent were originally based on the historical British/European model, reflecting their colonial contexts. This model filtered down to the student–supervisor situation as well, in terms of both the hierarchical/patriarchal relationship between the two parties and of style, responsibilities and expectations. It was also essentially a 'hands-off' model with little meaningful interaction between supervisor and student. The model worked adequately in the northern context where the student body represented a considerable degree of homogeneity in terms of educational background, culture, national identity and socio-economic status. The model is less appropriate today, and is becoming less and less so in contexts such as ours, which are characterised by a host of complicating factors. This presents a challenge to postgraduate study and supervision, requiring of us a mind shift in negotiating the territory, both of the research process and the relationships undergirding it.

Issues to consider in supervisor–student negotiations

Among the issues to consider in negotiating an MOU are the following:

Relationship

- A mutual commitment to maintaining communication and agreeing on the mechanisms to do so.
- Identifying and discussing mutual roles and responsibilities.
- Establishing and maintaining appropriate boundaries.
- Aiming for compatibility. Obvious mismatches in personality and style put the whole process in jeopardy, but once committed, it is important to make the most of the relationship.
- Sensitivity to the personal situation of a student, for example, financial problems, domestic issues, health problems or being a foreign student.
- Sensitivity to cultural difference. This is critical to developing a good working relationship between supervisor and student. Cultural sensitivity does not mean making assumptions that are patronising and based on stereotypes. Conflict can easily arise out of ignorance of respective cultural norms, which may filter into academic performance, either as supervisor or student.

Thesis

- Agreeing on a realistic thesis timeframe, which includes short-term targets.
- Sensitivity to language issues, especially oral and written communication skills in a second language, and plans to address these.

Practical and administrative issues

- Agreement on the frequency and nature of meetings and feedback on written work.
- Plans relating to co-supervision.
- Strategies to manage conflicts.
- Discussion about student funding needs and how these will be met.
- Commitment to publishing and issues pertaining to authorship with regard to co-authored publications.

Supervision meetings, submission of written work and effective feedback

Before the thesis writing process begins, a protocol for supervision meetings should be established and included in the MOU. Some disciplines and individual supervisors adhere to specific conventions when it comes to supervision meetings. Others are more flexible, accommodating a blend of supervision style and student needs. The following issues should be discussed:

- Supervision style and the frequency and duration of meetings.
- Responsibilities. Who initiates meetings? What is the meeting confirmation and cancellation protocol?
- Mutual expectations regarding the submission of, and feedback on, written work.

Example: student

- How far in advance of meetings should work be submitted?
- In what form and when can I expect feedback?
- How should I prepare for meetings?

Example: supervisor

- My comments should be addressed immediately.
- Do not submit uncorrected work a second time.
- What degree of knowledge do you have in the use of software, for example, MSWord and PDFs?

Arrangements for supervisor absences, for instance, sabbatical leave

- Electronic submission and feedback?
- Consultations with co-supervisor or alternative member of the supervision team?

Keep a log

- Record discussion and decisions made at meetings.
- Confirm by e-mail immediately after the meeting.
- Check on what was agreed before the next meeting.

Roles and responsibilities

Clarifying roles and responsibilities is at the heart of developing a good working relationship between student and supervisor, and this is the object of an MOU. In preparation for supervision workshops, we ask participants to interview two supervisors of their choice prior to the workshop, at least one of whom should have considerable experience as a supervisor. Participants should ascertain from them the following:

- How do you understand your role as a graduate supervisor?
- What have been your best experiences as a supervisor?
- What have been your worst experiences as a supervisor?
- Are there any non-negotiables in your supervision style?
- What advice would you give to a new supervisor?

Workshop participants report on their interviews (retaining the anonymity of the supervisors interviewed) and in the ensuing discussion the following points are noted:

◆ Points of similarity and difference in their approaches.

◆ Things that constituted both negative and positive experiences for the supervisors.

◆ Any apparently idiosyncratic features in supervision style.

◆ Issues or practices that participants wish to query.

◆ Major gleanings from the exercise.

The object of this exercise is threefold:

1 It inevitably highlights the fact that despite different styles of supervision, the core roles of the supervisor remain intact.

2 It raises issues that may need to be negotiated with the student at the beginning of the supervision process.

3 It shows that there are different, yet valid, supervision styles.

A useful exercise in clarifying responsibilities and expectations is the *Role Perception Rating Scale*.[7] This aims to determine the perceptions of both student and supervisor about their respective responsibility for a number of key areas in thesis production and supervision. It has proved helpful in negotiating the MOU.

◆ Twelve items are set out in a table, listed as paired statements, one on the left and the other on the right, with a scale of 1–5 down the centre.

◆ Each expresses a standpoint regarding responsibility which supervisors and students may take on a particular issue:

• A score of 1 comes down on the side of it being entirely the supervisor's responsibility, while a 5 allocates all responsibility to the student.

• A score of 2–4 indicates that the responsibility should be shared and therefore negotiated.

◆ Supervisors and students will not agree on all their scores. The value of the exercise is to identify, at the outset, those issues which need to be discussed, since they represent areas of potential conflict.

◆ The exercise gives the student a clue as to the supervisor's style and gives the supervisor some idea of what sort of student he or she is taking on.

---

7   This exercise is based on the Role Perception Rating Scale from the booklet, *Tracking Postgraduate Supervision* (1995), developed by members of the Queensland University of Technology Supervision Evaluation Project Team. Available at www.rsc.qut.edu.au/studentsstaff/training/workshop_materials/2006/Resources/tracking_supervision.rtf. Accessed 18 July 2013.

Example:

It is the supervisor's responsibility to identify a research topic for the student	1	2	3	4	5	It is the student's responsibility to identify a research topic

Different supervision styles

Supervision styles may be influenced by differences in personality and, to some extent, the nature of the discipline, but the following points are, nonetheless, important and should be discussed fully:

- Some styles give more responsibility to the student and others to the supervisor.

- Whatever the style, supervisors should guide rather than prescribe, advise rather than interfere, and encourage independence and growth rather than make the student dependent.

- There are two poles regarding supervision styles: the supervisor who is product-driven and the supervisor who is process-oriented. The former is more common in the sciences, where thesis production tends to be linear, the latter in the humanities, where research is more discursive and where research and writing happen simultaneously, with several chapters being worked on at once. But individual supervisors themselves in all disciplines tend to lean more to one side or the other.

- The 'hands-on/hands-off' spectrum. Some supervisors work closely with students, wishing to meet regularly—some as often as weekly. Others are content to meet with the student once or twice a year and will not initiate meetings. The supervisor's style should be identified by the student (perhaps by consulting previous students) and discussed when drawing up the MOU.

- The role and style of the supervisor will change during the course of supervision, going through different phases—overseer, guide, intellectual sparring partner, pastor, devil's advocate (towards the end, seeing the thesis through the eyes of the examiner) and student's advocate (dealing with examiners' reports and assessment committees).

- Aim for partnership. The best supervisor–student relationships are those that flourish to the mutual benefit of both parties.

Supervisor responsibilities[8]

The supervisor's primary task is to guide and inspire students to help them reach their full scholarly potential. With this in mind, the supervisor has a responsibility to:

---

8 Informed by 'Postgraduate supervision: Guidelines for students, faculty members and administrators', Faculty of Health Sciences, UCT (adapted, with permission, from a student handbook from the School of Graduate Studies at the University of Toronto).

- Initiate a discussion with the student on the MOU as early as possible.

- Help the student formulate the research topic and proposal, and develop a plan for the production of the thesis.

- Ensure that necessary practical arrangements are made to facilitate the research, for example, funding, laboratory space, access to equipment and other resources.

- Help the student understand rules, policies, procedures and deadlines in the university as they pertain to graduate dissertations, and give the student some perspective on the process as a whole.

- Keep records of meetings and decisions taken, and provide effective and timely feedback.

There are certain issues that affect some disciplines more than others. For example, in laboratory-based research, where the student will be working full-time, it is the supervisor's responsibility to: arrange office and laboratory space; organise for the availability of major equipment and access to other research facilities; discuss funding needs up front and, with the student, to make plans to address these.

Certain things are not normally the responsibility of the supervisor, for example, editing spelling, grammar and style—except to direct the student to where she or he can get help where this is appropriate. This does not mean that a supervisor should not assist where he or she feels it is appropriate and necessary. One possibility is to provide detailed comment on such matters after receiving the first piece of written work. A few pages should be sufficient to help the student see what is required. However, where students are studying in a second or third language, the situation is more complex and many supervisors feel bound to assume a capacity-building role with their students in terms of their written communication skills.

Student responsibilities

One of the things that cripples graduate study is lack of initiative by the student and failure to accept responsibility. For the student–supervisor partnership to work optimally, the student has certain obligations, which should be addressed in the discussion of the MOU. Among these are the following:

- Become familiar with the rules, policies, procedures and deadlines in the university, department and faculty. If you are uncertain about any area, discuss this with your supervisor.

- Prepare a research plan and timetable in consultation with your supervisor as a basis for the programme of study.

- Meet with your supervisor regularly and report on progress and results.

- Where applicable, establish a supervisory committee with the assistance of your supervisor (some departments and faculties may require this).

◆ Keep supervisors informed on how you can be contacted, and of any significant changes that may affect the progress of your research.

◆ The need to obtain ethics approval for certain types of research—notably that involving human or animal subjects—has become more stringent than in the past. As ethics clearance is never given retrospectively, ensure that approval is obtained or that it is not required before embarking on data collection.

◆ Where applicable, acquire the necessary health and safety skills required to undertake the proposed research.

◆ The model of PhD currently adopted in South Africa is such that the degree is usually conferred on the basis of writing—and in some cases also defending—a full thesis, usually of about 80 000 words in length.[9] This indicates the enormous weight placed on communication and writing skills, bearing in mind that at least one, and in some institutions three, of the examiners will be external to the university and probably from abroad. The point is that if your skills in these areas are lacking, steps should be taken at the outset to address the situation. Many universities have Writing Centres designed specifically to assist in this area.

◆ Take responsibility for backing up your computer files to prevent loss of data and written work.

◆ Maintain good records of each stage of the research.

◆ Discuss problems with your supervisor and heed advice, and never bypass the supervisor by making an independent decision (this is particularly important in experimental research).

◆ Be honest, respectful, responsible and informative.

HOD responsibilities

Heads of Departments (HODs) play, or should play, an important role in the supervision process of graduate students. Many supervisor responsibilities depend on the support and sometimes the initiative of the HOD. This may vary in different universities, but generally the HOD has the responsibility to:

◆ Appoint supervisors, even if the process is managed by a departmental or faculty committee.

◆ Convene supervisory committees where required.

◆ Consult supervisors on matters affecting them.

◆ Ensure that supervisors understand their responsibilities such as implementing the MOU.

---

9 This applies even in cases where previously published articles are included. Some universities provide for a creative component as part of the examinable material in a PhD. Here the length of the written component is less.

- Manage conflicts that might arise between supervisors and students.

- Support supervisors who are having difficulties in their supervisory role.

- Refrain from making unjustified demands on supervisors, such as allocating them more students than they can properly manage, or a disproportionate number of weaker students.

- Give academic staff who are equipped to supervise, the opportunity to do so, and encourage and enable those who are not thus equipped to obtain the necessary mentorship and training.

Co-supervision, team supervision and consultancy

At our university every graduate student must have a designated supervisor approved by the faculty and who is a permanent academic staff member there, or an emeritus professor approved for supervision of a particular student. This may differ between institutions, but there will, nevertheless, be various mandatory procedures for the appointment of supervisors. It is sometimes necessary or prudent—and in some departments compulsory—to appoint a co-supervisor. Ultimately, however, it is the supervisor who assumes full responsibility for the supervision process.

Formal co-supervision may be indicated in the following circumstances:

- When local supervision of a project is required in the physical absence of the supervisor—for example, when the supervisor is away for long periods such as sabbatical.

- When a supervisor is unable to provide all the guidance needed. This may be because the study is interdisciplinary or includes sections that are beyond the research competence of the supervisor, such as expertise in a particular method.

- When an institution, faculty or department has its own rule requiring co-supervision.

- For first-time supervisors requiring mentoring in the craft of supervision. Increasingly this is becoming mandatory—and for good reason.

Certain factors must be kept in mind:

- The supervisor and co-supervisor should meet and agree from the outset on their respective roles, and they should liaise regularly with each other and the student.

- The student should be kept fully informed of any decisions and should normally be party to such discussions.

- Decisions about respective roles should be included in the MOU.

- Careful negotiation is required for interdepartmental/interfaculty co-supervision.

◆ The student should inform the supervisor of any meetings with the co-supervisor, indicating what was discussed and the outcomes.

◆ The co-supervisor should not recommend changes to the dissertation, beyond the parts that have been designated for co-supervision, without first discussing these with the supervisor.

◆ There is usually very little remuneration for external co-supervisors, their participation depending mainly on goodwill. This can sometimes lead to complications. Be sure to find out what (if any) remuneration is available for co-supervision and do not presume that a sense of collegiality will suffice!

Group/team supervision is common practice in some contexts. Usually this means that more than one person is supervising a group of students, and it ensures that there is always someone on hand to assist the student. It is also a means of load sharing, and in some departments—notably in the sciences—it is common practice for post-doctorates to be involved. This does not obviate the need for a designated supervisor, and neither should it mean that a student be denied adequate one-on-one meetings. It does, however, complement his or her role and provide a back-up in the supervisor's absence. (Refer to Chapter 14, Excursus, for proposed alternative models of supervision.)

Consultancy is a useful option when a supervisor feels that a student discussion with an expert on a specific topic is warranted. The supervisor should discuss this with the student and approach such a colleague to arrange a meeting. This is not a formal arrangement and no remuneration is usually involved.

Supporting students

Being a graduate student, especially when engaged in writing a doctoral dissertation, can be a lonely and sometimes depressing experience. It also creates practical needs. Faculties, departments and supervisors need to provide a supportive environment within which students can pursue their work. Supervisors should ensure that their students are aware of what is available and assist them wherever necessary:

◆ *Accessing resources*. Student funding needs are a priority, as well as matters of space, equipment, computers etc.

◆ *Induction and orientation* of research students, especially those coming from other institutions and countries.

◆ *Training courses* as necessary—research methods, library search skills, data management tools, etc.

◆ Setting up *networking opportunities*—departmental, institutional, inter-institutional, web, international contacts.

- Encouraging students to participate in *conferences, colloquia,* etc. and making this financially possible for them.
- Exploring the possibility of *conducting research abroad* in areas and at institutions appropriate to the study.
- Cultivating a research culture in the department by arranging *postgraduate peer-review seminars.*
- Encouraging student research *support groups.*

But do not make students over-reliant on the supervisor. They should be encouraged to take initiative and act independently, although assistance should be offered in negotiating difficult periods. Peer support, especially from those who are nearing completion, is very useful in helping them know where they are in the process and encouraging them to persevere.

Research ethics in thesis writing

Addressing issues relating to integrity in research (research ethics) is a presupposition in responsible supervision and should be addressed in the conversation around the MOU and appropriately included in the final document. Issues such as plagiarism and the falsification of data should be addressed. As with all research, before postgraduate study commences it is important to ascertain whether ethics clearance will be required and to obtain this. In the PhD context, research ethics includes but is more than obtaining the necessary clearance for a project. Quality assurance requirements place an increasing onus on institutions to ensure that research procedures are ethically executed. (Refer to Chapter 14.)

Moving on

Having covered the preliminary issues in the PhD process from the perspective of both student and supervisor, I move on in Chapter 13 to focus on the early stages of thesis production.

WRITING A THESIS
THE PREPARATORY STAGES

Introduction

It has been suggested that there are at least three critical steps in setting out on the PhD journey:[1]

1 Getting started.
2 Getting organised.
3 Dividing the huge task into less formidable pieces and working on those pieces.

These steps may seem obvious, but for many people they represent great barriers to writing a thesis. Taking the steps is both psychologically and logistically empowering. It is part of all good research strategy.

Getting started

Doing a PhD is ultimately about writing. The degree is awarded for the thesis and not for the project per se, so you should get started by writing something as soon as possible. This applies regardless of the area in which you are working or the type of project being undertaken. A particular temptation for those working in disciplines that are not writing-oriented is to procrastinate in starting to write, and this should be dealt with as soon as possible. Remember, writing is an iterative process and early efforts are rather like rough, unhewn but potentially beautiful gemstones.

Right at the beginning you will have an idea of where the study will go—a 'gut feeling' about what needs to be done, what you will find, and how you are going to get there. So begin with a draft outline of your thesis; put in as much detail as possible at this stage, even though you know that things will change. This provides something tangible to work with and will become your working document. Your supervisor will be thrilled to see something *written*! You should include:

◆ Your hypothesis or the question you are asking or the problem you have identified, that is, the 'gap' that you are seeking to fill.

◆ Possible chapter headings and sub-headings.

◆ Notes on the methods you will use.

---

1   Material in this section draws on Wolfe, J. (1996; modified 2006). 'How to write a PhD thesis', www.phys.unsw.edu.au/~jw/thesis.html#outline. Accessed 3 February 2014. I am also indebted to participant contributions at local supervision workshops.

- Figure titles, if appropriate, for the type of study.

- What you think you will find or what conclusions you think you will reach.

Scientific or scholarly writing is not a natural talent for most people. It needs to be cultivated, and this takes time and practice. Initial efforts to write are often clumsy, not least because thesis construction requires a particular type of writing—different from anything else. So the sooner you embark on the task, the sooner you will be able to start the process of gradual refinement—and one barrier to the production of your thesis will have been removed.

Getting organised

For some people being organised comes naturally. Others find it more difficult. Wherever you lie on the spectrum, becoming *appropriately* organised for writing a thesis is a challenge. There are certain basic things that can smooth out the process.

Get organised on your computer

- Begin with *opening a series of sub-folders and files* in a folder called 'Thesis':
  - general ideas
  - article/book summaries
  - thesis abstract
  - a file or sub-folder for each chapter
  - references/bibliography.

- *Title* and *date* each version of what you write and save it so that 1) like items are grouped and 2) you recognise the latest version. Be discerning about what you keep and what you delete (you may later decide that a previous version is better).

- When summarising an article or book/chapter, *write it up on your computer* immediately. Avoid being left with files full of handwritten summaries that never quite made their way into the thesis conversation!

- Don't stint on *file names*. Although it may look clumsy, descriptive titles help to identify the content of files. This applies particularly to material saved in the 'ideas' folder, which will not have a central theme.

Systematically back up your work. This prevents catastrophes when computers crash or are stolen, or hardcopy material is lost. Back up in several places: a flash drive or Dropbox; send yourself e-mails with attachments; scan documents that are available only in hard copy.

Efficient storage. This is important for *non-electronic material* such as artefacts and other materials, as well as documents, which for some reason or other may not be scanned.

Save bibliographic data. Consider using one of the bibliographical data management programs such as Citation, Endnote, Reference Manager or the newer Mendeley and Zotero. Most of these programmes are expensive but some institutions have site licences, providing access to all students and staff. *Mendeley is available free online.* Whether you use one of these packages or not, it is critical to keep an up-to-date list of all literary sources used, and to accurately capture publication details at the time of use. This prevents a scramble at the end when you have to produce a bibliography or list of references.

Time management. This refers to the effective use of the time available to you for thesis writing. Nurture habits and develop rhythms, which include regular times for writing. This sometimes means creating time—where a thesis is concerned, time will never come knocking on your door!

Commit yourself to *writing* something every day. Set specific blocks of time for administrative responsibilities. There will *always* be administrative tasks to which you have to attend—they keep coming. Allocating time for these frees up other time for research and writing. Both administrative build-up and thesis neglect should be avoided, and this requires good strategising.

Dividing the task into smaller, less formidable pieces

This is necessary to avoid the paralysis that results from feeling overwhelmed by a formidable task, which can hinder many people from even entering the starting blocks of a PhD.

Writing a thesis is, indeed, a long and difficult task, but it can be accomplished by taking *one step at a time*. Break the task down into *constituent parts*, and identify specific steps, comprising both a *time* and an *activity* component. *Set short-term targets*; for example, begin with a literature search to ascertain what work has already been done in the area and what gaps are discernible. This could, in some disciplines, be done in about six months.

Breaking up the PhD process into manageable blocks with short-term, often incremental, targets is arguably the most empowering accomplishment in the beginning stages of the journey. This takes us to the next section, which focuses on the development of a coherent PhD research plan.

Developing a research/project plan

There are several reasons why a research plan is necessary for graduate study, and why it should be developed as early in the process as possible. *Quality assurance* procedures in the higher education sector monitor student throughput rates. *Financial constraints* have an impact on the time available to most people for graduate study. The *psychological impact* of having a plan, breaking the project down into manageable chunks, and identifying an end point to the process is empowering to both student and supervisor.

Despite differing timescales between a Master's by course work and mini-dissertation, a research Master's dissertation, or a PhD, the point is to see *how the project can be managed in the designated time*. A study plan, which includes *short-term targets* and which is built into the MOU, becomes a reference point to measure progress and to ensure timely completion.

Beginning the discussion

Discuss what is *feasible and practical* in terms of expectations. This will relate to personal and financial considerations and to the nature of the research being undertaken (field-work may require a longer period than a text-based piece of research, as might waiting for the results of experiments or engaging in a longitudinal study). It also relates to student capacity and whether the study is full- or part-time.

Having ascertained how much time is available and necessary, plan with a *possible graduation date* in mind and work back from there. Begin with the submission deadline for that graduation and incorporate the component parts of thesis production within a timeframe.

From registration to graduation (PhD)

An important step in developing a research plan would be to identify the different stages of the project, what needs to happen at each stage, and how long each process requires.

Example:

Stage 1: Preliminary steps to be taken within the first six months:

- identification of a possible supervisor
- initial conversations with supervisor
- literature search relating to proposed topic
- exploring funding opportunities (if not done previously)
- provisional registration (if this facility exists)
- writing of proposal
- ethics approval as appropriate
- approval of proposal by faculty or relevant institutional board, and final registration.

Something similar might be prepared for subsequent stages of the project.

The PhD project: Identifying a topic and framing a question

We have noted that some students start out with a clear idea of what they want to research. This may result from working in a research team where different aspects of a larger project need to be researched, or where recent research has revealed a gap in knowledge that needs to be filled. Or the idea may have evolved over time, possibly as an outcome from a previous study or through being part of a regular departmental seminar.

But many students require assistance to arrive at or fine-tuning a suitable topic or project for their PhD. The role of the supervisor in this case is to help the student move from:

- an area of general interest to a broad topic
- a broad topic to a more focused one
- a focused topic to a research question (or problem)
- a question that interests the student to its wider significance.[1]

In doing so the following factors need to be considered:

- availability of local expertise and resources for doing the research
- the supervisor's competency to supervise the topic
- suitability of the topic, whether for Master's or doctoral research
- the student's passion for the topic
- the student's competency in methods and techniques required for the project.

It is useful for the supervisor to have a few topics on hand related to his or her own specific area of interest.

What are the criteria for a PhD?

Almost universally, a PhD is awarded for an *original and significant contribution to knowledge*. Understandably, students are concerned about whether their study meets these criteria, and many supervisors fail to invite a conversation about this.

While *originality* in a PhD is crucial, it is not always easy to define. There is no stipulation about the *way* in which a PhD study should be original, or of the *extent* of the originality. This is good news for the student!

A number of ways have been identified in which a study might be original:[2]

- By providing a new angle on a previously researched problem.

---

1   See Booth, et al, *The Craft of Research*, Ch. 3, 40–55.
2   Phillips & Pugh, *How to Get a PhD*, 63, 64, drawing also on the work of Francis, J.R.D. (1976). 'Supervision and examination of higher degree students', *Bulletin of the University of London*, 31: 3–6.

- By providing a single new observation.

- By bringing new evidence to an old issue or taking a particular technique and applying it in a new area.

- By carrying out empirical work that has not been done before or making a synthesis that has not been made before.

This suggests a certain ambiguity in the meaning of originality, but also that it is not really difficult to be original. It is sufficient to take a small, incremental step in understanding. Patrick Dunleavy suggests that originality has one of two sources, which encapsulate all the possibilities: 'the discovery of new facts or the exercise of independent, critical power'.[3]

Defining a *significant* contribution to knowledge is more challenging, and might have slightly different meanings in vertical disciplines (where knowledge builds directly on what has gone before) than it does in others, where knowledge is discursive and has more scope for organic growth. One guideline is that, in both, *intellectual maturity and critical depth are more important than the scale or scope of the research findings*. It is the critical depth that is crucial for the ultimate question: 'What difference does this make?'

The important thing is to carry out the work and communicate it in such a way that the examiners are convinced of the study's originality in the sense of a contribution to knowledge in the field. Implied in this are the student's familiarity with other work being done in that particular field and hence with the relevant literature, and the ability to distinguish this from, and relate it to, the new contribution made by the current study.

Developing a proposal

We saw that one of the benefits of provisional registration is that it gives the student formal access to supervision during the early stages of identifying a project or conceptualising a topic and developing a proposal. The proposal-writing is a critical exercise, and in some disciplines will require several drafts. This will help the supervisor to assess further the ability of the student and discern particular needs, and it will help the student to clarify what it is he or she intends to do, and how this can be achieved.

The proposal is a project-planning document intended to:

- Indicate the focus for research.

- Set out the aims of the research project.

- Indicate how the student intends to achieve these aims.

- Provide a benchmark against which progress is measured and adjustments made.

---

3   Dunleavy, P. (2003). *Authoring a PhD: How to plan, draft, write and finish a doctoral thesis or dissertation.* Basingstoke and New York: Palgrave Macmillan, 49.

Proposals may need to be revised as research and writing proceed, and it is good to revisit them from time to time. If the research leads in directions that are significantly different from what is in the proposal, it may be necessary to modify it and even change the title of the thesis. This will require official approval and, in some cases, resubmission to the ethics committee.

Proposals vary in length and sometimes in scope, and the student and supervisor should be familiar with institutional/faculty requirements. Normally a Master's proposal is 5–10 pages (depending on whether it is a minor or full dissertation), and a PhD proposal is 15–20 pages. In principle, length should be determined by the content deemed necessary for the purpose. In some of the science disciplines, a proposal can be developed in a relatively short period of time—as little as six weeks. In other disciplines the process might be longer (up to six months) and more involved, particularly where there is a strong conceptual–theoretical element or complex methodological issues.

The content of the proposal

The emphasis placed on different aspects of the proposal will vary according to discipline, and students are advised to consult examples of research proposals in their own discipline. Generally the proposal should contain the following:

◆ **Title.** Although provisional at this stage, the title should be chosen with care, as any major change may require faculty approval. A thesis title should give a clear indication of what the study is about, but should not be longer than necessary.

◆ **A brief description of the project or area of research**, locating the proposed research in its wider context.

◆ **The research question/problem.** This provides the focus for the dissertation. What is it that you as the student wish to investigate? This should be a crisply stated single question or problem, which could then be fleshed out in a number of sub-questions.

◆ **Rationale.** Provide some information about why you have chosen this particular research area. This may be from theoretical interest or it may have emerged out of issues of practice or scientific advance. In either case, you should indicate what contribution the completed project might make to our understanding of the field. In other words, what difference will it make?

◆ **Literature review** (and/or the equivalent in disciplines in which other sources are fundamental, for example, judgments in law). You need to have read sufficiently in your field to justify the research question. The literature review is intended to locate the dissertation in relation to the most significant literature and other developments relating to the topic of the thesis. It has the broad aim of familarising you with the theoretical and empirical work that could inform the study, clearly locating it in this corpus of work. The literature referred to here should have a direct relation to the problem being addressed in the thesis.

◆ **Conceptual/theoretical framework.** This section is critical to some disciplines and far less relevant to others. It involves a brief discussion of the theoretical basis of the dissertation. Some of its key terms, drawn from the relevant theory, may be mentioned and defined. What perspectives do you bring to the project? Not all studies place the same emphasis on an explicit theoretical base (deductive approach). Some focus on broader empirical engagement, so that new theory will emerge out of the study (inductive approach).[4] In this case, an analytic framework needs to be developed, defining concepts, demonstrating links between these, and indicating how the concepts will be recognised in the data. The fact that the conceptual framework may not be so clear-cut at the beginning, especially in qualitative research, is itself a conceptual framework.

◆ **Research methods.** In some disciplines and types of study, the methods are clear-cut and simple. For example, in the sciences with laboratory-based research or the humanities with text-based research, the methods section of the proposal (and thesis) will be fairly short and straightforward. In other disciplines, notably those engaging in certain types of empirical studies, this section is critical and requires much more detailed attention, particularly where ethical issues come into play. Research methods indicate how the research design will be implemented, so that appropriate methods are vital.

◆ **Research design.** Developing a research design, of particular significance in empirical research, involves crucial decisions about how the research is to be conducted in order to make the project both meaningful and manageable.[5]

The following questions may be helpful in preparing this section:

- How will the research be structured in order to answer the question/s?
- What approach will be used, for example, qualitative or quantitative?
- Why is this the best way to go about answering the question/s?[6]

◆ **Data collection and analysis.** Specify how the data will be collected and analysed, why particular tests are employed, and how the data will be used.

◆ **Research ethics.** Should the project involve working with human or animal subjects, ethics approval should be obtained before the research begins. Verification of ethics clearance should be submitted with the proposal. (Note: as ethics clearance is never given retrospectively, data collection should not commence before approval has been granted.)

---

4   See English, *Professional Communication*, 242.
5   For examples of research design, refer to Mouton, *How to Succeed*, 143–180.
6   English, *Professional Communication*, 247.

- ◆ **Thesis structure.** Provide a preliminary outline of the thesis, indicating possible chapters, etc.

- ◆ **Timeline.** Provide a short research plan to indicate how the research will be conducted and the dissertation completed in the required time.

- ◆ **Select bibliography/list of references.** Whereas the literature survey relates to the topic very specifically, the select bibliography gives an indication of the broader sources to be used in the research. This will provide a basis for the final bibliography in the dissertation and should therefore be kept up to date and expanded as a separate file during the research and writing of the dissertation so that no bibliographical information is lost. However, disciplinary conventions differ and some studies require a 'List of references' (only those sources that have been *cited*) rather than a 'Bibliography' (all sources that have been *consulted*), or sometimes both.

Thesis structure

The structure and production of a dissertation will vary between fields and disciplines.

- ◆ In some, matters of literary style may be of greater importance than in others.

- ◆ In some there is more scope for creativity than in others, though all require some creative and imaginative input.

- ◆ In many disciplines the thesis develops in a linear way, while in others it can be a more organic process.

- ◆ But all dissertations should strive for clarity of expression, logical development and readable style.

Most disciplines have their own conventions for the structure of a thesis. Although these are not imposed on a PhD student, individual supervisors or departments may wish the student to adhere to them. Often, such conventions have evolved as the most effective way to present all the material required for the particular type of study being undertaken, so it is unwise for a student to deviate too far from the pattern of presentation or thesis structure that is normative in the discipline. To get an idea of 'what works' a student should, at the outset, *read other good theses* available from the library. Supervisors should be able to recommend these.

While in theory arriving at a thesis structure might be straightforward, in practice it requires skill. Table 13.1 identifies the various components of a thesis, which help to structure it. Although it reflects the science model, the questions covered may be packaged differently to apply to humanities, law and other studies as well.[7]

---

7   www.uq.edu.au/student-services/phdwriting/phfaq05.html. Accessed 26 July 2013.

Table 13.1: Pointers to structuring a thesis

Why am I doing it?	Introduction
	Significance
What is known?	Review of research
What is unknown?	Identifying gaps
What do I hope to discover?	Aims
How am I going to discover it?	Methodology
What have I found?	Results
What does it mean?	Discussion
So what? What are the possible applications or recommendations? What contribution does it make to knowledge? What next?	Conclusions

Thesis structure should be considered from the perspective of both the reader and the author. For the reader, the structure should *make the thesis accessible*, with a chapter sequence that is logical and well organised. For the author, the thesis structure should *sustain the progress of the research*, keeping the argument on track and facilitating the development of the author's approach to the topic.[8] For both, the 'storyline' should be clear from start to finish.

A thesis typically contains three types of material, which might be described as the lead-in, the core (the actual contribution to knowledge) and the lead-out sections. These sections parallel the three parts of a scholarly article: introduction, body and conclusion. Although there is no set formula for a correct balance, certain guidelines may be useful in structuring a typical 80 000-word thesis, bearing in mind that they *are* guidelines and therefore not prescriptive:

Lead-in material/opening chapters

- Sets the stage: frames, highlights and sets up the core material to make it accessible and understandable.
- Helps readers to appreciate the usefulness and originality of the work.
- Contains the background and motivation for the research (usually the introduction), literature review, methods and research design.
- Usually no more than three chapters/50–60 pages.
- It is critical to process material before writing this section to avoid the wordiness that betrays a poor grasp of the issues and knowledge of techniques.

---

8   Dunleavy, *Authoring a PhD*, 43. Much of what follows in this section draws on Chapter 3, 'Planning an integrated thesis: The macro-structure', 43–75.

- Undue protraction of this stage leads to a slow-starting thesis, which sounds alarm bells to examiners (suggesting lack of clarity in what you want to do).
- Material included in these chapters should be on a 'need to know to appreciate your contribution' basis,[9] rather than a 'tell it all' basis. *Remember*: not all work done at the beginning of the study is included in thesis itself.

PERSPECTIVE

At the beginning of my own PhD, my supervisor insisted that I spend time study-ing and understanding a particular historical council, which took place in 451 CE. After a time I proudly presented him with about 20 pages on the topic, only to be met by this comment: 'Right, now that you understand a critical part of the context of your thesis, extract the essence, put the rest aside and continue.' In retrospect I saw that this groundwork was essential for the study to help me grasp the real issues at stake, but that it did not warrant a place in the thesis itself.

Lyn Holness

Core of the thesis/middle chapters

- This should normally comprise about five-eighths of the thesis.
- Has a high research value-added[10] content.
- Comprises the actual contribution to knowledge, therefore contains the most substantively new, different sections of your research.
- Reports on primary research and presents new and distinctive arguments.
- Exact structure of this section varies according to the type of study.
- *This is the make-or-break section* for awarding a doctorate.

Lead-out material/concluding chapters

- Normally one or two chapters, including the conclusion.
- Brings the study together, integrating and restating the findings in a concise and decisive way.
- Using the thesis abstract as a guide, make sure that the introduction and con-clusion tally.
- Be aware of questions that have arisen during the study and/or ones that are still to be answered.
- How can the work be taken further and what are its practical implications?

---

9   Dunleavy, *Authoring a PhD*, 61.
10   The contemporary business term 'value-added' is increasingly used in a variety of spheres to refer to extras or additions which add quality, going beyond what is expected, to provide something new.

- ◆ *Word of caution*: when acknowledging 'limitations of the study' be aware that examiners have a sharp nose for laziness 'interpreted differently'!

The arrangement and size of these component parts is what gives the thesis its final shape or structure—the 'storyline' or showing how the plot emerges. Among his useful suggestions on thesis structure, Dunleavy cautions about the following:

- ◆ Do not 'end-load' the thesis, that is, do not make the first and third sections disproportionately large in relation to the core section.

- ◆ As far as possible, keep the three components in distinct blocks so that material is not scattered around your thesis, requiring the reader to piece bits together.

- ◆ Carefully choose a 'strategy of explanation' that shows your work to its best advantage.

Of course, there will be variations in thesis structure from discipline to discipline and study to study, and the suggestions above deliberately omit labelling, that is, naming chapters. But it is possible to extract generic principles that apply to the structure of most theses or dissertations. To reiterate: *do not discount the importance of consulting examples of good theses in the same research area to get an idea of style and structure.*

Methodology

Methodology plays a central role in some disciplines, a critical basis for all further discussion. The entire study stands or falls on selecting and implementing the appropriate methods. Here the methods section occupies a prominent place at the beginning of the thesis, and all that follows refers back to it. At the other end of the spectrum are those disciplines in which methodology plays a relatively minor role. These are mainly the text-based disciplines, where in some cases the method used only becomes evident at the end and is summed up in the conclusion. In such disciplines it has even been suggested that people who spend too much time on methodology possibly don't have much else to say. The danger here is that methodology receives too little attention and that the study consequently lacks direction and coherence.

Whatever the situation in your discipline, three things are important:

1　Methodology is crucial, and examiners look for clarity and accuracy. The method identifies the 'how' of the thesis.

2　The student must be familiar with the conventional methods of her or his discipline, and be competent in the particular one/s selected for the study. In some cases it might be necessary to take a research methods course in preparation for the project.

3　The student must demonstrate competency in the methods used. The degree of competency in the student manifests itself in subtle ways to an examiner, as early on as the opening chapter of the thesis.

A NOTE ON 'METHODOLOGY' AND 'METHOD'

While these two terms are frequently used interchangeably, there are subtle differences between the two. Methodology is the science of the way we go about doing things. From an academic perspective, it is the overarching framework, which encompasses the various elements involved in doing research. This includes research design and methods. Methodology is the theory behind the activities of sampling, collecting and analysing data. Method is a subset of methodology. Further down in the methodological hierarchy, as a subset of method, are the in-struments used—questionnaires, experiments, etc.

Conclusion

The aim of chapters 12 and 13 has been to set the stage for the project, which will culminate in the writing, examination and finally graduation of a thesis. We move on to this in Chapter 14.

ELEVEN PRACTICES OF EFFECTIVE POSTGRADUATE SUPERVISORS[11]

Foundations

1 Ensure that the partnership is right for the project.

2 Get to know students and carefully assess their needs.

3 Establish reasonable, agreed expectations.

4 Work with students to establish a strong conceptual structure and research plan.

Momentum

5 Encourage students to write early and often.

6 Be available for regular contact and ensure high-quality feedback.

7 Get students involved in the life of the department.

8 Inspire and motivate.

9 Help if academic and personal crises crop up.

Final stages

10 Take an interest in students' future careers.

11 Carefully monitor the final production and presentation of the thesis. (Note: this may apply in some but not all contexts.)

---

11 Adapted from James, R. & Baldwin, G. (1999). *Eleven Practices of Effective Postgraduate Supervisors.* Centre for the Study of Higher Education and the School of Graduate Studies, University of Melbourne. Full booklet available at www.cshe.unimelb.edu.au/publications.html. Accessed 7 May 2015.

THE WRITING PROCESS
SUBMISSION AND EXAMINATION

Thesis writing differs between disciplines, the most notable difference being between the humanities and law, on the one hand, and the sciences, on the other. In the former the actual thesis construction or writing process is in place from the outset and, as noted, often a thesis grows organically to a certain point. In the sciences—natural, applied and, to some extent, the social sciences—data collection and analysis occupies a major part of the process and only when enough material has been obtained does the process of 'writing up' begin. But even here, the discipline of actually *writing* should be in place from the beginning. There is always something to write when producing a thesis.

There are certain things that are generic to all good thesis writing, albeit with nuances of emphasis and convention according to discipline. The same applies to the examination process: choice of examiners, what they look for in a thesis, and how they score it are common across the disciplines.

Strategic and stylistic issues in thesis writing

We consider now some of the guidelines for thesis writing:

- **Titles, sub-titles and headings.** These are of great importance both to attract attention and to give a clear indication of what follows. In thesis writing, titles and headings should not be gimmicky. You are not trying to sell a book with an alluring title.

  - **Thesis title.** This should not be longer than necessary, but long enough and explicit enough to show exactly what the thesis is about. A main title followed by a colon and further explanation is effective.

  - **In-text titles and subtitles.** As far as possible these should be short and to the point. Allowing for differences in disciplinary conventions, overuse of titles and subtitles can fragment the work, particularly when the thesis is of a more theoretical and discursive nature.

- **Writing style.** With regard to writing style, students will fall somewhere on a spectrum. At one end are those whose research is tied up with actual writing. Here concept, argument, theory, etc. play a significant role. Words are important. These students love the process of writing, and are often reluctant to practise word economy. At the other end of the spectrum are those, mainly from the sciences and commerce, for whom writing narrative does not come naturally. They are far more comfortable with bullet points, graphs and tables than they are with writing a coherent paragraph. Both groups need to keep the reader, that is, the examiner, in mind, remembering that effective written communication of process, findings, summation and suggestions is the essence of a good thesis. Having recognised this, there are additional pointers to good writing style in what follows.

- ◆ **Sentences and paragraphs.** The initial impact created on the reader of a thesis (notably the examiner) is crucial, creating immediate impressions of the work.

  - For this reason the first sentence of a thesis or chapter is critical, as is the first paragraph. Careful attention should be given to its construction.

  - As a general rule, sentences should be reasonably short. Each should contain one idea, building on the previous sentence and preparing for the next.

  - Even when a complicated point is being made, it is usually possible to break a sentence up into at least two shorter, less cluttered sentences.

    For example:

    'The results of the survey were compromised by poorly prepared question-naires, and, in addition, many people were not at home when the researcher called and some could not read English.'

    Reads more effectively as:

    'The results of the survey were compromised on several points. Question-naires were poorly prepared, many people were not at home when the researcher called, and some could not read English.'

  - As with sentences, each paragraph should flow logically from the previous one, leading to the next. Each should develop one theme rather than try to cover more ground, the theme being introduced by a 'topic sentence'.[1] The idea of linking words, sentences and paragraphs (known as segues) is crucial to the flow of the thesis.

  - Use simple words in preference to complicated ones, but do not be simplistic.

  - Each discipline and field has its own vocabulary. Do not substitute or explain the meaning of terms that belong to the language canon of the discipline, for example, technical terms in biochemistry or ecclesiastical terms in theology.

- ◆ The issue of **'voice'** is increasingly making its way into academic discourse.

---

1   English, *Professional Communication*, 18.

- There is a growing awareness that no study is entirely objective. Why are certain questions asked and not others? Why are certain methods or tests selected and observations made and not others? It is because the researcher has made decisions in this regard, and these become the filter through which the research passes. There is always a subjective element, no matter what the discipline.

- Disciplinary conventions differ, and in some there is more openness and opportunity for the writer to locate her- or himself in the study than in others.

- There are also other aspects to 'voice' that come through in a thesis. For example, it is more effective to use active than passive language: 'a delay in data gathering was caused by heavy rain' should be replaced with 'heavy rain caused a delay in data gathering'. The latter is crisper and less cumbersome.

◆ **Chapters.** These are the building blocks of a thesis, and to hold together they must be carefully structured internally. Chapters should be divided into shorter component parts, linked by a common theme. Four elements should be included at the start of each chapter:

1 A chapter title.
2 An introductory 'high impact' element, designed to attract the reader's attention.
3 A piece of text moving from the introductory statement to some discursive comment on the chapter's main themes, leading into
4 A set of signposts to the chapter's main sections.[2] This suggests that at any stage in the chapter a reader will know exactly what the chapter is about.

NOTE

THE 'EMERGENCY STOP' ...[3]

It is helpful to think of the 'emergency stop' test when reading a thesis chapter. As a driving instructor might unexpectedly issue an emergency stop instruction to a learner driver, so we can imagine a random, unannounced instruction to a reader to stop reading at some point in a thesis chapter. Without looking at it again, the reader of a well-constructed chapter should be able to explain:

- the main theme or themes of the chapter

- the aim of the chapter

- the number of sections to the chapter

- what can be anticipated after the point at which reading was halted.

2 Dunleavy, *Authoring a PhD*, 91.
3 Dunleavy, *Authoring a PhD*, 98–100.

> A well-constructed chapter is not a mystery tour, with a vague title, an unclear focus and a meandering from one theme to the next, throwing up new elements or themes on every other page.

- **Chapter abstracts.**[4] A useful strategy is to write a brief abstract of each chapter or section, especially in the final drafting stages. This should encapsulate what you really want to say and will therefore help to keep the writing of the chapter on track instead of going off on a tangent. This is also helpful if the dissertation has to be reduced in size. (Chapter abstracts are not necessarily for inclusion in the final thesis.)

- **Introduction and conclusion.** The introduction and conclusion of your thesis are critical (as they are in all scholarly writing). Although neither can be finally written until the thesis is complete, it is helpful to keep notes and write rough drafts early on, anticipating what might be included in the final draft. This ensures several things:

  - These become *aides-mémoire* of material that you think should be included in these sections;

  - In the case of the introduction (which may include much of what was in the original proposal), it serves as a guide when writing the thesis, and in the case of the conclusion, it helps keep the thesis focused on the likely outcomes of your research as it develops.

  - The conclusion is where 'future work' could be mentioned in the closing section. This indicates awareness that all research is part of a continuum and never self-terminating.

  Always keep in mind that the examiners will read your introduction with care to find out what you are attempting to achieve, and they will read your conclusion with equal care to see whether or not it tallies with your introduction and indicates clearly and succinctly what you have achieved or proved.

- **In-text referencing.** Among the challenges in writing a thesis is to discern where acknowledgement is required for a particular concept or principle, and where it might safely be omitted. The following might be helpful:

  - Omitting a reference would apply when what is being said is so familiar to every researcher in the field, having found its place in the seminal discourse, that no acknowledgement is necessary. In physics, for example, dynamics systems do not require a citation of Newton, while in Christian studies no explanation for the term 'synoptic gospels' is appropriate.

---

4   Based on seminar material by John W. de Gruchy.

- *Acknowledging the source*, which applies more commonly, is necessary when using an observation, making a generalisation or citing a result that is not your own. It is also necessary when the current argument builds directly on what has preceded it, taking knowledge a step further or adding a new dimension to an existing insight. This is particularly important in disciplines that are vertical, that is, where results build on results that, in turn, have been built on previous results. Physics is an example of a vertical science.

Good referencing is critical to the validity of an argument, checking the foundations on which additions build and tracing them back to a level that is judged to be reliable.[5]

- **Quotations.** In some disciplines quotations are common,[6] but there are important guidelines for their use:

  - As far as possible avoid long quotations. If they are necessary, paraphrase parts or break them up with comment.

  - Quotations of more than three lines should be indented. Do not use longer quotations than necessary.

  - Quote accurately and ensure that references are correct.

  - Quotations must link in clearly with the flow of the discourse; they must make the point better than you can and add authority to what you are saying; they should not introduce tangential themes.

  - They must not 'talk to each other', that is, appear side by side without adequate comment.

  - Wherever possible, quote from original, not secondary, sources. This is responsible scholarly practice.

NOTE

QUOTING FROM SECONDARY SOURCES

The risk of quoting from secondary sources is twofold. First, the quoted section may contain errors. Second, the context in which the original author was speaking is often lost, so that the section is quoted in support of something quite different from or secondary to that which the original author intended by it.

- **Tables, graphs, etc.** These should be used appropriately and clearly labelled. A word of caution here: do not become so absorbed in perfecting graphics that you fritter away time, that could be used more profitably on thesis content. On the other hand, do not present graphic material shoddily. A balance is required.

---

5   Wolfe, 'How to write a PhD thesis'.
6   Use of quotations is related to the conventional referencing style of the particular discipline.

PART 4

- ◆ **Appendices.** This is a useful way of including material that adds value to the thesis but which does not warrant a place in the thesis itself. Appendices usually provide additional details on something referred to in the text. One advantage of using appendices is that they do not contribute to the word count.

- ◆ **An excursus.** An excursus accommodates an essential tangential discussion which gives the reader a greater appreciation of a point being made but without disrupting the flow of the thesis. These are more substantial than footnotes and are usually situated between chapters or sections. They should be used sparingly and only on the recommendation of the supervisor, and they should not be too long. The end of the excursus should bring the discussion back to the point at which it started. An excursus is included in the word count.

- ◆ **Bibliography/references.** For the examiner the bibliography or list of references is a 'window' to the student and the thesis. This should contain all the literary sources that were used in the research, but *only* those that were used. In some disciplines the reference list will be limited to those works actually cited in the thesis. Where a bibliography is required, indicating works both consulted and cited, you should be able to explain, if questioned, the inclusion of any book or article in the list (in other words, what has the work contributed to the thesis?).

- ◆ **Writer's block.** This is bound to happen at some point in the writing process. It is normal and not necessarily a cause for alarm. Reasons for writer's block may vary and the following strategies might be useful:

  - Move on to another section to avoid being bogged down by digressions, perceived gaps, lack of confidence, boredom, etc., and return to the problem sections later.

  - Set manageable, short-term writing targets (and reward yourself in some way when they are reached).

  - Sometimes it is appropriate to take a short physical and mental break from the thesis—perhaps go for a walk or watch a movie.

- ◆ **Writing for examiners.** As the process reaches its final stages, you should begin to write with potential examiners in mind. What is important at this stage is that the supervisor begins to read the thesis through the eyes of an examiner as well. This presupposes that she or he has begun to think about possible examiners, and it means a shift in the role the supervisor plays for this penultimate stage. Enter the devil's advocate!

Before we move on to the selection of examiners, a few additional issues relevant to the thesis need to be addressed.

Thesis abstract

You could see the abstract as a tool to control the flow of ideas throughout your thesis. A well written abstract links in a logical way the reasons for the research, your aims, how you went about achieving them and their significance.[7]

A thesis abstract, usually 300–400 words, is included at the beginning of the thesis. The immediate purpose of this is to orient the examiner to the work, giving him or her a bird's-eye view of the thesis as a whole. It is the first thing the examiner will read, a mini-thesis that should stand alone and be understood apart from the thesis itself. The abstract is also the first thing any potential reader will look at, and may be the deciding factor in whether someone reads your work or not. Bear in mind, too, that it is the abstract alone that will pop up in any electronic search for work undertaken in your particular area.

Typically, students leave the writing of the abstract until last and then scramble to put it together in time for submission. But a draft abstract can be a useful tool as a working document to maintain focus throughout the process. Tenses will change ('it is antici-pated' would become 'it was found'), but this does not detract from the value of a working abstract (a pocket thesis).

A word of caution: do not use telegraphic phrases or acronyms and abbreviations in the abstract, and do not repeat information given in the title.

The elements of an abstract[8] are summarised as follows:

1 **What was done?** (What ideas, notions, hypotheses, concepts, theories or thoughts were investigated?)

2 **Why was it done?** (What was the rationale for the study?)

3 **How was it done?** (How did you do the work? What data were generated and used? What was the origin of the data? How were data gathered? What tests, scales, indices or summary measures were used? In other words, how was the analysis and/or synthesis done?)

4 **What was found?** (What were the conclusions and what were the significant findings?)

5 **What is the significance of the findings?** (What difference does it make? What's next?)

Publishing and the thesis

There are three issues to be addressed concerning publications in relation to a PhD: publishing in the course of the research; including previously published material in a PhD; and publishing out of the completed PhD.

---

7   www.uq.edu.au/student-services/phdwriting/phfaq15.html. Accessed 26 July 2013.
8   Refer to www.uq.edu.au/student-services/phdwriting/phlink08.html. Accessed 20 January 2015.

Publishing while doing a PhD

A difference between the humanities and science streams (both in their broadest sense) is that publishing along the way is more common in the sciences than it is in the humanities. A particular nuance here is that when PhD students in the humanities *do* publish it is usually alone, whereas in other disciplines, publications out of the PhD project are co-authored by student and supervisor. In the latter case it is the supervisor's responsibility to discuss authorship issues (refer to the MOU) and to explain the review process.

Inclusion of previously published material

We noted earlier that in the South African system a PhD is awarded for a successfully examined thesis. This does not preclude the inclusion of previously published material, and in some disciplines it is common. Individual universities will have guidelines, but certain rules usually pertain:

- The articles must be worked into a thesis that addresses a particular question, and which has an integrating introduction and conclusion.

- The sections of the thesis must cohere with the role of each article, and how it fits in, as identified in the introduction.

- In the event of co-authored papers, the precise role of the PhD applicant in each paper must be specified.

- There is often a limit to the amount of published material in relation to new material that can be included.

Publishing from the completed thesis

It is expected of every PhD student, and in some disciplines Master's as well, to publish from the thesis. We have referred to publishing during the process, but for many students publishing will follow graduation. This may take various forms: a monograph; chapters reworked as journal articles or book chapters; a summary in article form of the main ideas of the thesis. Whatever the case, commitment to publish should be built into the MOU at the outset.

Upgrades

In some universities it is possible to upgrade from a Master's to a PhD degree during the research process. Similarly, a PhD may be downgraded to a Master's if the student is not producing material of the requisite quality for a PhD or if, for any reason, he or she no longer has time to complete a PhD. In the case of an upgrade, the procedure may be similar to this:

- A supervisor who considers a student's work to meet, or have the potential to meet, PhD requirements may apply through the HOD for an upgrade.

- Requests for upgrades must be made prior to submission but usually after at least one year of registration.

- Upgrades are more common in the sciences, where the extent of the contribution to knowledge can become clear early on and where students are usually already grounded in scientific method/s.

- There are some supervisors who contend that a Master's is a necessary stage in the process of becoming a researcher, and so are reticent to recommend upgrades.

- A downgrade, on the other hand, may ensure that the student obtains a degree (usually a second Master's) rather than abandoning the study.

Notes on intellectual property[9]

In addition to points made in the earlier discussion of intellectual property, there are additional perspectives that relate directly to graduate study.

Ownership of data

It occasionally happens that for one or other reason a Master's or PhD student leaves before completing the degree. Who, then, owns the data? The unequivocal answer is that the data belongs to the institution. It is normally left with the supervisor in the form of raw data, laboratory books, weekly reports, etc. Typically the supervisor sets another student to work on the project, carrying it on from the point at which the original student left off. The second student proceeds, under the direction of the supervisor, to gather more data and to redevelop the project. A publication may ensue, usually bearing the names of both students (and anyone else involved in the project). However, the data collected by the original student may not form part of a thesis. (This section is of particular relevance in the sciences.)

Plagiarism[10]

Plagiarism is a tricky subject because it has to do both with research ethics and trust. It can happen unwittingly (usually through ignorance) or knowingly (in defiance or in the hope that it will not be detected). It happens with students and with fully fledged researchers, and has led to some notable legal tangles.

> **'COPY AND PASTE' HAZARDS ...**
>
> '... in a world where we move data around so easily, students get odd ideas of ownership ...'[11]

---

9   De Gruchy & Holness, *The Emerging Researcher*, 150, 151.
10   This section is informed by material from seminars presented by Karin de Jager.
11   Booth et al. *The Craft of Research*, 201. See also 201–204.

For a supervisor to suspect plagiarism and to challenge a student is a serious situation, which should be addressed with urgency but also with wisdom. Plagiarism today is not just a matter of lifting passages of text from a book or article and using them as your own, but also—and increasingly—of taking material from the Internet. Many journals today are accessed online and often there are no authors cited. In such a case the title of the article, journal name and issue (where relevant), the full URL, and date of access should be provided as a reference.

Here are some guidelines for both students and supervisors:

◆ The student should be fully aware of what plagiarism is, why it is a serious academic offence, and what consequences might result if it is committed. This requires that both student and supervisor are well informed on both the issues at stake and university policy, and it should be included in the MOU. Most universities will have a student declaration with regards to plagiarism.

◆ Students should meticulously acknowledge each of the sources used, irrespective of whether they are quoting from another work, paraphrasing what someone else has written or borrowing ideas from elsewhere. This should be done immediately to avoid losing track of the sources of information.

◆ Students should be familiar with referencing conventions in the particular discipline.

◆ Drawing attention to suspected plagiarism should be done with tact and sensitivity, but also with firmness, allowing the student the chance to acknowledge the fault and deal with it appropriately.

◆ If the student denies any fault, he or she should be reminded of what is at stake and on what grounds the subject has been raised. From a supervisor's perspective, the student should be given space in which to deal with the matter if, in fact, he or she is guilty.

◆ Plagiarism is not always easy to detect. There are now electronic tools that help to identify potential acts of plagiarism (for instance, Turnitin), but these have limited use because they are entirely dependent on databases with publications in the field. A useful technique is 'string-searching'; keywords or phrases are typed into a search engine and all references checked out.

◆ A supervisor may realise that a certain passage or section in the dissertation has been lifted from a familiar text, but this is seldom the case. Usually a supervisor has to rely on his or her own intuition—become suspicious when the 'voice', style or content of a passage does not tally with what they have come to expect of a student. In some cases it may help to ask a colleague, preferably someone familiar with the student, to read the sections that have aroused suspicion.

◆ If a student is found guilty of plagiarism in the examination process, not only will the thesis be disqualified, but the competence and integrity of the supervisor will obviously also be questioned. The student should be made aware of this.

WHAT IS PLAGIARISM?[12]

Whenever you do written work you must differentiate between your own ideas and those that you did not think of yourself but which you have read elsewhere—in particular you must distinguish what you have *written* from what you are *quoting*.

You commit plagiarism in written work when you use another person's words, ideas or opinions without acknowledging them as being from that other person. You do this when you copy the work 'word for word' (verbatim) or submit someone else's work in a slightly altered form (such as changing a word to another word with the same meaning) *and* you do not acknowledge the borrowing in a way that shows from whom or where you took the words, ideas or reasoning.

You must provide references whenever you quote (use the exact words), para-phrase (use the ideas of another person, in your own words) or summarise (use the main points of another's opinions, theories or data). It does not matter how much of the other person's work you use (whether it is one sentence or a whole section), or whether you do it unintentionally or on purpose; if you present the work as your own without acknowledging that person, you are committing theft. You are taking someone else's work and passing it off as your own. Because of this, plagiarism is regarded as a very serious offence and carries heavy penalties.

If another student gives you one of his or her past assignments, you may not copy it and hand it in as your own; you are not allowed to do this. It is another form of plagiarism. While academic staff will teach you about systems of referencing, and how to avoid plagiarising, you too need to take responsibility for your own academic career.

Student declaration

1. I know that plagiarism is wrong. Plagiarism is to use another's work and pretend that it is one's own.
2. I have used the .... convention for citation and referencing. Each contribution to, and quotation in, this essay/report/project/ .... from the work(s) of other people has been attributed, and has been cited and referenced.
3. This essay/report/project/ .... is my own work.
4. I have not allowed, and will not allow, anyone to copy my work with the intention of passing it off as his or her own work.
5. I acknowledge that copying someone else's assignment or essay, or part of it, is wrong, and declare that this is my own work.

Signature _____

---

12 Excerpts from 'Avoiding plagiarism: A guide for students'. University of Cape Town Senate document. www.uct.ac.za/depts/records; www.uct.ac.za/uct/policies.php. Accessed 13 March 2013.

Appointment of examiners

The supervisor should begin thinking of possible examiners about two-thirds of the way through the thesis. A typical process may be along these lines:

- Supervisors may/should ask potential examiners if they are willing to undertake the task. This helps facilitate the process of their appointment by the appropriate institutional authority.

- The supervisor recommends the names of potential examiners to the HOD who, in turn, submits the names to the faculty or institutional higher degrees board. This requires suitable motivation, especially if the examiner recommended has not been used for this purpose previously.

- In the case of our institution (and each will have its own policy), for a Master's dissertation two examiners are appointed, and a further one is appointed as a substitute should the need arise. At least one should be external to the university. In the case of a PhD, three examiners are appointed, and a further two are
appointed as substitutes. They should all be external to the university, and preferably international.

- Whatever the details of an institution's examination policy, the aim should be for objective, scholarly and fair review of the work such as will uphold the institution's reputation in the broader academic community and give credibility to the graduated student.

What follows are some guidelines for supervisors in making recommendations:

- Examiners should be established authorities in the discipline/field.

- They should not be opposed ideologically to the position adopted by the student, or methodologically in reaching conclusions.

- If the dissertation is interdisciplinary in nature, the examiners should be sympathetic to and competent in such research and collectively embody the necessary skills needed for the examination.

- Examiners should have some knowledge or awareness of the institution's examination process and what is required of them. This is particularly important when selecting examiners from overseas where the system is different, for example, the United States.

- In some cases it is unwise to select examiners who are completely unfamiliar with the local context in which the thesis was written; for example, many students are writing in a second or third language.

- It is advisable to nominate examiners whom the supervisor knows and in whom she or he has confidence for the task. Once nominated, the assessing body will assume that those nominated are the best suited. This can have serious consequences in the examination process if there is disagreement among the examiners. At that stage, in the case of a negative report, it is not possible for the supervisor to argue that an examiner was not suitable.

◆ It may be institutional policy that candidates are not permitted to know the names of their examiners and should play no role in their selection. In this case, the process is confidential until the final outcome has been formally communicated to the student, at which time, should the examiners have agreed to this, their names may then be made known to the student. Each institution will have its own policy in this regard.

◆ Once recommendations are made and examiners appointed, it is inappropriate for the supervisor to have contact with them in connection with the thesis.

◆ The designated institutional authority, having approved the nominations, invites those recommended to become examiners, informs them of the procedures and takes the process forward.

Thesis submission

Both those new to supervision and those doing PhDs should understand the submission and examination process for a PhD. General principles remain fairly constant for the PhD model currently employed in South Africa and many other contexts. What follows is based loosely on South African institutional processes, but the material is easily adaptable to situations elsewhere. Supervisors and students should check on the processes in their own universities, bearing in mind that processes sometimes change. Students should be referred to the relevant offices for documents that are useful or necessary in preparing, completing and submitting their dissertations.

When is the thesis ready?

◆ In short, the thesis is ready when the supervisor is convinced that it is as good as the student can produce and that additional time spent on it is not likely to improve its quality.

◆ However, it is ultimately the candidate's responsibility to decide when s/he is ready to submit. Institutions may have a minimum mandatory period of registration for both Master's and PhD degrees, but there may also be provision to submit without the supervisor's approval (this is not usually advised, even when allowed).

◆ The normal and highly preferable way is for both supervisor and student to reach agreement on the matter. Sometimes a supervisor may feel that the thesis is not yet ready for submission, and that further work is necessary. After consid and money has been spent on it, it is obviously unwise to submit until it is reasonably believed that the candidate will be successful. Or the supervisor may feel that a particular student has done the best he or she is capable of, and that further work is psychologically, academically or financially neither possible nor warranted. At some point closure is necessary.

Letting it go

Many students have difficulty in finally letting the thesis go! Deadlines are useful. A student who does not have a deadline or is thinking about postponing it, should take note of this: *a thesis is an extensive work. It cannot be made perfect in a finite time. It will not contain the final word on any subject.*

There will inevitably be things in it that you could have done better and there will inevitably be some errors. No matter how many times you proofread it, there will be some things that could be improved. Set yourself, as the student, a deadline and stick to it. Make it as good as you can within that time, and then hand it in! Be familiar with your faculty and institution's cut-off dates for graduation.

Submission

- Take note of submission deadlines.
- Students and supervisors should be familiar with submission requirements; for example, the letter of intention to submit, containing relevant information.
- Make sure that acknowledgement is received.

The examination process

Examiners are typically given six weeks to examine a thesis and submit their reports and recommendations. Each university will have a set of guidelines for examiners, plus a report form indicating possible grades. In the South African system this would be:

For a Master's:

1. Award degree with distinction.
2. Award degree.
3. Award degree after specific changes are made to the satisfaction of the supervisor.
4. Invite candidate to revise and resubmit for examination.
5. Do not award degree.

For a PhD:

1. Award degree with minor typographical changes.
2. Award degree with specific changes, made to the satisfaction of the institutional doctoral board.

3   Invite candidate to revise and resubmit for examination.

4   Do not award the degree.

Some institutions require a *viva* in which the PhD student defends her or his thesis orally before a committee appointed for this purpose. In some faculties or institutions, candidates may be required to summarise their work in the form of a *journal article* or *formal conference paper* in order to qualify for graduation.

What is the examiner looking for?[13]

With regards to the thesis as a whole, the examiner is required to ascertain the following:

- A thesis must be satisfactory with regard to literary style and presentation.
- It must show that the candidate has understood the nature and purpose of the investigations, is sufficiently acquainted with the relevant literature, has mastered the methods of research appropriate to the topic and their application, and is capable of assessing the significance of their findings.
- A PhD thesis must constitute original research and is expected to make an original contribution to the field.

An examiner should take note of the following when considering the individual thesis components (the emphasis on different components may vary with discipline):

- The importance of the topic dealt with in the thesis is persuasively motivated.
- The research field has been properly delimited and the research problem and key questions clearly formulated.
- The literature review is critical, discriminating and up to date.
- The candidate's conceptual understanding of the approach to the topic and the topic itself is adequate.
- The argument for the theoretical approach adopted is convincingly presented.
- The research design has been fully motivated and the research methodology properly mastered.
- The study is clearly focused and the work as a whole is systematic, logical, well structured, balanced and clear.
- The claims made throughout the study are substantial, coherent, founded, consistent and persuasive.
- The candidate has been selective, critical and independent in his/her engagement with secondary sources.
- The candidate has made effective use, where relevant, of the data or illustrative material to support the development of the argument.

---

13   Adapted from the 'Guidelines for examiners', University of KwaZulu-Natal (UKZN).

- The conclusions are relevant and the interpretation and discussion of the findings satisfactory.

- The level of expression conforms to academic discourse.

- The text is properly organised in terms of chapter divisions and length, paragraphing, indentation and numbering, and the layout of the study is acceptable (title page, table of contents, appendices, abstract, quality of typography).

- The referencing system is consistent throughout and the bibliography complete.

Dealing with examiners' reports

Once examiners' reports have been received and considered in line with institutional processes by the relevant institutional assessing body, the supervisor will be informed of its decision, which is then communicated to the student. The supervisor discusses the reports with the student and sets out how corrections will be managed. Especially in the case of a PhD, it is rare that no corrections are required. Corrections may take one of the following forms, depending on the examiners' reports:

- Minor corrections to the satisfaction of the supervisor.

- More significant changes to the satisfaction of the supervisor and the institutional assessing/awarding body.

- A revision of the thesis and resubmission for examination; this is usually sent only to the dissenting examiner (in the absence of consensus in the reports).

For a student, receiving examiners' reports is a nail-biting experience! It is usually dreaded and may result in huge relief—or in devastation. Both outright failure (which is rare) and the request to revise and resubmit the thesis for examination are extremely difficult for both student and supervisor. There may even be an element of recrimination. While a failure is final and difficult, in the case of a 'revise and resubmit' it is critical for both student and supervisor to approach the situation positively and constructively.

A useful strategy for corrections is for students to tabulate every criticism and requirement of the examiners and to sign off when each has been addressed. With any more contentious issue, and particularly with revision and resubmission, the supervisor's input on how strategically to respond is vital. Because revision of a thesis is a substantial undertaking and there is usually a time limit to accomplish this, the student will rely heavily on the supervisor's logistical and emotional support in establishing a project plan to meet the requirements timeously.

Beyond supervision

Depending on the student's motivation for doing a Master's or PhD degree and future plans, as well as university expectations, supervisors have responsibilities beyond actual supervision. They should:

- Plan and arrange funding for the student to present at a conference, and assist with networking whenever possible.
- Discuss career options and help in the preparation of appropriate CVs if requested.
- Provide letters of reference to ensure the student's professional development.
- Encourage students, where applicable, to prepare and keep a structured portfolio.
- Encourage students who have not already done so to publish from their theses.

Conclusion

As with most of the topics covered in this book, there is a great deal of reference material available on supervision, providing a range of perspectives on each topic. What we have done in this chapter, and in Part 4 as a whole, is to provide an introduction to postgraduate supervision, as much with the intention of identifying what is involved in the process as with addressing the issues themselves. You, the reader, are urged to make use of any resource, human or textual, which will enhance your capacity to supervise Master's and PhD students in the writing of their dissertations.

EXCURSUS

Complementary models of supervision[14]

Currently, South Africa produces 26 doctoral graduates per million of the total population. The target that was set for 2014 has increased this number to between 100 and 120.[15] However, it is acknowledged that '*working only within existing systems*, and taking into account available capacity' there is no way that this could materialise in the foreseeable future.[16]

The traditional approach to supervision—that is, a single supervisor taking on one-to-one supervision—means that only a limited number of doctoral students can be served if the quality of supervision is to be maintained. Yet it is unlikely that in South Africa the number of available supervisors or the availability of resources will increase significantly in the short term.

In addition, the postgraduate pedagogical and administrative landscape is changing. The postgraduate student population is more diverse in terms of academic preparation, language proficiencies, modes of learning and purposes for taking on doctoral studies. Graduates are expected to have a greater variety of skills and attributes, and with more interdisciplinary and transdisciplinary research being undertaken, there is a need for greater flexibility in models of postgraduate studies, and greater co-ordination of effort. *It is therefore prudent to be looking at alternatives to the traditional one-on-one model of supervision.*

Traditional one-on-one model (1 student : 1 supervisor)

There will (and must) always be space for this model, wherein the individual student-researcher is 'apprenticed' to the individual supervisor who guides the independent research of the student. The value of this model lies in the personal, direct aspect of academic development. The disadvantage is that it is not an efficient model for rapidly increasing PhD production.

There are alternative (complementary) models of supervision that should be considered and adopted. The models below all rely on some form of distributed supervision, which means that the supervision is shared among peer students or among supervisors working as a team. In addition, these models are strengthened by scaffold-ing in the form of fixed structures, group seminars, journal clubs, writing circles and routines, which—because they are shared—reinforce commitment.

---

14 Prepared by Nelleke Bak.
15 Mouton, J. (2011). 'Doctoral production in South Africa: Statistics, challenges and responses', *Perspectives in Education*, 3 (29): 13–29.
16 ASSAF Consensus Report. (2010). *The PhD Study: An evidence-based study on how to meet the demands for high-level skills in an emerging economy.* Pretoria: Academy of Science of South Africa, 107 (author's emphasis).

The following is a brief overview of the advances and drawbacks of some complementary models of supervision.

Student cluster models (2 or more students : 1 supervisor)

A student cluster model of two or more students being supervised together on a shared topic can circumvent the ubiquitous problem of isolation experienced by the student in the 1 : 1 model.

◆ Group models draw on the productive processes in a collaborative learning environment.[17] Learning through interaction is a demonstrably powerful mode of learning which also helps to create a sense of strong community.

◆ Group discussions provide opportunity for students to externalise—and thus clarify—their thoughts with peers and supervisor.

◆ Group models enhance enculturation, increase networking and create a motivating space for skills development.[18] And, importantly, group models mitigate some of the human and other resource constraints. This model of supervision is already used in the natural and applied sciences, but is being increasingly adopted in other disciplines as well.

Student cluster model 1: Cohort supervision

A cohort group consists of students all starting at the same time at the same level and progressing through the programme at the same rate. There are numerous advantages in adopting this model: there are economies of scale in that the supervisor can take the group through the same necessary steps of generic training; shared deadlines help to motivate production of writing; and students who are working in the same theoretical field can piggy-back on each other's research through sharing key articles, sparking new insights and getting peer feedback. Potential disadvantages are that it demands great group management skills from the supervisor, and individual students may feel that there is not sufficient individual focus on their specific research topic in group discussions.

Student cluster model 2: Group supervision

Whereas the cohort group consists of students all at the same level and same stage of work, group supervision consists of students at different stages of their research and different levels. The commonality of the group is that all the students are working on a

---

17 Clark, A. (1996). 'Economic reason: The interplay of individual learning and external structure', in J. Drobak & J. Nye (eds). *The Frontiers of the New Institutional Economics*. San Diego, CA: Academic Press, 269–290, and Clark, A. & Chalmers, D. (1998). 'The extended mind', *Analysis*, 58 (1): 7–19.

18 Puntambekar, S. & Kolodner, J.L. (2005). 'Toward implementing distributed scaffolding: Helping students learn science from design', *Journal of Research in Science Teaching*, 42 (2): 185–217.

similar topic or a large, funded research project. The advantages of this model are that students are members of a research team, drawing on and contributing to the same body of literature and following shared research methods. Students in earlier stages or on lower levels of study learn from those who are further in their research. Opportunities for students to learn from each other through peer guidance and for co-publishing are increased. A potential disadvantage is that it can lead to a production line of research with little scope for individual innovation.

Student cluster model 3: Pyramid or network model of supervision

Under the guidance of a senior supervisor, one postdoctoral fellow guides two or three doctoral students, who, in turn, mentor a limited number of Master's students. This community-of-scholars model, within a structured environment, provides multilevel supervision and initiates doctoral students and postdoctoral fellows into being supervisors themselves. This model optimises resources and maximises the available supervisory capacity.

Supervisor cluster model (2 or more supervisors : 1 student)

Often one supervisor cannot be expected to provide all that is needed all of the time to all of the students. A group of supervisors guiding one student enables a range of expertise to inform the student's work, shares the supervisory load, exposes the student to a variety of academic styles, thinking and debates, enables the student to build up a broader network of academic contacts, and, through the on-going conferment among the supervisors, protects the student from possible supervisor abuse. With the growth in joint degrees and international student mobility programmes, a networked supervisors model is becoming more appropriate.[19]

Supervisor cluster model 1: Co-supervision (2 supervisors : 1 student)

Co-supervision is a well-established practice to bring in additional expertise on a topic, as well as to initiate novice supervisors into the supervision process. Recent developments in technology have broadened the availability of co-supervisors. Via various audio-visual, media-conferencing software packages, multiple parties can now confer online with ease and at no or little cost. In addition, the shift towards inter disciplinary and transdisciplinary research programmes makes co-supervision an attractive option in which expertise from various disciplines can be brought to bear on the thesis project.

---

19   Hattingh, B. & Lillejord, S. (2011). 'A networked pathway to the PhD: The African–Norwegian case of productive learning cultures', *Perspectives in Education*, 29 (3): 100–110.

Supervisor cluster model 2: Supervisory committees (multiple supervisors : 1 student)

With supervisory committees, the student is guided by three or four experts, each with his and her own specialisation. Individual supervisors can serve on several supervisory committees because their input is limited to their specific area of expertise. Supervisory committees can also draw on the expertise available in industry and business, where there are large numbers of staff members with PhD qualifications.[20]

Complementary and alternative models of supervision entail economies of scale and provide a shared and firm structure within which the student progresses. The anticipated outcomes are that more PhD students can be supervised, that the throughput rate can be increased by reducing the time-to-degree period, and that those who choose a career in academia will be in a position to replicate the model and accommodate their own increased number of PhD students.

---

20   Nerad, M. (2011). 'What we know about the dramatic increase in PhD degrees and the reform of doctoral education worldwide: Implications for South Africa', *Perspectives in Education*, 29 (3): 1–12.

CONCLUSION
GROWING THE NEXT GENERATION OF RESEARCHERS

Writing this book has provided an unparalleled opportunity to reflect on the multiple dimensions, challenges and opportunities of research development in our context at this time in history. It has also foregrounded a number of features of UCT's Emerging Researcher Programme (ERP) which are perhaps not always fully appreciated, either by participants or facilitators. Interestingly, most have to do with aspects of heterogeneity inherent in the programme—initially a potential challenge but in reality an asset. The university's research capacity-building vision was, from the start, a generic, centrally managed and structured, institution-wide initiative reaching out to early-career academics in all faculties and academic departments. For the first six months, the ERP operated in a single stream, but when it became apparent that in certain respects the needs and experience of 'scientists' and 'social scientists' differed, we operated in two streams for some of our activities. Within both streams there was, and continues to be, a coming together of and exchange between individuals from different disciplines and different cultures, and across a wide age spectrum.

Among the most rewarding outcomes of our seminars and workshops is the fruit born of conversations struck up between *researchers from diverse disciplinary backgrounds* in both formal meeting rooms and in social spaces. Whether the focus is supervision training, writing for publication or grant writing, evaluation sheets invariably reflect appreciation of the opportunity for cross-fertilisation of ideas and experience, and of the exposure to a variety of disciplinary perspectives on a range of issues. It is especially gratifying to report a number of modest collaborative initiatives between emerging researchers that have resulted from such interaction. Although this was never an intention of the ERP, exposure to disciplines other than one's own in the early-career stage shows serendipitous potential in the fostering of the interdisciplinary consciousness that is becoming critical in a mutating research environment.

A second unexpectedly enriching feature of the ERP is the *cultural mix of participants* at any one event, invariably reflected in the conversation. A single question can evoke a metaphorical meander from a Cameroonian colleague, an incisive, word-economic, no-frills response from a visiting German scientist, and a bold, gesticulating interjection from a colleague immersed in local township theatre. Discussions also reflect disciplinary culture and convention, at times provoking heated, yet collegial, debate, impressing alternative perspectives on participants.

Not all emerging researchers are young. Some have entered academia late: women having raised families; men and women leaving school to work, studying part-time over many years. Others take up academic posts after years of professional experience. The ERP, while having much to offer this group, has also gained enormously from their maturity and the wisdom that comes from life experience. Younger researchers—sometimes a generation apart from these colleagues—have also benefited. So, while an explicit goal of the ERP is to 'fast-track' the career paths of young researchers, providing opportunities to develop skills, to reach targets and have experiences that might otherwise take years in coming, there is also a qualitative underpinning of the programme provided in part by ERP participants who are older and have a rich store of wisdom and knowledge to share.

This book has been written in Africa and for Africa. Here, despite the urgent need to grow a new generation of researchers, there is an abiding respect for age. So it is fitting that we close with some wise and encouraging words drawn from the experience of an emerging researcher who is at the same time a grandmother.

MPOE JOHANNAH KEIKELAME'S STORY

Kgomo ya morago e ya tsena mo sakeng.
(The ox that walks behind also gets into the kraal.)

Maybe you will be surprised as to why I am using the idiomatic expression above. It is because I was born and bred on a farm … on my parents' farm. I am also an African Motswana woman. I carry all these things that make me who I am into my life—even, genuinely so, into my research and my work. I have witnessed and learned 'how and when' each ox entered the kraal. Some were quick, some were very slow … like me. But it does not matter when and how. What matters is that through persistence and endurance, anyone can eventually enter the kraal. Here I mean you will reach the GOAL that you have set for yourself … I have one too—which is to enter the kraal.

In 1990, I registered for my honours degree and I had to present a research question before writing a proposal. I was also working full time as a registered nurse and midwife and I was in charge of the blood bank. I realised that there was a shortage of blood supply and I wanted to know why we had this problem. Now, here, was the opportunity where it would be easier for me to do my project because it was work which was relevant to my job and which would therefore be supported by management. The results would help us to understand the cause of the problem and to find strategies to address it. The project was therefore *feasible in terms of the resources* I had. Another important thing, which I want to share with you, is that I had an *interest in the topic*. Because of that, I kept some notes on comments that donors and non-donors made during blood-donation sessions. These helped me to have an idea of the *kind of questions to ask* when I collect the data. This project was published in 1995. I was the second author; my supervisor was the first author.

Now here are some of the things that motivated me in my research journey—and by the way, I am still working towards entering the kraal. I had a desire to publish my Master's thesis project and I wanted to be the first author. So I invited my co-supervisor to publish with me because I needed support from an experienced researcher. This was a learning opportunity for me. The process was challenging. What motivated me were the encouraging comments from reviewers. I worked hard to address the issues they raised. The paper was accepted for publication. Well, don't despair if some of your articles are rejected or when reviewers' comments and editors' decisions are unfavourable. I had such an experience too. My third paper was rejected but accepted for publication as a letter to the editor. I was disappointed by this outcome and rejected the decision. I consulted with other colleagues on the matter and informed them of my decision. Some thought that I was not behaving like a 'true scholar'. Others said that I should submit it elsewhere, advice on which I acted. My co-authors were also supportive of the decision that I took. The paper was accepted elsewhere—not as a letter to the editor. Advice and support from others is very important ... but the decision is yours ...

Something else I have learned: do not spurn opportunities when they come your way even if you think you do not have time. Make use of them because you get exposure and you are able to network. Here is what happened with me. I was invited as an international speaker. I was invited to contribute to a book on global conversations on epilepsy. I was invited to review articles for two international journals. I responded positively to each of them. There are many ways of entering the kraal. Take opportunities; don't turn them down. Research and publishing take a lot of commitment—especially when you do a PhD through publication, as I am doing.

I have an auto-immune condition—sometimes I experience fatigue; my pace of work becomes slow ... just like the ox that I told you about. Listen to your body. There is nothing wrong when you realise that you need to pause ... I did so too in 2007 because of ill-health and also because I am older ... I am an older ox ... I am a wife, a mother, grandmother and mother-in-law, and I am also working full-time. What did I do? I kept on reading about my topic. My research question has never changed. I think this helped because I could have confused myself—not actually knowing what I want to do. I think that what is also important in this journey is to have a very supportive supervisor—like the one I have. He is always excited about my work ... he tells others about it ... this is another thing that motivates me. You can make your research journey an exciting one, too, despite all odds ... Don't forget that you have to drive yourself too ... in order to enter the kraal that I told you about. I am looking forward to hearing your story.

MEMORANDUM OF UNDERSTANDING

This is the framework of a typical Memorandum of Understanding. It should be adjusted to accommodate issues relevant to disciplines/faculties/institutions.

This document, which is intended to ensure a mutually productive process of supervision, should be completed early in the supervision process. Each year, an additional memorandum must be completed before the student renews registration.

MEMORANDUM OF UNDERSTANDING (MOU)

Name of graduate student: ....

Signature: ....

Name of supervisor: ....

Signature: ....

Date: ....

Part A: Details of candidate and supervisor

Full name of student: ....

Qualifications: ....

Student's experience, giving particular attention to research experience and mastery of second language, as may be relevant.

Thesis title: ....

Personal particulars:

Student number: ....

Current address: ....

Email: ....

Telephone number(s): ....

Supervisor:

Full name: ....

Department: ....

Co-supervisor, if any:

Full name: ....

Department: ....

Institution: ....

Part B: Expectations

1   The supervisor must set out what is expected of the student, including, an assessment of the time to be spent on each phase of the thesis, frequency of supervision and progress reports, travel arrangements (where necessary) and interim publications (if intended). ....

2   Supervisor's plans to provide for her/his absences, if away for more than two months during the next three years. ....

3   Courses and classes: list any course or workshop that the student should attend in order to assist in writing the thesis. ....

4   Financial arrangements for duration of study: specify any financial assistance, by way of bursaries and salaries, to support the student. Should the student terminate studies, or fail to make satisfactory progress to the extent that reregistration is denied, will s/he be contractually obliged to repay any bursary?

5   The student's expectations of the supervisor. ....

    Supervisor's comment.   ....

6   The student must set out a plan for the project, including a detailed time commitment.   ....

    Supervisor's comment.   ....

7   Publications: (Full details should be noted) ....

8   Meetings and feedback on written work: ....

Part C: Observations (if any) by the Chair of the Higher Degrees Committee

Signed................. Name.. Date ....

Once seen by all parties, copies of this document must be returned to the student, supervisor and Faculty Office.

Memorandum of Understanding Annual Supplement: Review, plans and budget

This supplement consists of three schedules, which must be completed at or before the start of the second, and each subsequent year.

Schedule 1 is a report by the supervisor (with optional comments by co-supervisors) on the candidate's work to date, a recommendation by the supervisor that registration be renewed (or that this be refused on the grounds of inadequate progress), and the response of the candidate to the report and recommendations. It is primarily an opportunity for the candidate and supervisor to take stock of progress.

Schedule 2 is a plan of work for the year ahead.

Schedule 3 is a budget for the year ahead, with additional details covering supervisor availability, expected outputs from the work and any special arrangements.

▌ REFERENCES

Books and journal articles

Achebe, C. (1964). *Arrow of God*. Oxford: Heinemann African Writers Series.

Alberts, B. (2013). 'Impact factor distortions', Editorial, *Science*, 340, 17 May.

Altbach, P. & Salmi, J. (eds). (2011). *The Road to Academic Excellence: The making of world-class research universities*. Washington, DC: The World Bank.

ASSAF Consensus Report. (2010). *The PhD Study: An evidence-based study on how to meet the demands for high-level skills in an emerging economy*. Pretoria: Academy of Science of South Africa.

Boas, F. (1919). 'Scientists as spies', *The Nation*, 797, 19 December.

Bolker, J. (1998). *Writing Your Dissertation in Fifteen Minutes a Day: A guide to starting, revising and finishing your doctoral thesis*. New York: Henry Holt & Company.

Booth, W.C., Colomb, G.G. & Williams, J.M. (2003). *The Craft of Research*. 2nd edition. Chicago, IL: University of Chicago Press.

Boughey, C. (2012). 'Linking teaching and research: An alternative perspective', *Teaching in Higher Education*, 17 (5): 629–635. Online 29 October 2012. www.dx.doi.org/10.1080/13 562517.2012.725528. Accessed 21 October 2014.

Boyer, E.L. (1990). 'Enlarging the perspective', in *Scholarship Reconsidered: Priorities of the Professoriate*, Ch. 2. Carnegie Foundation for the Advancement of Teaching: Special Report.

Brew, A. (2003). 'Teaching and research: New relationships and their implications for inquiry-based teaching and learning in higher education', *Higher Education Research and Development*, 22 (1): 3–18.

Center for the Study of Human Rights. (1994). *Twenty-five Human Rights Documents*. New York: Columbia University Press.

Clark, A. (1996). 'Economic reason: The interplay of individual learning and external structure', in J. Drobak & J. Nye (eds). *The Frontiers of the New Institutional Economics*. San Diego, CA: Academic Press.

Clark, A. & Chalmers, D. (1998). 'The extended mind', *Analysis*, 58 (1): 7–19.

Costello, A. & Zumla, A. (2000). 'Moving to research partnerships in developing countries', *British Medical Journal*, 321: 827–829. www.bmj.com/content/321/7264/827. Accessed 20 October 2014.

Davis, M. (1997). *Scientific Papers and Presentations*. San Diego, CA: Academic Press.

Day, A. (2007). *How to Get Research Published in Journals*. Aldershot: Gower Publishing.

De Gruchy, J.W. & Holness, L. (2007). *The Emerging Researcher: Nurturing passion, developing skills, producing output.* Cape Town: UCT Press.

Dietz, A.J., Jansen, J.D. & Wadee, A.A. (2006). *Effective PhD Supervision and Mentorship: A workbook based on experiences from South Africa and the Netherlands.* Amsterdam and Pretoria: Rozenberg Publishers and Unisa Press.

Dunleavy, P. (2003). *Authoring a PhD: How to plan, draft, write and finish a doctoral thesis or dissertation.* Basingstoke and New York: Palgrave Macmillan.

Echezona, R.I. & Ugwuanyi, C.F. (2010). 'African university libraries and Internet connectivity: Challenges and the way forward', *Library Philosophy and Practice*, September. www.webpages.uidaho.edu/~mbolin/lpp2010.htm. Accessed 4 March 2012.

English, J. (ed.). (2012). *Professional Communication: Deliver effective written, spoken and visual messages.* Cape Town: Juta.

Epstein, D., Kenway, J. & Bode, R. (2005). *Writing for Publication.* London: Sage Publications.

Evans, L. (2012). 'Leadership for researcher development: What research leaders need to know and understand', *Educational Management, Administration and Leadership*, 40 (4): 423–435. Originally published online, 25 April 2012. www.ema.sagepub.com/content/40/4/423. Accessed 20 April 2015.

Francis, J.R.D. (1976). 'Supervision and examination of higher degree students', *Bulletin of the University of London*, 31: 3–6.

Germano, W. (2005). *From Dissertation to Book.* Chicago, IL: University of Chicago Press.

Gibaldi, J. (2003). *MLA Handbook for Writers of Research Papers*, 6th edition. New York: The Modern Language Association of America.

Gibbons, M. (2013). 'Change and reflection', *ACU Bulletin*, 179: 3–7.

Haarhoff, D. (1998). *The Writer's Voice: A workbook for writers in Africa.* Johannesburg: Zebra Press.

Hart, C. (2001). *Doing a Literature Review: Releasing the social science research imagination.* London: Sage Publications.

Hattingh, B. & Lillejord, S. (2011). 'A networked pathway to the PhD: The African–Norwegian case of productive learning cultures', *Perspectives in Education*, 29 (3): 100–110.

Henson, K.T. (1995). *The Art of Writing for Publication.* Boston, MA: Allyn and Bacon.

Imperial College, Research Office. (1993). 'Managing projects', *Nursing Research*, 42 (1), January/February. www3.imperial.ac.uk/researchsupport/managingprojects/managingbudget. Accessed 26 November 2013.

Jowi, J.O. (2011). Report on ANIE conference: 'Africa: Universities rethink internationalisation', *University World News*, 86, 10 November. http://www.universityworldnews.com/article.php?story=20111120095222860. Accessed 20 April 2014.

Katz, J.S. & Martin, B.R. (1997). 'What is research collaboration?' *Research Policy*, 26: 1–18. www.sussex.ac.uk/Users/sylvank/pubs/Res_col9.pdf. Accessed 3 March 2015.

Kessel, F. & Rosenfield, P.L. (2008). 'Towards transdisciplinary research: Historical and contemporary perspectives', *American Journal of Preventative Medicine*, 35 (2), Supplement: S225–S234.

Kotecha, P. (ed.). (2012). 'Internationalisation in Higher Education: Perspectives from the Global South', *SARUA Leadership Dialogue Series*, 2 (2): 49–58.

Macfarlane, B. (2007). 'Defining and rewarding academic citizenship: The implications for university promotion policy', *Journal of Higher Education and Policy Management*, 29 (3): 261–273.

Max-Neef, M.A. (2005). 'Foundations of transdisciplinarity', *Ecological Economics*, 53: 5–16.

Mouton, J. (2004). *How to Succeed in your Masters and Doctoral Studies: A South African guide and resource book.* Pretoria: Van Schaik.

Mouton, J. (2011). 'Doctoral production in South Africa: Statistics, challenges and responses', *Perspectives in Education*, 3 (29): 13–29.

Nerad, M. (2011). 'What we know about the dramatic increase in PhD degrees and the reform of doctoral education worldwide: Implications for South Africa', *Perspectives in Education*, 29 (3): 1–12.

New, M. & Morrell, R. (2013). 'Draft report on the URC Task Team on Interdisciplinary and Transdisciplinary Research at UCT', University of Cape Town.

Novotny, H. (2006). 'The potential of transdisciplinarity'. First published in *Interdiscipline*, May 2006. www.helga-novotny.eu/downloads/helga_novot_b59.pdf. Accessed 13 April 2014.

Oxford. (2002). *South African Concise Oxford Dictionary.* Oxford: Oxford University Press.

Phillips, E.M. & Pugh, D.S. (2003). *How to Get a PhD: A handbook for students and their supervisors*, 3rd edition. Maidenhead: Open University Press.

Pietsch, T. (2013). 'Academic networks, internationalisation and empire', *ACU Bulletin*, 179, June: 18, 19.

Pietsch, T. (2013). *Empire of Scholars: Universities, networks and the British academic world, 1850–1939.* Manchester: Manchester University Press.

Puntambekar, S. & Kolodner, J.L. (2005). 'Toward implementing distributed scaffolding: Helping students learn science from design', *Journal of Research in Science Teaching*, 42 (2): 185–217.

Ramtohul, R. (2003). 'Academic freedom in a state-sponsored university: The case of the University of Mauritius'. *Journal of Academic Freedom*, 3: 1–21.

Rao, J.V. & College, A.V.N. (n.d.). 'Culture through language in the novels of Chinua Achebe', in *African Postcolonial Literature in English: In the postcolonial web.* www.postcolonialweb.org/achebe/jrao1.html. Accessed 10 May 2014.

Repko, A.F. (2008). *Interdisciplinary Research: Process and theory*, 2nd edition. London: Sage Publications. www.sagepub.com/upm-data/43242_1.pdf. Accessed 23 October 2013.

Robson, C. (2002). *Real World Research,* 2nd edition. Oxford: Blackwell Publishing.

Rose, R. (2010). 'Writing a book is good for you', *European Political Science*, 9: 417–419. www.palgrave-journals.com/eps/journal/v9/n3/full/eps201018a.html. Accessed 27 August 2013.

Rugg, G. & Petre, M. (2004). *The Unwritten Rules of PhD Research*. Maidenhead: Open University Press.

Sawyerr, A. (2004). 'African universities and the challenge of research capacity development', *Journal of Higher Education in Africa*/RESA, 2 (1). www.codesria.org/IMG/pdf/8-SAWYERR.pdf. Accessed 11 February 2013.

Selby-Harrington, M.L., Donat, P.L. & Hubbard, H.D. (1993). 'Guidance for managing a research grant', *Nursing Research,* 42 (1), January/February. www.ahrq.gov/professionals/clinicians-providers/resources/nursing/funding/grants/grant-management.html. Accessed 26 November 2013.

Stock, P. & Burton, R.J.F. (2011). 'Defining terms for integrated (multi-inter-trans-disciplinary) sustainability research', *Sustainability*, 3: 1090–1113; doi: 10.3390/su3081090; 1098. www.mdpi.com/journal/sustainability. Accessed 25 October, 2013.

Strunk, W. Jnr. & White, E.B. (2000). *The Elements of Style*. London: Penguin Books.

Terras, M. (2012). 'The impact of social media on the dissemination of research: Results of an experiment', *Journal of Digital Humanities*, 1 (3), Summer 2012. Available at www.journalofdigitalhumanities.org/1-3/the-impact-of-social-media-on-the-dissemination-of-research-by-melissa-terras/. Accessed 11 February 2013.

Turok, N. (2012). *From Quantum to Cosmos: The universe within*. London: Faber and Faber.

Zanna, M.P. & Darley, J.M. (1987). *The Compleat Academic: A practical guide for the beginning social scientist*. New York: Random House.

Zeleza, P.T. (2012). 'Internationalisation in higher education: Opportunities and challenges for the Knowledge Project in the Global South', *Internationalisation in Higher Education: Perspectives from the Global South*, SARUA Leadership Dialogue Series, 4 (2): 4–28.

Zeleza, P.T. & Olukoshi, A. (2004). *African Universities in the Twenty-first Century*, Vol. 1: *Liberalisation and Internationalisation*. Dakar: CODESRIA.

Zell, H.M. (1998). *A Handbook of Good Practice in Journal Publishing*, 2nd edition. London: International African Institute.

Web sources

Armstrong, C. (2007). *How to Develop Successful Networking Skills in Academia*. www.jobs.ac.uk/careers-advice/working-in-higher-education/573/how-todevelop-successful-networking-skills-in-academia. Accessed 20 May 2013.

Bart, M. (2013). 'To promote a congenial workplace, invest in people', *Faculty Focus*, 5 October. www.facultyfocus.com/articles/academic-leadership. Accessed 5 November 2014.

Belmont Report. (1979). www.hhs.gov/ohrp/humansubjects/guidance/belmont.html. Accessed 15 August 2013.

Budapest Open Access Initiative, 14 February 2002. www.budapestopenaccessinitiative.org/read. Accessed 3 March 2015.

Cipriano, R.E. (2012). 'Faculty collegiality as a synergistic agent', *Faculty Focus*, 15 August. www.facultyfocus.com/articles/academic-leadership. Accessed 25 April 2014.

Columbia University Libraries, Copyright Advisory Office. (n.d.). 'If you cannot find the owner'. www.copyright.columbia.edu/copyright/permissions/if-you-cannot-find-the-owner/. Accessed 5 March 2015.

Dar es Salaam Declaration on Academic Freedom and Social Responsibility of Academics. (1990). www1.umn.edu/humanrts/africa/DARDOK.htm. Accessed 25 April 2013.

De Jager, K. (2009). *Handbook on Citation and Related Matters*. Centre for Information Literacy, University of Cape Town. www.open.uct.ac.za/bitstream/item/.../09_Citation_Handbook_ccd.doc? Accessed 28 April 2015.

Elsevier. (2015). 'How to write a scientific paper: A general guide', for *Oral Surgery, Oral Medicine, Oral Pathology and Oral Radiology*, A9–A11. www.oooojournal.net/article/S1079-2104(05)00320-3/fulltext. Accessed 3 March 2015.

Gordimer, N. (1988). 'Review of Chinua Achebe's *Anthills of the Savannah*'. www.nytimes.com/1988/02/21/books/a-tyranny-of-clowns.html. Accessed 10 May 2014.

Helsinki Declaration. (1964, amended 1975, 1983, 1989, 1996, 2000, 2002, 2004, 2008), www.wma.net/en/30publications/10policies/b3/. Accessed 20 August 2013.

Hugo, G. (2013). ACU Perspectives speech on 'International migration and higher education in Australia', 27 March. www.acu.ac.uk/news/view?id=49. Accessed 20 June 2013.

James, R. & Baldwin, G. (1999). *Eleven Practices of Effective Postgraduate Supervisors*. Centre for the Study of Higher Education and the School of Graduate Studies, University of Melbourne. Full booklet available at www.cshe.unimelb.edu.au/publications.html. Accessed 1 May 2007.

Materu-Behitsa, M. (2003). 'The Database of African Theses and Dissertations (DATAD)'. www.codesria.org/pdf/mary_Materu_Behitsa.pdf). Accessed 12 February 2013.

Montreal Statement on Research Integrity in Cross-Boundary Research Collaborations. (2013). www.wcri2013.org/Montreal_Statement_e.shtml. Accessed 20 August 2013.

Priem, J., Taraborelli, D., Groth, P. & Neylon, C. (2010). 'Altmetrics: A manifesto'. www.altmetrics.org/manifesto/. Accessed 26 January 2015.

Queensland University of Technology, Supervision Evaluation Project Team. (1995). *Tracking Postgraduate Supervision* booklet. http://www.rsc.qut.edu.au/studentsstaff/

training/workshop_materials/2006/Resources/tracking_supervision.rtf. Accessed 18 July 2013.

Shekman, R. & Patterson, M. (2013). 'Science policy: Reforming research assessment', eLife 2013, 2:e00855. www.ascb.org/SFdeclaration.html. Accessed 28 April 2015.

Singapore Statement on Research Integrity. (2010). www.singaporestatement.org/statement. html. Accessed 5 August 2013.

Smith, H. (2011). 'Relationships between teaching and research'. www.ucl.ac.uk/calt/ support/cpd4he/resources/research_teaching. Accessed 6 February 2014.

Suber, P. (2004). 'A very brief introduction to open access'. www.legacy.earlham.edu/~peters/ fos/brief.htm. Accessed 3 March 2015.

Taylor & Francis, Author Services. (n.d.). 'Working with proofs'. www.journalauthors.tandf. co.uk/production/checkingproofs.asp. Accessed 3 March 2015.

The Lancet. (n.d.). 'Statements, permissions and signatures'. www.thelancet.com/lanpsy/ information.../statements-permissions-signatures. Accessed 5 November 2013.

The Linux Information Project. (n.d.). www.linfo.org/peer_review.html. Accessed 25 April 2014.

Thomas, D. (2007). 'Reviewers, and how not to kill them', in *Writing a Book,* Part 7, www. pragdave.pragprog.com/pragdave/writing_a_book/index.html. Accessed 22 April 2015.

University of Birmingham. (n.d.). 'Benchmarks for Academic Citizenship'. www.intranet. birmingham.ac.uk/hr/documents/public/pdr/academic/citizenship-benchmarks.pdf. Accessed 3 November 2014.

University of Cape Town. PC 01/2011. *Authorship Practices Policy.* www.uct.ac.za/about/ policies/. Accessed 5 November 2013.

University of Cape Town Senate document. (n.d.). 'Avoiding plagiarism: A guide for students'. www.uct.ac.za/depts/records. www.uct.ac.za/uct/policies.php. Accessed 13 March 2013.

University of Melbourne. (n.d.). 'Academic honesty and plagiarism'. www.academichonesty. unimelb.edu.au/plagiarism.html. Accessed 8 January 2015.

University of Southampton. (n.d.). 'Impact and dissemination of research findings'. eResarch Methods series. www.erm.ecs.soton.ac.uk/theme8/impact_and_dissemination_of_the_ research_findings.html. Accessed 26 March 2013.

Wolfe, J. (2006). 'How to write a PhD thesis'. www.phys.unsw.edu.au/~jw/thesis. html#outline. Accessed 3 February 2014.

Yallow, R. (n.d.). 'Responsible conduct research: Mentoring'. www.ccnmtl.colombia.edu/ projects/rcr_mentoring/foundation/index.html. Accessed 27 April 2015.

▌ INDEX

Entries are listed in letter-by-letter alphabetical order. Page references in *italics* indicate where you will find information in tables.

A

abstracts 138–139, *159*, 225
academia 3–38
academic
    citizenship 10–11
    environment, distinguishing features of 9,
        11–20
    freedom 9–13
    integrity 9
    networking 15–18
Academic Ranking of World Universities
        (ARWU) 29, 30
access
    initiatives, African Library Consortia 67–70
    licences 92
achievable objectives 137
acknowledgements 88, *159*
ad hominem promotions 99, *101* , 103–104
administration, core function of academic 5
Africa
    academic disciplines in 43
    access to research information in 65–66
    perspective, international collaborative
        research 58–60
    response to internationalisation 28–29
African theses, database for 76
aims 135, *136*, 136
altmetrics 182–183
animal subjects, research with 82–83
anti-circumvention clause 92
appendices, thesis 224
apprenticeship xvii–xviii
argument, structuring 163–164
art of research 63–64
article processing charges (APCs) 180
articles, legal 162
Arts and Humanities Citation Index® 71
assessment in scholarly research 146
Association of Commonwealth Universities
        (ACU) 68, 78
Academy of Science South Africa (ASSAf) 188
authorship 86–89
    requirements, journals 88
    issues, grants management 143–144
    journal article *159*
Automated Rights Management (ARM) 92

B

Belmont Report 21
benchmarking 24, 33–44
Berne Convention 90
bibliographic
    data management 77, 208
    data saving 208
    references, thesis 224
bibliography *159,* 214
bibliometrics 30–31, 52, 53–54, 177
blogging 19
body of article 159
    IBC model 159
    IMRAD formula 159–160
Bologna Process 28–29
book
    proposal 170–171
    review, legal 163
bookmarking sites 19
books
    accreditation 165–166
    and scholarly articles, relationship between
        166–168, *168*
    basics of 165–168
    chapters in 151
    contract negotiation 173
    editing 151
    editorial process 173
    launching and marketing 174
    not considered research output 166
    publication 151, 152–155
    scholarly 165
    scope of 168
    situations indicating writing of 168
    types of 165
    writing 165–174
Boolean searching 74–75
brackets, Boolean operators 75
Budapest Declaration 179

C

case note 160–162
chapters
    abstracts 222
    in books 151
    thesis 222

citation 208
    count 148
    indexes 71
    rates 176
Citation Index® 175
coaching xvi–xviii
co-authorship 52
code of ethics 80–81
coherence 38, 39
cohort supervision 237
collaboration 42
    co-authorship and 52
    reasons for 50–51
    what it is 51–52
collaborative research 27, 55, 49–54
collaborators 51–52
collegiality 9, 13–15
computer management 207–208
conceptual framework, thesis 213
conclusion 159, 222
conference paper 120–124
    feedback 124
    post-submission 151
    preparation 121–122
    pre-peer review 151
    presentation 120, 123–124, 126–127
    proposal/abstract 121
    title 120
    topic 120
    proceedings 151
    participation 117–118
conferences
    DHET accreditation of 72
    KPIs of research 99, 101–102
    networking 16, 119, 152
    organisation 119–120
    participation, KPIs of research 99, 100, 101,
        101–102
    peer review 12, 151
    planning for 118–119
    reasons for presenting at 117–118
    sabbaticals 116
    selecting 118
    timing of 119
    types of 118–119
Constitution of the Republic of South Africa 10
consultancy 203–204
contract negotiation, publishing 173
contribution, weighting in collaborative research
    54
contributor–guarantor method 88
co-productions and co-publication, implications
    of 55
copyright 90–93
co-supervision 203–204, 238

Council for the Development of Social Science
        Research in African (CODESRIA) 59
counselling xvi–xviii
craft of research 63–64
creative disciplines 147
credit, assignation of 86–89
cross-disciplinary research 47
cross-fertilisation 53
curriculum vitae (CV) 105–107, 132
Dar es Salaam Declaration on Academic Freedom
        and Social Responsibility of Academics
        9–10

D
data
    analysis 84–85, 213
    bibliographic management of 77
    collection and processing, ethics 83–84
    ownership of 227
Database of African Theses and Dissertations
        (DATAD) 76
Department of Higher Education and Training
        (DHET)
    accreditation criteria 165–166
    accredited journals 71, 177–178
    research evaluation criteria 149–150
digital
    footprint 18–19
    information, copyright and 92–93
    shadow 18–19
    sources, acknowledgement of 93
Digital Rights Management Systems (DRMSs) 92
discipline-based research 27
disciplines, academic, breach of 42–45
discussion
    IMRAD formula 160
    journal article 159
dissemination strategies 181–183
dissertation see thesis
double dipping 135
Dramatic, Artistic and Literary Rights Organisa-
        tion (DALRO) 92
duplication of outputs 39–40

E
early-career researcher 109–110, 153, 154–155
editing books and journals 151
electronic networking 16
e-libraries 77–78
Emerging Researcher Programme (ERP) xiii,
        xv–xvi
engaged scholarship 5
enquiry-based learning 8
error 83–84

ethics 20–22, 79–80
    approval for research with human subjects
        81–82
    clearance, grant project 132
    code of 80–81
    data collection and processing 83–84
    guides to 80–81
    of publishing 85–86
    relationships and 80
    thesis writing 205–239
    websites 80–81
examiners, PhD 230–231, 234, 224
exception, copyright 90–91
excursus 224

F
face-to-face networking 16
fair-dealing assumption 90–91
fraud 83–84
funders 134, 137, 141
funding *see also* grants
    agency 129–130
    applications, institutional protocols 139
    applications peer review 12–13
    availability for PhD 194
    cycles 130
    databases 130
    sabbaticals 116–117
    securing, KPIs of research 98 100, *101*

G
Gantt chart 142–143
global
    and local 33
    competitiveness 25
    information environment 66
    research partnerships 32
Global Development Network (GDN) 68
Global South
    effect of colonial past on 43
    international partnerships 32
    international research landscape and 25–33
gold route, open-access publishing 180
Google Scholar 19, 70, 77, 177
grant
    application, waiting period 142
    implementation 142
    management 140–144
    project, ethics clearance 132
    -writing, principles of 129–140
grant proposals
    abstract 138–139
    aims 135, *136*, 136
    budget for 134–135
    CV preparation 132
    demonstrating planning 130

    funders' instructions 134
    goals 135, *136*, 136
    identifying a funder 129–132
    marketing of project 131–132
    objectives 135, *136*, 136–137
    outcomes 135, *136*, 137
    outline 139–140
    outputs 135, *136*, 137
    presentation 133–134
    principles of writing 140–144
    project description 141–142
    review guide 140
    reviewers' reports on 139
    terminology 135–137
    title page 137–138
    -writing, principles of 129–140
grants
    availability 129–130
    feasibility 131
    funders of 131–132
    management, reporting 144
    principles, project management 140–144
    principals, responsibilities of 140–144
    KPIs of research 98, 199, *101*
    renewal 144
    securing 129–140
graphs 223–224
green route, open-access publishing 180
group supervision 237–238
guarantors 88

H
Heads of Department (HOD), responsibilities of
    202–203
Helsinki Declaration 21
hierarchies, collaborative research 55–56
h-index 31, 148, 175–177
human subjects, research with 81–82
humanities
    and sciences, differences 187, 191
    integration of scientific data 44–45

I
IBC model 159
impact
    factor (IF) 31, 148, 175–176
    of research 148, 175–183
    rating application 38
IMRAD formula 159–160
information skills training 70
informed consent 81–82
Institute of Scientific Information (ISI)
    listed journals 71
    Web of Knowledge 176, 177
institutional
    protocols, funding applications 139

repositories, research visibility 180
integrationist approach 45
integrative knowledge 45
integrity in research 20–22
intellectual
    integrity 20–22
    property 89–92, 227
interdisciplinary research 42–59
international
    collaborative research 54–57
    journals 153
    partnerships 31–33
    research landscape 25–33
    theses 76
International Convention on Economic, Social
    and Cultural Rights 21
International Network for the Availability of
    Scientific Publication (NASP) 67–68
internationalisation 24, 25, 26–33
    African response to 28–29
    effects of 27–29
    intra-African 28
Internet
    effective use of 72–77
    material types of 72–73
in-text referencing 222–223
intra-African internationalisation 28
introduction
    IBC model 159
    IMRAD formula 159–160
    journal article 159
    thesis 222

J
journal articles
    and books, relationship between 166–168,
        168
    components of 159
    disciplinary perspectives 159–160
    publication 150
    scientific research and 147
Journal Citation Reports 176
journal lists, locating 71–72
journals
    editing 151
    editors and publishers of 152
    instructions to authors 152
    online 152, 153
    open access 153
    print 152, 153
    specialist 153
    targeting appropriate 152
    types of 152,
    what to avoid when writing 153–154
junior researchers and authorship 87–88

K
key performance indicators (KPIs) 98–99
keywords 159
knowledge
    economy 25
    production 6, 8
    -transmission, teaching as 7

L
law publishing 160–164
leadership, core function of academic 5
legal
    article 162
    book review 163
    online commentary 162–163
    research, publishing 160–164
libraries and librarians 65, 70
limitation, copyright 90–91
literature review 159, 212–213
logic, structuring argument 163

M
macro-planning 99–100
Master's degree 189–190, 232–234, 226–227
measurable objectives 137
Memorandum of Understanding (MOU) 87, 89,
        143–144, 187, 194, 195–196, 209
Mendeley 19, 77, 182
mentoring xvi–xx, 71
method
    and methodology 218
    IMRAD formula 160
    thesis 217
methods, journal article 159
micro-planning 97–98
mobility
    early-career researchers and 109–110
    staff and students and 28
monograph/dissertation, thesis published as 166,
        168–170
Montreal Statement 21
multidisciplinary research 47–48
multiple supervisors 239

N
names, inclusion and ordering 55, 86, 88
narrative description, rating application 38–39
national library consortium 66
National Research Foundation (NRF)
    institutional processes 141
    ranking system 33–44
    ratings 99, 101, 104
    research evaluation criteria 147–148
NEPAD STI policy e-library 77
networking 9, 15–18, 126, 152
network model of supervision 238

New Academic Practitioners' Programme
  (NAPP) xviii
Nexus database 76
non-electronic material, storage 201–208
non-textual outputs 147, 148

O
obiter dicta 161
objectives 135, *136*, 136–137
omnibus journals 153
one-on-one model, supervision 236–237
online
  commentary, legal 162–163
  journal platforms 69—70
  journals 152, 153
  presence 9, 18–20
open access
  journals 153
  publishing 179–181
  resources 69–70
originality 149
orphan works 91
outcome-oriented research 7
outcomes 135, *136*, 137
outputs 39–40, 135, *136*, 137

P
partnerships, international 31–33
passivity 94
patents 147
peer review 9, 11–13
  assessment in scholarly research 148
  conference proceedings 151
  criteria 156
  DHET research evaluation criteria 149
  functions 155
  in a university 11–13
  in publishing 155–158
  process 155–157, 166
  problems 13
  rating system 35
  reviewers' comments 156–158
permissions to reproduce 90, 91–92
personal
  issues, accommodation of 99, *101*, 104–105
  research, benchmarking 38–44
PhD
  and Master's, differences 189–190
  appointment of examiners 230–231
  criteria for 210–211
  embarking on 181–205
  examination process 232–234
  feedback 197–198
  funding for 194
  KPIs of research 98, 100, *101*
  readiness for 193

registration 193, 211
  student perspective 193–195
  supervisor's perspective 191–193
  submission of written work 197–198
  upgrade from Master's to 226–227
plagiarism 85–86, 227–229
planning 94–108
  effective 96–97
  macro- 99–100
  micro- 97–98
  realistic 96–97
  reasons for 95–96
  short-term 97–98
  targets 97–98
  template 99, 100, *101*
policy, structuring argument 163
political factors for collaboration 51
popular articles, publication 151–152
post-conference submission of papers 151
poster presentations 125–127
postgraduate student, authorship and 89
postgraduate supervision *see* supervision
power relations 7, 9, 87
pre-acceptance review process 172
pre-conference peer review 151
principal investigator (PI)
  authorship issues 143– 144
  communication 144
  continuation and future grants 144
  financial management grants 143
  personnel management 143
  project management 142–144
  reporting and accountability 141
  responsibilities 141–144
  time management 142–143
  waiting period and grant implementation 142
  institutional and agency support 141–142
principle, structuring argument 163
print journals 152, 153
professional
  body, legal submission to 163
  development, KPIs of research 99, *101*, 103
  relationships, networking 15
project
  management, grants 142–143
  terminology 135–137
proofs, working with 158
proposal, thesis *see* thesis proposal
provisional registration facility 193
publication profile 176
publications, peer-reviewed 98, *101*, 102
publisher
  sourcing 171, 172
  working with 171, 172
publishing 147–174
  conventional 147

assessment of research impact 148
disciplinary perspectives 159–160
ethics of 85–86
in science 159–160
legal 160–164
process 171
scholarly *see* scholarly publishing
types of material 150
while doing PhD 226
pyramid model of supervision 238

Q
QS World University Rankings 29, 30
quality
    assurance 24, 34
    rating application 38
quotations 223

R
race, evolutionary ideas of 59
ranking systems 29–30
rating system *see* researcher rating system
ratio decidendi 161
rationale 212
recruiting academics 31
referees *see* reviewers
reference list 214
Reference Manager 77, 208
reference sources, assessing 72–73
references
    bibliographic, thesis 224
    journal article *159*
referencing, in-text 222–223
relationships, ethics 80
reliable objectives 137
replication of outputs 39–40
research
    and study leave *see* sabbaticals
    art of 63–64
    assessment of 310–312
    assistant's and student's position, collaborative
        research 54–55,
    bases xvii
    benchmarking 33–44
    boundaries, crossing 42–59
    capacity xiv
    collaborative 27
    core function of 5
    craft of 63–64
    description of 38–44
    design 63, 213
    development grants, peer review 12–13
    development, personal 64
    dissemination strategies 181–183
    ethics 213
    evaluation criteria 147–148

feasibility 131
focus 27, 107–108
funding, collaboration 32, 50
grants *see* grants
impact 148, 175—183
information, access to, Africa 65–66
information and management 66–78
integrity 20–22, 79–93
interdisciplinary *see* interdisciplinary research
key performance indicators 98–99
landscape 24–41
legal 160–164
libraries' place in 65
measurement of 30–31
methods 213
narratives 38–39
nature of 7
ongoing 40
opportunities, optimising 109–128
outcome-oriented 7
output 39–40, 98, 147
plan 208–209
planned future 40
planning *see* planning
profile developing 63–78
publishing *see* publishing
question/problem, thesis 212
rating application 34–44
reports, publication 151
scientific, merit of 131
story 38–44
teaching and, relationship 6–9
training, collaboration and 51
understanding-oriented 7
visibility institutional repositories 180
research visits 99, 101–102, 127–128
    documenting and reporting on 128
    KPIs of research 99, 101–102
    preparing for 127
    reasons for 127
    value of 127–128
Research Professional Africa (RPA) 77–78, 130
researcher rating system
    adapting for personal research benchmarking
        38–44
    how it works 34–36
    limitations and challenges 37
    strengths and weaknesses 36–37
researchers
    development xiv
    early-career 48–49, 109–110, 153, 154–155,
        194, 240–242
results
    IMRAD formula 160
    journal article *159*
review articles 151

reviewers 11–12, 132–133, 139, 172
Role Perception Rating Scale 199–200
role-play 191

S
sabbatical
   proposal 113–115
   report 117
sabbaticals
   conference participation 116
   follow-up 117
   funding and study leave 116– 117
   KPIs of research 99, *101*, 103
   outcomes and outputs 117
   planning 110–117
   preparation 112–113
   reasons for granting 111
   study leave 116–117
   supervisor and 198
   time and place 115–116
   travelling abroad 115–116
San Francisco Declaration 31, 148, 177, 182
scholarly article and book, relationship between
   166–168, *168*
scholarly publishing 149–174
   functions 149–150
   motivation for publication 149–174
   writing books *see* books writing
scholarly visibility, collaboration 51
Science Citation Index® 71
science
sciences
   and humanities, differences 187, 191
   publishing in 147, 159–160
self-
   archiving articles 180
   -assessment of research outputs 39–40
   -knowledge 96–97
   -plagiarism 85–86
sentences and paragraphs, thesis writing
   220–221
Shanghai system 29, 30
sharing of knowledge 53
short-term planning 97–98
Singapore Statement 21
SMART techniques 137
social media
   online presence 19
   publication 151–152
   research dissemination 182
social responsiveness, function of academic 5
Social Sciences Citation Index® 71
social taboos 75
South Africa Department of Higher Eduction
   see Department of Higher Education and
   Training (DHET)

South Africa researcher rating system *see* rating
   system
South African National Research Foundation *see*
   National Research Foundation (NRF)
South African theses 76
speaking and listening, collaborative research 56
specialisation, collaboration and 50
specific objectives 137
spelling, American and British 75
staff
   conditions, rethinking of 27
   mobility 28
storage, non-electronic material 201–208
stretching oneself 97
student
   cluster models 237–238
   -focused knowledge-production, teaching
     as 7
   mobility 28
   responsibilities of 201–202
   support for 204–205
study leave *see* sabbaticals
subject encyclopaedia 73
subsidy
   earning 165–166, 177–178,
   issue, academic publishing 149
   policy 178
supervision
   co- 203–204
   meaning of 190
   meetings 197
   models of 188, 236–237
   postgraduate 187–205
   KPIs of research 98, *101* , 102
   relationship 191
   training 187
   workshops 191
supervisors
   absences 198
   and data analysis 84–85
   authorship and 89
   choice of 194
   cluster model supervision 238–239
   eleven practices of effective 218
   responsibilities of 198–200, 235
   negotiations with -students 197–198
   relationships with students 197
   styles 200
supervisory committees 239
support relationships xvii–xviii

T
tables, thesis 223–224
targets planning 97–98
teaching
   and research, relationship 6–9

core function of academic 5
    models of 7
    –research nexus 6–9
team supervision 203–204
terminology
    American and British 75
    project 135– 137
theoretical framework, thesis 213
theory, engaging with 163–164
theses, searching for 75–76
thesis 190
    abstract 225
    methodology 217
    proposal 211–214
    publication arising from 150
    published as monograph 166, 168–170
    publishing 225–226
    structure 214–217, *215*
    submission 231–232
    supervisor-student negotiations 197
thesis writing
    discussion 209
    identifying topic 210
    preparation 206–218
    process 209–214, 219–239
    research ethics 205
    research plan 208–209
    stages of 209
    strategic and stylistic issues 219–224
    time management 208
Thomson Reuters
    Academic Ranking of World Universities
      (ARWU) 29, 30
    Web of Science 30
thread, research 39
time
    available, assessment of 99–100
    management 97–98, 142–143, 208
timed objectives 137
timeline 214
title *159*, 137–138, 212, 219
transdisciplinary research 27
transfer of knowledge 53
truncation symbols 74–75
trust 83–84
twitter 19

U
UCT
    'Afropolitan' vision xiv
    New Academic Practitioners' Programme
      (NAPP) xviii
underlying theme, research 39
understanding-oriented research 7
universities
    and intellectual enterprise 22–23
    evolving functions of 25–26
    management, challenges to 288
    purpose of 6
    rankings 29–30
university library 65, 70
university rankings 29–30
upgrade from Master's to PhD 226–227

V
values, structuring argument 163
virtual presence 18–20

W
waiting period, grant application 142
wildcard symbols 74
writer's block 224
writing style, thesis 219–220

XYZ
Zotero 19